CONFLICT AND CONCILIATION
IN IRELAND 1890–1910

CONFLICT AND CONCILIATION IN IRELAND
1890–1910

Parnellites and Radical Agrarians

PAUL BEW

CLARENDON PRESS · OXFORD
1987

Oxford University Press, Walton Street, Oxford OX2 6DP

Oxford New York Toronto
Delhi Bombay Calcutta Madras Karachi
Petaling Jaya Singapore Hong Kong Tokyo
Nairobi Dar es Salaam Cape Town
Melbourne Auckland

and associated companies in
Beirut Berlin Ibadan Nicosia

Oxford is a trade mark of Oxford University Press

Published in the United States
by Oxford University Press, New York

© Paul Bew 1987

British Library Cataloguing in Publication Data
Bew, Paul
Conflict and conciliation in Ireland
1898—1910: Parnellites and radical
agrarians.
1. Ireland—History—1901—1910
2. Nationalism—Ireland—History
I. Title
322.4'2'09415   DA960
ISBN 0-19-822758-2

Library of Congress Cataloging in Publication Data
Bew, Paul.
Conflict and conciliation in Ireland, 1898—1910.
Bibliography: p.
Includes index.
1. Ireland—Politics and government—1901—1910.
2. Ireland—Politics and government—1837—1901.
3. Nationalism—Ireland—History.   4. Land tenure—
Ireland—History.   5. Parnell, Charles Stewart,
1846—1891—Influence.   I. Title.
DA960.B48   1987   941.5082'1   86-28578
ISBN 0-19-822758-2

Typeset by Joshua Associates Limited, Oxford
Printed in Great Britain by
Billing & Sons Limited, Worcester

FOR JOHN PATRICK

Acknowledgements

IT is a pleasure to thank those friends who have helped sustain me during the preparation of this book. Jim Donnelly and Roy Foster, notwithstanding their very heavy schedules, read and commented most helpfully on my earlier drafts. I owe much to their exceptional generosity. In James Loughlin's case, I benefited both from his own interesting ideas on the 1880s and his remarkable knowledge of the Dublin archives. Professors David Miller, Lewis Warren and Cornelius O'Leary all gave the project their sympathetic backing. I gained a great deal from my friend Henry Patterson's knowledge of Ulster politics in this epoch. It was Brendan Clifford who initially drew my attention to the All for Ireland League.

The first draft was written while a visiting lecturer at the University of Pennsylvania. I should like to thank Dr. Denis J. Clark, executive director of the Samuel Fels Foundation and President of the Philadelphia Centre for Irish Studies for his enthusiastic support and interest. It is a special pleasure also to thank Perry Curtis of Brown University for his informed and perceptive observations on my earlier work. Perry Curtis, and in different ways, David Fitzpatrick and Don Jordan, have shaped my work in recent years more than they know. The original inspiration has, however, its roots in Edward Norman's stimulating course on the 'Home Rule Debate' in Cambridge in 1970/71. My greatest debt is to my wife Greta Jones who, despite her own heavy involvement in teaching and writing, did more than anyone to keep this project on course.

Finally, I should like to thank the librarians and archivists of the British Library, the National Library of Ireland, the Public Record Office both in London and Belfast and the State Paper Office in Dublin Castle. They dealt with an enormous flow of requests with great patience and courtesy. I owe a special debt also to the manuscript rooms of Trinity College Dublin and University College Cork. In my own city, the Linenhall Library, and the two university libraries of Queen's and Ulster, were essential, as always, to my work.

Belfast   PAUL BEW
May 1986

Contents

List of Maps

Abbreviations

BL	British Library
CSO	Chief Secretary's Office, Registered Papers
FJ	*Freeman's Journal*
HC	House of Commons
HL	House of Lords
IP	*Irish People*
IT	*Irish Times*
IWI	*Irish Weekly Independent*
NLI	National Library of Ireland
PRO	Public Record Office of England, Kew
PRONI	Public Record Office of Northern Ireland
SPO	State Paper Office, Dublin Castle
TCD	Trinity College Dublin

See also list of newspapers in bibliography.

1. Ireland

Introduction

Bear in mind ... the policy of another school in the party, who have
wanted in Parnell's day and since to oppose every concession through
the fear that, by lessening the area of grievances and the opportunities
for agrarian agitation you lessen the dynamics of the national cause.
There is a certain plausible narrow case for their theory. But Parnell's
policy was based on a wider and deeper conception of the forces of
nationhood, which do not depend altogether on economic considerations, agrarian or otherwise.

T. P. Gill to J. E. Redmond 12.6.1902, NLS MS 15,190(1)

THE Irish 'Land War' of 1879–82 was characterized by a rare combination of social and political forces which endowed Irish nationalism
with a sense of excitement and purpose it was not to recover until after
the Easter Rising of 1916. In many respects, these years of the Land
League crisis represent the decisive turning point in Anglo-Irish
relations. The struggle, as it was internationally perceived, of over
500,000 Irish tenants—mostly Catholic and nationalist—against less
than 20,000 'alien' landlords—mostly Protestant and unionist—proved
to be of compelling importance. British political leaders did not have
to take either the demand for an Irish peasant proprietorship or a
Dublin parliament too seriously in the mid-1870s; by the mid-1880s
the inevitability of peasant proprietorship was conceded by both
major British parties, whilst the leadership of one of them, the
Liberals, was committed to some form of Irish self-government. The
key figures on the Irish side were Charles Stewart Parnell, the
charismatic Anglo-Irish leader of the Irish parliamentary party and
Michael Davitt, the plebeian product of the insurrectionary Fenian
movement: Davitt's principal achievement was to bring Fenianism—
which had previously been largely uninterested in social issues prior
to the achievement of full independence—into the mainstream of Irish
peasant life.[1] Much of the militancy of the peasantry in the west of
Ireland was due to the influence of a radicalized neo-Fenianism.
Paradoxically, this fusion of social activism and nationalism in the

[1] T. W. Moody, *Davitt and Irish Revolution 1846–82*, Oxford, 1982.

land agitation—such was its political charge—helped to reduce the hostility of the Catholic Church to popular nationalism. Indeed, many parish priests acted as leaders of the 'Land War' in the localities, whilst a section of the hierarchy somewhat reluctantly followed suit.

Unfortunately for Irish nationalism, the striking unities of 1879–82[2]—the apparent 'identity' of the land question and the national question; neo-Fenians and parliamentarians forming a bloc with priests; small and larger tenants aligned together against landlordism backed up by British power—proved to be a temporary phenomenon. The structural fragility of the Land League alliance played a decisive role here:[3] the class divisions of the popular movement (involving rural bourgeoisie, middle and poor peasantry and agricultural proletariat), proved ultimately debilitating. Moreover, these social divisions were reinforced by profound political differences: the neo-Fenians had supported the objective of 'peasant proprietorship' as a means to national independence. They had assumed that once the peasantry were mobilized behind this slogan they would meet with unbending resistance from the 'landlordist' British government: in fact, they were met by the partial, but substantial reform of the 1881 Land Act. Though he may have made significant pro-Fenian gestures, Parnell's own priorities lay elsewhere.[4] He aspired to satisfy the tenantry on terms which were not disadvantageous to the landlords— the whole process to be subsidized by a generous contribution from the British Treasury. Parnell hoped that this would open the way for landlord acquiescence (or perhaps even co-operation) in the nationalist project. As F. S. L. Lyons has observed: '[Parnell's] favourite nos-

---

[2] S. Clark, *Social Origins of the Irish Land War*, Princeton, 1979; K. T. Hoppen, *Elections, Politics and Society in Ireland 1832–85*, Oxford, 1984.

[3] W. E. Vaughan, *Landlords and Tenants in Ireland 1848–1904* (Studies in Irish Economic and Social History, 2) Dundalk, 1984, 30–9; R. V. Comerford, *The Fenians in Context: Irish Politics and Society 1848–82*, Dublin, 1985, 223–50.

[4] *An Phoblacht*, 8 March 1930, in an article 'Memories of Kilmainham', carries this interesting passage: 'It is not generally known that Parnell took the Fenian oath. Strolling through Dublin one day immediately after the signing of the Kilmainham Treaty, he met a Land League organiser from the west, they were on their way to Trinity College library to look up some data on Griffiths land valuation when their conversation turned to the question of physical force versus constitutionalism. They continued their talk in a quiet manner, then in that singularly incongruous setting, and at Parnell's own suggestion, he was sworn a Fenian—with the proviso that his doing so would be kept a secret during his lifetime. The man who swore Parnell in lies in far off Colorado in an exile's grave.' Paul Bew, *C. S. Parnell*, Dublin, 1980, *passim*. See also the same author's *Land and the National Question in Ireland 1858–82*, Dublin, 1978, 60–3, 108, 152, 226–8 and 259, for the reconciliation theme.

trum in these critical years was to bring the younger and more progressive landlords into the Home Rule movement so as to give it sufficient cachet to convince British legislators in London.'[5] Parnell's personal vision was as incapable of fulfilment as the neo-Fenian one; in consequence, he was forced to implement a series of 'pragmatic' adjustments, notably the 'alliance' with British liberalism, which bitterly disillusioned some of the republican pure spirits. Many former Fenians were lastingly integrated within conventional Parnellism—but some turned to brutal and bloody acts of terrorism.

By 1886 it was tragically clear that the years of land war and subsequent home rule crisis had intensified the identification of Catholicism and nationalism. Above all, Unionists had succeeded—and they were helped in this by injudicious nationalist tactics—in stigmatizing the programme of the land movement, which had substantial initial appeal for the Protestant tenantry of north-east Ulster, as merely the cover for nefarious separatist objectives.[6] It was only after his fall from grace and the O'Shea divorce scandal that Parnell felt able to venture a strong statement of conciliation on the subject of Ulster opposition, for while he remained the leader of the united nationalist contingent such arguments would have been highly divisive. In his heyday, as Lyons has observed, Parnell 'never seems to have asked himself what he meant by the "Irish nation" or the "Irish race" which he claimed to lead, and the idea that Ireland might possibly contain two nations, not one, apparently never entered his head.'[7] Lyons concludes of Parnell's position on Ulster Unionism that he 'never came remotely within reach of developing a constructive approach to the potentially lethal threat it represented.'[8] In Belfast in May 1891, an isolated Parnell did, however, declare: 'It is undoubtedly true ... that until the ... prejudices of the minority, whether reasonable or unreasonable are conciliated ... Ireland can never enjoy perfect freedom, Ireland can never be united.'[9]

[5] F. S. L. Lyons, 'The Land War', *Irish Times*, 12 May 1979.
[6] Paul Bew and Frank Wright, 'Agrarian Opposition in Ulster 1848–87', 205–27, in Sam Clark and James Donnelly (eds), *Irish Peasants: Violence and Political Unrest 1780–1914*, Madison, 1983; see also the forceful analogous essays by Brian Walker, 'The land question and elections in Ulster 1868–86', 230–68, in the same volume and F. Thompson, 'Attitudes to Reform: Political Parties in Ulster and the Irish Land Bill of 1881', *Irish Historical Studies* vol. XXIV, 1985, 327–40.
[7] F. S. L. Lyons, *Charles Stewart Parnell*, London, 1977, 623.   [8] Lyons, ibid.
[9] Bew, *Parnell*, 127–31: for a more cool assessment of this speech, see J. P. Loughlin, 'Gladstone, Irish Nationalism and the Home Rule Question 1882–1892' (Trinity College, Dublin, Ph.D., 1983), 459–63.

In the meantime, however, the nascent Unionist bloc had decisively emerged in north-east Ulster—taking its impetus from the Home Rule panic of 1885–6 and the Third Reform Act of 1884; this last gave the sectarian force of the Orange Order a particular power—not because a majority of the electorate were Orangemen but because a majority of the new potential Unionist electorate was perceived to be. The General Election of 1885 further revealed the deep-rooted sectarianism of Irish politics: the nationalists won every seat with a Catholic majority—which meant every seat in the three southern provinces but two (the Dublin University seats) and half those in Ulster.

It is often remarked of Parnell that he seemed not to have an introspective side; what is less often remarked is that this was true of the movement he led as well. The remarkable upsurge of Parnellite nationalism, largely due to the exploitation of the land question, was too sudden and too dramatic to leave much time for speculation on the meaning of the national soul. Rarely has a vigorous nationalist movement had so little room for nationalist ideology. Under Parnell everything was in movement and the problem of politics was to overcome the dangerous obstacles repeatedly thrown up by the more or less permanent crisis: Forster's coercion; the Phoenix Park murders; the Liberal split over Home Rule; the Pigott 'forgeries'; and finally, the O'Shea divorce court revelations. But in the long sterile period following Parnell's fall the ideologists were given their chance to come forward to interpret the implications of the Land League revolution. They did so, it will be argued, in most cases with a notable disregard for Parnell's own views.

In the two decades which followed Parnell's fall there was a widespread assumption in Ireland that some kind of self-government was an inevitability. But popular certainty on this point was combined with widespread uncertainty on others: how generous would the measure of independence be? Would the Ulster Unionists be included within the new Ireland? Which local elite would predominate when the British finally left? Would the Anglo-Irish 'ascendancy' be able to retain any of their influence? All groups—all shades of nationalist and unionist opinion—were plagued by doubts and confusions concerning British intentions. All found it difficult to influence the British state in any decisive way.

The period also sees interesting changes in British government policy towards Ireland. It sees the high point of 'constructive Unionism' first under Gerald Balfour as Irish chief secretary (1895–1900) and

George Wyndham (1900–5). The Conservative government in 1898 democratized Irish local government and in 1903 implemented the major land purchase proposals of the Wyndham Act. Wyndham's subsequent ambitious projects of Irish devolution floundered on the opposition of both 'diehard' Unionist and Nationalist opinion. Some of this conservative strategy had been motivated by the (vain) hope that it might be possible to 'kill' home rule with 'kindness'. After 1906 the Liberals were in power; despite their earlier Gladstonian commitment to the Irish cause they were profoundly unwilling or unable to offer Home Rule. The moral uncertainty of this position again made it relatively easy for the Irish party to extract important concessions— town and evicted tenants; agricultural labourers; and above all higher educational interests (the Catholic university bill of 1908) all benefited. The most notable of these reforms, however, was the neglected Birrell land act of 1909. Throughout these years, the Irish parliamentary party remained the principal voice of nationalist aspirations. In particular, after the founding of Sinn Fein in 1900 it was plagued by 'purist' critics calling for a withdrawal from the London parliament, but it was to be 1917 before these critics would be able to launch an effective electoral challenge. These new radical nationalists have recently been the subject of scholarly research;[10] the focus here, however, will be on the 'old men' of the Irish parliamentary party; on the processes by which hegemony was lost, rather than those by which it was won.

This is not to deny the importance of the new 'Irish Ireland' currents. When the massively influential Irish language revivalist Father Eugene O'Growney died in 1903, the *Freeman's Journal* (the principal organ of constitutional nationalism) described his funeral thus:

We question if there has ever seen in the Irish capital such a significant procession as this ... Father O'Growney was triumphantly carried to the Broadstone by a generation that is only growing into manhood, that is breast high for his idea and ideals. The Parnell funeral was one intensive sob for a great leader fallen in his prime, and the MacManus funeral was a political demonstration meant to give the warning note to the Fenians; but yesterday's function took the character of both. It was a requiem and tocsin combined.[11]

---

[10] Tom Garvin, 'The anatomy of a nationalist revolution: Ireland 1858–1928', *Comparative Studies in Society and History*, forthcoming.
[11] *FJ*, 28 September 1903.

The *Freeman* neglected, however, to acknowledge that the 'Gaelic Revival' (the Gaelic League was founded in 1893) was bound to have a powerful, albeit unspoken, Catholic complexion, given the ways in which it attempted to utilize the Irish past; hence, the hostility which it attracted from even 'liberal' Unionists. The new nationalism of the 1890s and 1900s was open to the charge of being increasingly exclusive, introspective and intolerant: the emotional mirror image, albeit understandably, in certain important respects, of the 'imperialism' which it sought to displace. The 'new nationalism' was contemptuous, as its key figure Arthur Griffith put it, of the 'cosmopolitan heresy of our time.'[12] Griffith further explained: 'When we say we love Ireland we do not mean by Ireland the peasants in the fields, the workers in the factories, the teachers in the schools, the professors in the colleges—we mean the soul into which we were born and which was born into us . . . the Ireland that stretches back to Emain Macha.'[13]

The 'whole tenor' of the Gaelic League's argument was that Irish nationalism stood or fell by its cultural identity: 'an idea, moreover, that did not include, and could not be shared by . . . the aliens of north-east Ulster, who had broken the continuity of the Irishness of Ireland.'[14] But it is important also not to exaggerate the significance of the 'Gaelic revival'; as the Unionist *Northern Whig* pointed out, Irish speaking was actually on the decline in the 1890s—those who spoke Irish only fell from 38,192 to 20,953,and the bilingual grouping fell from 642,053 to 620,189[15]—and as the pro-Sinn Fein journal, *The Peasant and Irish Irelander* noted in 1907 the Gaelic League has 'not yet effected a lodgement in the countryside'.[16] Much the most significant political arena in Ireland in 1890–1910 was the Irish parliamentary party which was affected by diverse, relatively liberal influences as well as those of a more unsophisticated, elemental sort. The Irish party had two principal planks, 'Ireland for the Irish' and the 'land for the people'.[17] But what did these phrases mean? How were the Irish to be defined: in pluralist terms as Protestant, Catholic and dissenter or simply as Catholic? How precisely was the land to be divided amongst the people? These two interrelated questions set the context of this

---

[12] *Sinn Fein*, 26 April 1913 quoted in F. Ryan, *Sinn Fein and Reaction*, Dublin, 1984, 47. This text edited by M. O'Riordan for the Labour History Workshop.

[13] Ibid.

[14] D. G. Boyce, *Nationalism in Ireland*, London, Dublin, and Baltimore, 1982, 238.

[15] *Northern Whig*, 13 July 1902.

[16] *The Peasant and Irish Irelander*, 9 March 1907.

[17] Boyce, *Nationalism*, 270.

study: the objective of which is to illuminate the interaction of two opposing conceptions of Irish nationalism. The first of these conceptions, which is here labelled 'Parnellite' tended to seek a reconciliation with southern Protestant unionist and landlord opinion as the best route to Irish self-government. The second conception, the radical agrarian, saw little need for such a reconciliation; for radical agrarians, it was necessary for Irish nationalists to emphasize the need for renewed struggle and conflict with the traditional opponents of home rule. From 1898–1910 these two tendencies coexisted uneasily within the main organization of constitutional nationalism, the United Irish League, but over issues such as devolution and land reform they fought out an increasingly bitter battle. At stake for both sides were the most basic and fundamental assumptions about the nature of a self-governing Ireland. The latent question always remained: was Irish nationalism capable of being more than simply the expression of the grievances of the Irish Catholic democracy? As D. George Boyce has observed, the Home Rule movement faced a most important issue in these years: was it possible to mobilize behind a 'concept of nationalism' which spoke not in 'terms of conflict' but in 'terms of reconciliation'?[18] Irish political leadership in this period rhetorically embraced both 'conflict' and 'reconciliation'. John Redmond was capable of a certain strident tone: 'The more they fought against the Anglicization of Ireland, the more they cultivated a purely Irish public opinion racy of the soul, the more they taught the people to hate and despise the English government in Ireland the sooner they would get Home Rule in their country.'[19] On the other hand, however, in an address to Trinity College Dublin Historical Society in 1893 he hit a rather different note in calling for 'a government which must not be Celtic, which must not be Saxon—which should be Irish'.[20]

The period between 1890 and 1910 has not been subjected to the same degree of relentless revisionism which has characterized other periods of Irish history. Nevertheless, there is a growing conviction that this area requires new discussion. In particular, it is clear that the emphasis should be on the study of Irish nationalism *in Ireland*. In 1971 Peter Alter argued the case for more concern with the domestic—as opposed to the foreign affairs of the Irish parliamentary party.[21] In

[18] Boyce, *Nationalism*, 279.
[19] *Northern Whig*, 14 January 1902.
[20] *IWI*, 18 November 1893.
[21] *Die Irische National bewegung zwischen Parlament und Revolution*, München, 1971, 18.

1979 David Dickson spoke of the need for a 'redirection of research effort' to deal with the 'nature of life and social relations in the countryside which seemed to have altered in a number of subtle ways'[22] in this epoch. More recently still Sam Clark and James Donnelly have written: 'Not enough is yet known about the internal dynamics of the United Irish League at either the national or local level'.[23] Clark and Donnelly also see a particular need for a detailed analysis of the politics of the ranch war 1906–8.[24] The gaps in the existing literature are plain enough. Professor D. R. Gwynn, in his *Life of John Redmond* (1932), which remains the standard biography of the most important nationalist leader of the post-Parnell era, is concerned above all, as he later acknowledged,[25] to portray Redmond as one of the giants of the Westminster system. One effect of this is that Redmond's colleagues in the Irish party remain at best shadowy figures. There is little discussion of Redmond's distinctive political ideas—the demand for Home Rule is treated as a given. In particular, there is scant analysis of Redmond's conservatism or his relationship to Parnell. Parnell had given a particular weight to conciliation in his politics; yet nowhere does Gwynn pose the question of precisely where Redmond stood on this point. Equally serious, the book has little discussion of the one issue apart from self-determination which was of vital concern to the vast majority of Irishmen—the land issue. As A. C. Hepburn has noted, Gwynn's book virtually ignores the ranch war of 1906–8 and the Birrell land act of 1909: 'in order the more quickly to reach the dramatic political conflicts of the years 1910–14'.[26] Yet in this period the Irish farming society from which the nationalists drew the great bulk of their support was bitterly divided. There was on the one side, a large peasant class undertaking small or medium scale farming; on the other, a growing stratum of rich graziers. To be considered a grazier a man had usually to hold over 200 acres; though the United Irish League's newspaper was capable of dropping the figure to 100 acres when it suited a particular case.[27] More typically, a grazier's holding was probably between 400 and 600 acres; though

---

[22] Review of Sam Clark, 'Social Origins of the Irish Land War', *Studia Hibernica*, No. 19, 1979, 173.

[23] *Irish Peasants: Violence and Political Unrest*, Madison, 1983, 283.

[24] Ibid., 431.

[25] Denis Gwynn, 'John Redmond', *Studies*, vol. 45, 1956, 397.

[26] A. C. Hepburn, 'Liberal Policies and Nationalist Politics in Ireland 1905–10' (University of Kent, Ph.D., 1968). A brief note on historiography, 825.

[27] *Irish People*, 31 July 1900.

there was an elite grouping which held much more. It was possible to find these so-called 'ranchers' in every region of Ireland but they were particularly notable in three regions; the lowlands of North Leinster, including the counties of Meath, Westmeath, Dublin, Kildare and King's; the plains of East Connaught and North Munster, including the counties of Sligo, Roscommon, East Galway, Clare and Tipperary; the mountain pastures and boglands of West Connaught, including West Galway, Mayo and North-West Sligo and even parts of Donegal.[28] The graziers were frequently absentees and were often business or professional men who lived in neighbouring towns. The care of the cattle was usually delegated to herdsmen who lived on the land. In the west, these areas existed alongside tiny overcrowded holdings: in Westport Union—to give the most celebrated example of the period—over 4,000 families occupied holdings of less than £8 valuation while almost 100,000 acres were held by a mere 66 graziers, and 13 landlords used a further 52,000 acres for grazing purposes.[29] The nationalist Westport district council argued in May 1902 that the superficial area of the district would allow a fifty-acre holding for every family. But it is worth noting that the main centre of ranching was not Mayo but Meath. Furthermore, the ranching area of North Leinster as a whole contrasted sharply with the ranching areas of Connaught both in terms of the composition and extent of the peasant community. By the early 1900s, both a subsistence and a middle commercial peasantry were quite small numerically in the North Leinster area. But there was, however, a significant number of cottiers and labourers: making for in David S. Jones's words 'a highly polarised social structure'.[30]

The grazing community was composed of many different elements, both socially and politically. Some had, indeed, assisted in or benefited from the famine clearances of dispossessed cottiers in the years from the mid-1840s up to 1855: former middlemen, land agents or bailiffs, small town businessmen or even imported English or Scottish capitalist farmers. This was why Matthew Harris, a militant Land League radical, might place the graziers on a par with the landlords and describe their union with the bulk of the peasantry as the 'union of

[28] David S. Jones, 'Agrarian Capitalism and Rural Social Development in Ireland' (Queen's University, Belfast, Ph.D., 1978), 2–6, a sparkling thesis.
[29] Mary E. Daly, *A Social and Economic History of Ireland* (Dublin, 1981); *Mayo News*, 27 May 1902.
[30] Jones, op. cit., 10

the shark with the prey'.[31] Nevertheless, despite this forthright condemnation of the rancher, Harris had, in effect, to welcome these men into the Land League, though, equally characteristically, he was soon to regret this decision. Twenty-eight years later, the *Westmeath Independent* found it necessary to repeat the sentiments of Harris: 'The Irish landlord at his worst was no greater social sore than the grazier at his best.'[32] 'Bullockdom', and its attendant snobberies were roundly denounced on the nationalist side: 'It produced the Cawstle catholics, the shoneen priest, the shoneen magistrate, the shoneen prelate, the shoneen soldier of England, the shoneen foxhunter. The bullockdom of the land has furnished raw material for educational centres of denationalisation, where recruiting goes steadily on for the ranks of a materialistic imperialism, and where imitation of an inferior race is a cult.'[33] With such invocations it was hoped to exorcize a nagging doubt. For, as ranch warrior Laurence Ginnell more honestly told a nationalist audience in 1906, the 'ranch demon' has 'friends amongst yourselves'.[34] In 1916, a New Ross labourer denounced a local Sinn Fein critic of John Redmond who was accused of 'lassoing all the surrounding farms'. But, it had to be admitted even by this critic, that the rancher in case had an impeccable political pedigree. 'But I forgot, the rancher was a Fenian fifty years ago . . . Was he in jail in poor Forster's time. Yes.'[35]

It is clear that the tendency evident even before the land league had continued: the grazing stratum had continued to draw into its ranks the ambitious small and medium farmer, not to say shopkeeper, who was often at the same time a proud nationalist. Such developments had profound implications for the social cohesion of the nationalist bloc. In 1911 there were 328,473 Irish farmers, over 100,000 of whom farmed less than 10 acres; in addition there were 450,000 others working in agriculture. Some were labourers but the majority were 'relatives assisting', 'son or daughters hanging on in the hope of inheritance, or more slightly because there was nothing else to do'. There was plenty of room for manœuvre for politicians who wished to exploit the passions of the land hungry—even priests acknowledged that their congregations 'forgot their prayers' and fell into a 'blue funk'

[31] Bew, *Land*, 102.
[32] *Westmeath Independent*, 5 January 1918.
[33] *Sinn Fein*, 2 February 1907.
[34] PRO CO 903/13/45; *Irish Times*, 15 October 1906.
[35] *New Ross Standard*, 7 January 1916.

whenever the possibility of acquiring some new land arose.[36] The landlords may well have been psychologically disoriented by the increasingly nationalist texture of Irish life: but even after the Wyndham Act of 1903 they retained an important influence on Irish agrarian affairs. Indeed, the Land Act of 1903 may actually have buttressed the positions of the landlords by making them more financially secure, enabling them to pay off debts and generally to lower their expenses.[37] As one of the Wyndham Act's sponsors, the conciliatory Earl of Dunraven wryly observed, the 1903 Act had helped to 'pluck' many of the diehard landlords 'out of ruin'.[38] However, the most notorious remnant of landlord power—the principal target from 1900 onwards of the nationalist rural rhetoric—was the 'eleven months system' an explicit form of competition in untenanted land. Untenanted land, that is to say land directly held by the landlord on which he created no formal tenancy, constituted 10.1 per cent of the total area of Irish agricultural land. It consisted mainly of demesne land or home farms adjoining it, but it also included out farms and bog and mountain tract suitable only for rough grazing. The landlords employed the eleven month period for letting this land because they were not legally bound to recognize tenant right on such holdings—the Gladstone land acts of 1870 and 1881 applied only to yearly tenancies. In periods of cattle price boom, the landlords also found that this system enabled them to charge the highest rents the market could bear. The reliance of the grazier (and shopkeeper-grazier) upon the eleven months system became all the more crucial as a result of the sharp decrease of supply in marketable land from tenants; indeed, after the 1903 Wyndham Act, the coming of peasant proprietorship effectively destroyed the market in small peasant farms. Hence the dilemma for the grazier; the UIL bitterly stigmatized the 'eleven months' man as the ally of the landlord—some, at least, of this land had its origin in sorrowful evictions and clearances in previous generations—but where else was the ambitious man, who was very often a good nationalist, to get the land from if not from the landlord? Yet despite its obvious political importance, Gwynn does not raise this issue—essentially that of class division within nationalism—at all.

[36] Daly, op. cit., 61; *Roscommon Herald*, 24 October 1910.
[37] L. P. Curtis, 'The Anglo-Irish Predicament', *Twentieth-Century Studies* No. 4, November 1970.
[38] Dunraven to William O'Brien, 11 April 1910, NLI MS 8554.

Rather more surprisingly, and rather more significantly, similar lacunae may be found in the impressive work of F. S. L. Lyons. Lyons's discussion of 'Parnellism without Parnell' is effectively circumscribed by a rather limited definition of the distinctive features of Parnellism—essentially tight party discipline;[39] whilst his magisterial biography, *John Dillon* (1968), neglected to mention either the ranch war or its leading figure, Laurence Ginnell, despite that activist's interesting association with Dillon. It remains the case, however, that our understanding of the period has been profoundly shaped by the distinguished work of the late Dr. Lyons and that of his research students. Lyons himself in two major books, Sally Warwick-Haller in her thesis on William O'Brien,[40] and A. C. Hepburn, in his study of Liberal-nationalist relations, have provided suggestive and in most instances unchallengeable analyses based on the conventional sources for Anglo-Irish political history (political correspondence, police and official reports). The present work employs the same sources. In particular, the Davitt and Dillon papers which have only recently been made freely available to scholars have been utilized—as have older but very extensive collections such as the Redmond and O'Brien manuscripts. As far as police reports are concerned, an effort has been made to go beyond the occasionally bald and over-simplified summaries of the 'Intelligence Reports' series by utilization of the Chief Secretary's Registered reports housed in Dublin Castle. As for official reports, by far the most important piece of evidence is the Royal Commission on Congestion, which ran to eleven volumes and interviewed some 570 witnesses, taking two years to complete its enquiry. The Dudley Commission, as it became known, held 116 public meetings in different parts of Ireland and asked some 60,386 questions, receiving 'by no means short answers'. Augustine Birrell, then Irish chief secretary, told the cabinet, 'it is impossible to exaggerate its intrinsic importance, it marks a clear epoch in the history of the agrarian question'.[41] The present study has, however, also sought to exploit some new sources, in particular, the national and provincial press. Over eighty newspapers were employed in the

[39] The reference here is to F. S. L. Lyons, *The Irish Parliamentary Party 1890–1910*, London, 1951. The original Faber edition was reprinted in 1975 by Greenwood Press, Westport. Conn. See especially 255–6.

[40] Sally Warwick-Haller, 'William O'Brien and the Land War in Ireland 1877–1903' (University of Kent, Ph.D., 1980).

[41] PRO Cab 37/93/94283. 'The Dudley report on congestion in Ireland', 2 June 1908.

writing of this book, the majority of them based in rural Ireland. The intention here is to set the United Irish League firmly within its domestic 'grass roots' context, to study both its resources and constraints in the hope that this will permit a fuller understanding of the evolution of Irish nationalism. Above all, then, this work is a study of 'popular' politics rather than 'high' politics. It is an analysis of the Irish movement after Parnell—Parnellism without Parnell—but it is also an analysis of the fate of the Irish agrarian radical tradition.

I

The Legacy of Parnell

It cannot be disputed by any other than an extremely ignorant person that the average British Democrat is the fattest, best clothed, best housed and best paid Democrat in the wide world . . . every additional benefit now conferred on the British Democracy is another nail in the coffin of Home Rule.

Editorial in the *Parnellite* 18 February 1895

I think we should keep clear of any charge or even criticism that might throw the unionists who are working with us back to their party allegiance. It should be left to England to snub them; that should make them Irishmen.

Count G. N. Plunkett to John Redmond, 7 March 1897,
NLI Redmond Papers, 15220(6)

ONE of the most striking features of Parnell's politics was the relationship which he consistently assumed (or hoped) to exist between the land and the national question in Ireland. As his friend Andrew Kettle recalled: 'He was always very hopeless about the older landlords ever throwing in their lot with the people of Ireland but he expected that the young men would if the land question was settled by purchase.'[1] His brother, J. H. Parnell, explained in the same vein: 'I am certain my brother, C. S. Parnell, never intended to drive anyone out of the country, not even the landlords. It is quite a different thing to cut up legally the estates of the former landlords for the people, but not to drive away the moneyed individuals.'[2] The context is clear. C. S. Parnell accepted Sir Joseph McKenna's case[3] that Ireland had been overtaxed under the Union—it was therefore both good policy and an act of restitution for the London government to support a land

[1] Andrew Kettle, *Material for Victory*, ed. L. J. Kettle, Dublin, 1958, 34.
[2] *Irish Independent*, 7 January 1910; see also Roy Foster, 'Parnell and his People: The Ascendancy and Home Rule', *Canadian Journal of Irish Studies*, vol. 6, no. 1, 1980, 105–34.
[3] NLI, 15,203, McKenna to Redmond, 25 November 1894; *IWI*, 17 October 1897.

purchase scheme which was generous both to landlord and tenant in
Ireland. As Kettle put it to Parnell: 'By this course you will settle the
Land Question and draw the landlords to your side on the national
question.'[4] In Parnell's own highly optimistic words, he hoped to
'obtain the restoration of our legislative independence ... by the
union of all classes in Ireland'.[5]

In the 1890s, after Parnell's fall and death, these themes were rather
forgotten by the leadership of the anti-Parnellite majority within Irish
nationalism. Parnell had always been an explicit reformist; in a typical
speech at Westport in 1879 he declared:

You will say perhaps that many men have said that this struggling for
concessions in the House of Commons is a demoralising thing. Now I am as
confident as I am of my own existence that if you had men of determination
representing you, you could obtain concessions (hear, hear).[6]

Adding, equally typically:

I have always noticed that the breaking down of barriers between different
classes has increased their self-respect and increased the spirit of nationality
among our people. I am convinced that nothing would more effectively
promote the cause of self-government for Ireland than the breaking down of
these barriers between different classes.[7]

Against this, John Dillon, the dominant anti-Parnellite of the 1890s,
was suspicious of any reformist intent on the part of the British
government. This was a division which had its origins in the New
Departure era of 1878–9. Dillon, it is clear, feared lest settlement of
the land question reduce the support which the Irish peasantry gave to
nationalism. This emerged with absolute clarity in 1896,[8] when the
modest[9] Tory land reform of that year was discussed in parliament.
(The incoming Conservative government had been alarmed by the fall
in land purchase applications from 4526 in 1891 to a mere 1800 in 1895.
The government decided to provide additional funds for land
purchase and to relax somewhat the existing security and credit
arrangement. It was also decided to 'facilitate land purchase by the
Congested District Board'[10] by enabling it to borrow £500,000 from

---

[4] Kettle, ibid.
[5] Paul Bew, *Land and the National Question in Ireland 1858–82*, Dublin, 1978, 152.
[6] Ibid., 61.   [7] Ibid.   [8] *IWI*, 13 June 1896.
[9] Andrew L. H. Gailey, 'The Unionist Government's Policy Towards Ireland 1895–
1905' (Cambridge University, Ph.D., 1982), 22–8.
[10] Catherine Shannon, 'Arthur Balfour and the Irish Question' (University of
Massachussets, Ph.D., 1975), 104–8

the Treasury for its work of reconstruction in the west of Ireland.)[11] Dillon's fear that Home Rule might be killed by kindness was also visible in 1898 when the Tories democratized Irish local government.[12] William O'Brien, Dillon's most important supporter, was a more complex case. In a curiously neglected speech in Dromore on 22 November 1896 O'Brien had espoused some Parnellite themes. O'Brien was careful to explain that he spoke only for himself and not for the Dillonite leadership as a whole. Referring to the overtaxation issue, he recalled that we 'are still being robbed at a rate of two and a half million pounds a year.'[13] O'Brien then broached the question of the peasantry's efforts to buy out the landlords. For O'Brien the difference between the two sides was relatively small: 'the whole difficulty is summed up in about three or four years purchase'.[14] O'Brien concluded: 'For the sake of once and for all settling this great land question and of uniting all classes of Irishmen hereafter in a great national movement (loud cheers), I cannot say that it would not be money well expended if the difference was made up out of this great national fund.'[15] But O'Brien's argument did not make much impact. The *Freeman's Journal*[16] editorial the next day devoted itself to O'Brien's meeting at Dromore—without offering any comment on his most interesting theme. It was a suggestive silence—O'Brien had acknowledged that many fellow nationalists on the platform felt that landlords should receive only a 'quit rent'. Nor was O'Brien's audience captivated. His diary records: 'Broached for the first time a theory I have long brooded upon—that the only way of settling the land question is by a State Bonus, which would cover the difference between the price the tenants could afford to pay and the price that could encourage the landlord to sell . . . People listened rather bleakly and did not in the least understand.'[17]

Such a failure to apprehend O'Brien's meaning was perhaps hardly surprising. For some months before—on 3 May 1896—O'Brien, who had taken up residence in Mayo in 1895, had begun his last great commitment to agrarian radicalism, when he made a 'strong though

[11] For a discussion of the working of this aspect of the legislation, see CAB37/62/74324, G. Wyndham, 6 October 1902. Between the purchase of the Dillon estate in 1899 and the passing of the Wyndham Act of 1903, the Board bought 43 estates at a total cost of £570,000.

[12] *Irish People*, 1 June 1907.

[13] *Freeman's Journal*, 23 November 1896.

[14] Ibid.   [15] Ibid.   [16] Ibid.

[17] *Irish People*, 7 March 1906 reprint of O'Brien's diary, 23 November 1896.

not illegal speech' at Kilmeena, Co. Mayo, calling for 'the compulsory acquisition of large grazing farms for division among small farmers'.[18] O'Brien's subsequent involvement in western agitation ensured that the theme of conciliation, barring a few hints,[19] did not really surface in his politics until 1903. From this perspective, it is clear that the legacy of Parnell's most characteristic preoccupations fell hardly suprisingly to John Redmond, the leader of the embattled Parnellite minority of constitutional nationalists.[20]

In many respects, Redmond differed from Parnell; Redmond was, for example, a devout Catholic while Parnell had been a rather casual Protestant. The scion of a Catholic gentry family which had gained success in commerce and continental military service after dispossession in the seventeenth century, Redmond could draw on a tradition of family popularity ('love of the old stock' as the phrase went) and indeed political experience which was quite unusual for a young Parnellite lieutenant.[21] One pro-Redmond poet in the Waterford press expressed this admirably: 'Why vote for Redmond? Because he comes of good old stock, that in the dark days of Irish history was kind and considerate to the workers and toilers whose destinies lay in their keeping.'[22] Recalling the fact that Redmond could count among his ancestors priests of the penal era, another local observer was to conclude: 'Is it any wonder that the Redmonds were always Irish and Catholic?'[23] Partly on account of Redmond's 'Irish' and 'Catholic' beliefs, his support for Parnell after the O'Shea divorce court revelations had suprised many contemporaries. In other important respects also, Redmond's formation had been rather different from that of Parnell. In 1882, an Australian trip impressed him deeply; he was delighted to see the Irish play such a large role in the life of the colonies and this helped to reconcile him to the British empire.[24] Redmond demanded an Irish parliament for Irish affairs only and was happy to leave all matters of foreign policy to the imperial parlia-

---

[18] PRO CO 903/5, 5
[19] *IP*, 30 September 189(.
[20] For the activities of the anti-Parnellite majority, see F. S. L. Lyons, *The Irish Parliamentary Party 1890–1910*, London, 1951, 38–89; and the same author's *John Dillon*, London, 1968, 144–206.
[21] F. S. L. Lyons stressed this point in his contribution to the seminar held on the centenary of Redmond's birth, *Irish Times*, 8 October 1956.
[22] *Waterford News and General Advertiser*, 19 December 1918.
[23] *New Ross Standard*, 15 March 1918.
[24] D. R. Gwynn, op. cit., 53–4.

ment.[25] On 26 February 1895 in Cambridge, Redmond, striking a very suggestive note, described separation as not only 'impossible'—but also, and very much more controversially, as 'undesirable'.[26] As late as June 1891 Parnell had clarified a Wicklow call for 'legitimate freedom' with the remark: 'I don't mean separation from England or anything of that kind.'[27] But he was capable of referring to the physical force tradition as 'an imperishable force which ... gives me vitality and power'.[28] Even Redmond's most extreme utterances tended to be more discreet. His most militant speech—an excited reference at Navan on 8 December 1895 to driving the English government 'bag and baggage'[29] from Ireland—in substance goes no further than the demand for Irish control of Irish affairs. In later years Redmond became even less 'republican'. In May 1908 Redmond was interviewed by A. G. Gardiner. 'Our stake in the Empire is too large for us to be detached from it,' he said, 'the Irish people peopled the waste places of Greater Britain. Our roots are in the Imperial as well as the national.'[30] In October 1910 Redmond told the New York correspondent of the *Daily Express*; 'We do not demand such complete autonomy as the British self-governing colonies possess, for we are willing to abide by any fiscal system enacted by the British government ... once we receive home rule, we shall demonstrate our imperial loyalty beyond question.'[31] But these differences in formation and political tone should not hide the fact that Redmond was, in some rather important aspects, a faithful proponent of Parnellism.

At times, this was a weakness rather than a strength of Redmond's politics. Parnell's casual and uncomprehending attitude towards Ulster Unionist resistance to Home Rule had been one of the main flaws in his strategy. In 1891, it is true, a desperately isolated and opportunist Parnell made a number of dramatic appeals to his fellow

---

[25] Ibid., 55.

[26] *Workers' Republic*, 20 August 1898.

[27] Roy Foster, *Charles Stewart Parnell: The Man and his Family*, Hassocks, 1976, 210–11

[28] Parnell's speech 10 December 1890 quoted by Fred Allan, *Irish Weekly Independent*, 8 October 1894. Allan was one of those Fenians who moved into Parnellite politics in the 1890s, in general, though as Richard Barrett remarks 'partly because of the secrecy involved—Fenian-Parnellite relations in the 1890s' are more difficult to trace than might be expected'. 'The Policies and Political Character of the Parnellite Party 1891–99' (UCD, MA, 1983), 17.

[29] PRO CO 903/5/XC/A/25371; *Daily Independent*, 9 December 1895; *Fermanagh Herald*, 4 July 1917.

[30] *Irish People*, 26 May 1908.

[31] *FJ*, 5 October 1910; *Nationality*, 6 April 1918.

nationalists to pursue a policy of genuine conciliation of Ulster
Unionism, but for the previous ten years at least, Parnell had failed to
follow this advice in his own rhetoric. Redmond was similarly
unimpressive. In his speech on the second Home Rule bill, he tended
to reduce Ulster Unionism to Orangeism (and thus greatly under-
estimate it) while at the same time arguing that Unionists were
motivated by a profoundly justified sense of insecurity as to their
ability to survive once the unfair advantages granted to them by
history were removed:

This agitation against the Bill is promoted by a small minority of the
Protestants of Ireland. Large masses of the Protestants are, no doubt,
frightened by the Bill. I do not wonder at it. They have had in their hands for
generations a monopoly of all power and place and patronage. To be born a
child of the favoured race is to be provided for by some place or position of
emolument from one's cradle.[32]

Redmond revealed his own confusion by adopting a radically different
position a few weeks later—when he argued that the resourceful Ulster
folk would dominate an autonomous Ireland. Asked about Home
Rule, he replied:

I don't believe in the continuation of the present attitude of Ulster. After the
Bill is passed she may be sulky for a time, but when she finds that nobody
wants to injure her she will rapidly fall in line and take advantage of Home
Rule, and will be the most powerful influence in the government of Ireland. *By
her superior intelligence, education and other qualities, she will rise to the top*. This talk
about rebellion is rubbish; remember only one small corner of Ulster is
Unionist. There will be no rebellion, for there will be nothing worth rebelling
against. I remember Mr Parnell once saying that, as far as he had read the
history of the world, he never knew any nation to rebel except against a *real*
grievance, and that real grievance will be absent in this case. If the Irish
Parliament began to oppress Ulster, she would be perfectly right to rebel,
otherwise, she will not be so stupid and wicked.[33]

Equally revealing here is Redmond's lengthy correspondence with
William Mather, a Lancashire liberal MP, about a self-governing
Ireland: it ranged over many matters: the police; the judiciary;
education and imperial sovereignty. But, one aspect of the Home Rule
question, the Ulster problem, was treated with surprising brevity.
Relatively early in the discussion on 23 April 1892 Mather told

[32] D. R. Gwynn, *Redmond*, 37.
[33] *Black and White* quoted in *IWI*, 5 August 1893.

Redmond that one of the Ulster Unionist leaders had conveyed to him a fear that Ulster would be 'overtaxed' to support 'feckless' expenditure in the south.[34] But Redmond seems to have regarded such fears as beneath contempt—or at least the level of serious discussion—and appears to have infected Mather with the same idea. On 28 April, he wrote to Mather: 'As to Ulster I don't consider any special safeguards necessary at all.' On 1 May Mather replied: 'You will observe I mention no safeguards for Ulster at all.'[35] And so, with only a passing reference, the difficulty which was actually to prove most fatal to the Home Rule project was quietly buried.

Redmond's insouciance is all the more remarkable when the view of one of his small band of Parnellite MPs, William Field, is recalled. Commenting on the oppressive treatment of the Parnellite minority by the nationalist majority in this period, Field stated: 'They made social and business matters so bitter that I believe at the time it would have been impossible for us to live in Ireland but for the presence of a large number of Protestants in the community.' Field had duly noted: 'I think the first lesson the Irish people have to learn is that of toleration towards one another and fair play to minorities.'[36] Another Parnellite, Dr St Laurence ffrench-Mullen had said of the bigotry borne by the Parnellite minority that it 'had certainly broadened their conception of citizenship and deepened their views as to the right of free discussion in public affairs'.[37] Redmond, of course, was well aware of the deficiencies in the Irish capacity for toleration which these comments indicated. Nevertheless, in this period, he pushed the issue to one side.

But in other more creative ways Redmond did reflect Parnell's more consistent interest in the conciliation of those Irishmen (Ulster unionists apart) who stood outside the nationalist bloc. As Justin McCarthy noted Redmond, like Parnell, belonged to 'the country gentlemen order'. This fact, and the common interest thus generated, created a bond between Parnell and the Redmonds—a bond that had its own decided political significance. Quite simply, John Redmond and his brother, William, shared with Parnell an affection for the sporting life of the Irish squire. In his last more obsessive years, Parnell's enthusiasm here waned somewhat. Although always harbouring the hope of settling at Bushey, near Bray, he was rarely on his

---

[34] NLI MS 15206(1). See also J. P. Loughlin, 'Gladstone', 510/11.
[35] Ibid.   [36] *IWI*, 8 February 1896.
[37] *IWI*, 7 July 1894.

Irish estate (preferring Mrs O'Shea's villa at Eltham) and when he did
visit, his grouse bag was more likely to be full of rocks as he searched
for precious minerals. Nevertheless, in earlier more relaxed times a
bond had been formed with the Redmonds and the others. Willie
Redmond, John's brother, has left us a poignant recollection of a
shooting party at Parnell's Wickow home:

> I shall never forget the scene, Parnell lay upon the purple heather, dreamily
> looking down into the valley, towards the old barrack, while a couple of his red
> setters lay beside him . . . I remember that morning at Parnell's place well, and
> I am glad to think that of all the men there that day, not one ever turned a
> traitor.[38]

In John Redmond's case, the social position and pleasures he shared
with Parnell had other more profound implications for his politics,
implications beyond that of mere personal loyalty. As the Liberal
writer, Harold Spender, noted with sharp insight: 'Like all landlords
(Redmond) could not entirely put aside the clan feeling for his class.
There he was a true follower of Parnell. Right through the heart of the
nationalist fight, Parnell was always held back by a strain of sympathy
for the landlords.'[39] The implications of such an attitude on
Redmond's part only became fully apparent following Gladstone's
retirement in March 1894. As the British Liberal leadership under
Lord Rosebery reduced its commitment to the Home Rule cause,
Redmond, despite his slender forces—9 Parnellite MPs against
71 anti-Parnellites—felt free to develop a distinctive conservative
brand of nationalism. Redmond launched a number of vigorous
attacks on the reformist wing of British politics. He seemed to be
indifferent to the fate of the English 'toilers' in their 'struggle for
justice'. There was a certain sanction in Parnell's early speeches,
especially before 1881, for this sort of rhetoric, but it was not the wiser
and more considered Parnellite doctrine in the view of a worried
friend, T. P. Gill. 'Speaking in this way was one of the mistakes
Parnell admitted to me and he tried to avoid it in his later speeches,'[40]
wrote Gill to Redmond. Gill warned that such insults were 'gratuitous'
and 'unnecessary' and needlessly harmed the Home Rule cause in
England. But Redmond took such reproof lightly, for he appears to

[38] Ibid., 6 October 1894.
[39] Harold Spender, 'John Redmond: An Impression', *Contemporary Review*, vol. 113,
April 1918, 375/6.
[40] Gill to Redmond, 13 October 1893, NLI MS 15190.

have somewhat incautiously convinced himself that Liberal demoralization was such that the party could not within his own lifetime win an overall majority in a general election. In March 1895, for example, Redmond claimed:

The Liberals can never get back into power in our lifetime save by the vote of Nationalist Ireland, and that being so surely it is the Liberal party who ought to seek and cultivate our good graces, and not we who ought to go cap in hand begging for a continuance of our alliance with them.[41]

This was not an isolated comment, for Redmond returned to it again, well over a year later:

We believe that hanging on to the remnant of the Liberal party at the present time—the remnant of the Liberal party, which had practically renounced Home Rule, which probably for years and years will never be returned to power again, which in any case never can be returned to power in my belief, in our lifetime except by the aid of Irish votes—that policy of sacrificing everything to cling to this alliance is . . . a base . . . (and) foolish policy.[42]

These are dramatic but misleading declarations. They greatly underestimated the potential appeal of a revitalized British Liberalism. But on the basis of them Redmond drew up policy recommendations for nationalist Ireland. In general terms, he rejected the argument that the Irish cause and the cause of the 'British democracy' were identical. In a more particular sense, Redmond rejected the view that the Irish ought to support an immediate campaign to break the veto power of the House of Lords which stood in the way both of Home Rule and much progressive British legislation.

The most formal exposition of Redmond's view may be found in an article 'Home Rule: what has become of it?' he contributed to the *Nineteenth Century* in November 1894. It is a most lucid presentation of the essential points of the Parnellite case. In one graphic passage, Redmond explained his break with the fundamental assumption of much nationalist thought and practice since, at least, 1881: this was the assumption of an underlying unity linking the causes of the British democracy and Irish nationalism. It is true that Parnell gave the notion prominence in early 1881 for largely tactical reasons as a means of avoiding a revolutionary course of action.[43] Nevertheless, he could

---

[41] *IWI*, 16 March 1895.
[42] Ibid., 12 September 1896.
[43] Conor Cruise O'Brien, *Parnell and His Party 1880—1890*, Oxford, 1957, remains the best analysis of this conjuncture.

only have done so because the concept had reasonably wide acceptance. From 1882 onwards, there was a very obvious participation by
many Irish MPs in the struggle for 'progress' in British politics.[44]
Redmond now turned his back on this tradition with a vengeance. In
his view, it threatened to make the majority of Irish MPs a mere extension of an incoherent British Liberalism. Above all, he rejected the
burgeoning thesis that the struggle against the reactionary House of
Lords and the struggle for Home Rule were linked. For Redmond,
such a view entirely lacked basic political realism: 'Does anyone really
believe that without another revolution, the House of Lords could be
abolished within the next fifty years? And does anyone really believe in
the possibility of another revolution within the same period directed
against a fundamental part of a constitution under which English
liberty has been irrevocably established?'[45]

The great strong point in Redmond's article is apparent. He
insisted on the overriding need to achieve much greater explicit
support for Home Rule from both British politicians and the
electorate. 'What power has the House of Lords to resist the will of the
majority of the people of the United Kingdom in that matter or any
other, provided only that the expression of the people's will in
Parliament is the result of a clear mandate from the constituencies?'[46]
He answered his own question: 'It has none, and what is more has
never permanently or even for a long time persisted in the exercise of
such a power in the case supposed.'[47]

In Ireland, the anti-Parnellite majority argued bitterly against
Redmond. They pointed out that regrettable though the evolution of
Liberal policy might be, the only alternative was a Tory government,
unalterably opposed to the claims of Ireland. Granted Liberal
weaknesses on Home Rule, what was to be gained by savaging the
government? Would it not open the way for a repressive Tory government? Redmond had a number of answers to these questions, but
significantly they were not entirely consistent. On occasion Redmond
took refuge in a wild optimism: 'If the Tory party got into power I am
not so sure they would continue in their virtuous refusal of Home
Rule,'[48] Redmond declared in September 1894. In sharp contrast,
Redmond was capable of embracing a *politique du pire* in which 'Tory

[44] Alan O'Day, *The English Face of Irish Nationalism: Parnellite Involvement in British Politics*, Dublin, 1977, *passim*.
[45] 'Home Rule: What has become of it?' reprinted in *IWI*, 8 November 1894.
[46] Ibid.   [47] Ibid.   [48] *IWI*, 8 September 1894.

repression' was confidently invited, as it merely gave new vigour to the nationalist movement.[49]

For those who were unimpressed by this last alternative, Redmond offered a third and rather more low-key version of the nature of a future Tory government.[50] In this somewhat more realistic prospectus 'a Conservative government would not mean coercion because there would be no-one to coerce'.[51] It is obvious, of course, that Redmond's predictions were contradictory: the Tories might bring in Home Rule, they might repress Ireland or finally they might do neither and, perhaps, adopt a mildly conciliatory policy. But such inconsistency did not worry Redmond: all he had to argue was that any conceivable Tory government would be less debilitating for the Irish cause than a Roseberyite one.

In June 1895 these matters were brought to the test. The Rosebery government unexpectedly resigned, the deeply divided Liberals were defeated by the Tories in the ensuing general election. With the unexpected appointment of the 'dry, serious, rather academic'[52] Gerald Balfour to the office of chief secretary for Ireland, the Tories attempted a constructive Irish policy. Redmond welcomed the new approach which was apparent as early as the beginning of 1896. Reforms would never sap nationalist sentiment and were beneficial in themselves, in his view. Dillon, following Justin McCarthy's resignation before Parliament, was now installed as the leader of the majority. For Dillon the new Tory policy was an insidious attempt to 'kill home rule with "kindness".' It was a critical, even fundamental, divergence of outlook. But it was not the only issue to separate the two Irish leaders. For Redmond was attempting to forge alliances with forces in Irish society which Dillon regarded with the deepest suspicion.

In this, lies the final and decisive element in Redmond's strategy. His objective was clearly to reduce those tensions between Irishmen, more especially, in his perception, southern Irishmen, the existence of which gave so many British voters a reason (or excuse) to refuse Home Rule. It was a generous policy directed towards changing the whole terms of debate on the Home Rule issue. The dominant nationalist

[49] *IWI*, 8 November 1894.

[50] *IWI*, 14 July 1894. As in his remarks in support of J. H. Parnell's candidature for Meath, *IWI*, 6 June 1894.

[51] *IWI*, 12 September 1896. In this speech Redmond recalls his earlier predictions.

[52] Andrew L. H. Gailey, 'The Unionist Government Policy Towards Ireland 1895–1905' (Cambridge University, Ph.D., 1982), 18; Gailey's thesis, 9–99, gives the best analysis of Balfour's objectives.

strategy effectively accepted the existing definition of the issue, but sought to achieve victory by skilful manipulation of a favourable parliamentary balance of forces. Redmond, by contrast, sought to achieve Home rule by effecting a shift in English public (not just parliamentary) opinion. This was to be achieved by creating first a new and harmonious era of co-operation between different creeds and classes in Ireland.

Realignments (i) Sir Horace Plunkett

In the mid 1890s Parnellism was firmly placed in a ghetto within Irish politics. While he might extract amusement and a certain amount of comfort from the quarrels which wracked the anti-Parnellite majority—dividing the followers of Parnell's most bitter opponent, the 'clerical' Tim Healy, from the rest—Redmond knew that it was necessary to build up new alliances. As part of this strategy, Redmond became very interested in the manifold activities of a remarkable and engaging man, Sir Horace Plunkett, who represented the tory and unionist villadom of South Dublin in parliament. Since at least 1891, Horace Plunkett, then chairman of the congested districts board, had tried to open up lines of communication to prominent nationalists. He sought—through T. P. Gill—to have discussions with John Dillon on the congested districts question. Gill wrote to Dillon: 'It is his desire to see the problem of the congested districts approached as a neutral question on which Irishmen of different political convictions might come to some common view . . . I know this to be with him a sincere desire; he is an Irishman most earnestly devoted to the idea of doing good to his country uninfluenced by any political bias.' Gill went on to assure Dillon that he would have more in common politically and personally with Plunkett 'than perhaps either of you is likely at first . . . to imagine'.[53] But such optimism was not to be justified: Dillon's relationships with Plunkett were destined to be cool and distant and finally, openly hostile. But having failed to strike up a friendship with Dillon, Plunkett succeeded with Redmond.[54]

[53] Gill to Redmond, 14 August 1891, TCD Dillon papers 6754/536.
[54] Gill and Plunkett's historical reputations have suffered because of the brilliant satire at their expense to be found in George Moore, *Hail and Farewell*. Suggestive though it is on points of personality (self-importance in particular) it has to be said however that Moore is maddeningly vague on general questions of politics, see notably, his non-discussion, given a perfect opportunity, of western agrarian radicalism, page 566, of the 1975 Colin Smythe edition.

Somewhat surprisingly Redmond in 1895 urged a rising young journalist, E. Haviland Burke, editor of the *Parnellite*, not to oppose Plunkett's election for a South Dublin seat. Recalling the incident five years later, Burke wrote to William O'Brien: 'Redmond who didn't want Horace Plunkett opposed, never forgave me for persisting in the candidature—at the urgent invitation of the South Dublin National Representation Association—despite his advice to the contrary.'[55] Burke fought the election but was easily outpolled in a Unionist stronghold. Inevitably, though, Burke resented Redmond's action. In 1898–9, he was one of those Parnellites whose apparent disloyalty was to place severe strain on Redmond's leadership. It is clear therefore that Redmond took great risks for a political opponent, Plunkett, but why should he do so?

Plunkett was undoubtedly a unionist but he was committed to the improvement of Irish social conditions. Plunkett argued that Ireland's problems were essentially economic and not political, a case many nationalist found it difficult to accept. But Plunkett was still a difficult man to pigeonhole;[56] he did after all support some rather unconventional causes (for a Unionist MP for South Dublin)—the GAA, the Gaelic League and the campaign for a Catholic university. In August 1895 Plunkett produced 'a proposal affecting the general welfare of Ireland'. In this statement, Plunkett called for politicians of all parties to work together for the mutual and social advancement of the Irish people. Plunkett suggested that a committee should meet during the parliamentary recess, consisting of representatives nominated by the various tendencies, together with other prominent men who might be able to make a useful contribution. Plunkett received support from Redmond, some liberal Home Rulers and even some liberal Unionists. He was bitterly assailed both by mainstream Unionism and by mainstream nationalism. This did not stop the Recess Committee doing useful work as a pressure group. Redmond's Parnellite colleague, William Field MP,[57] amongst others had long been arguing the case for an Irish department of agriculture, and the Recess Committee made the establishment of such a department its prime

---

[55] E. H. Burke to W. O'Brien, 26 June 1900, O'Brien MSS, University College, Cork, AKA 59.
[56] P. Bolger, 'Horace Plunkett: An Anglo-American Irish Patriot', *Irish Times*, 29 March 1982. See also Cyril Ehrlich, 'Horace Plunkett and Agricultural Reform' in J. M. Goldstrom and L. A. Clarkson (eds.), *Irish Population, Economy and Society: Essays in Honour of the late K. H. Connell*, Oxford, 1981, 271–86.
[57] *IWI*, 8 January 1896.

objective. In 1899 they succeeded when the Department of Agriculture and Technical Instruction was set up with Plunkett as its head.

Redmond's collaboration with Plunkett was inevitably a rather fraught one, especially as Plunkett had a close political relationship with Gerald Balfour.[58] There were important problems of tone involved. Redmond, for example, as part of this enterprise had felt it necessary to put his name to a public statement which declared that the Irish farmer's methods were the 'most simple and barbarous in Western Europe.'[59] Words like these stung; indeed, almost a quarter of a century later, Redmond was still being upbraided for this observation.[60] What was, from one point of view, a simple social science observation, was from another point of view an insult to Ireland. Such an apparently 'neutral' conception as the improvement of agricultural productivity had its critics. As Redmond acknowledged at the beginning of 1897 in a *Nineteenth Century* article:

Even amongst the supporters of the Independent Nationalist or Parnellite party in this country there seems to be a few—a very few, however, as was shown in the recent convention of the party in Dublin—who fear those proposals on the ground that, at least, the improvements in agricultural methods with which some of these proposals are concerned would, in the end, lead to an increase in rents rather than anything else.[61]

Redmond here admitted the obstacles his policy faced—even amongst the Parnellite faithful. He had, indeed, been prepared to go to considerable lengths to impress Plunkett. There were many who doubted the wisdom of his strategy. His critics (notably John Dillon) asked—what was the point of trying to cover up essential political divisions? The spurious 'goodwill' generated by these bouts of co-operation was bound to disappear when the 'real' question of Home Rule again came on the agenda. Redmond replied that the 'real' question was not now on the agenda and was not likely to be so for the foreseeable future. In the meantime, it was worth trying to work with the more patriotic amongst the unionists. Nobody could be sure that such a policy would be successful. But there was no guarantee that the Dillonite alternative would work either. Indeed, there was another area of work where in Redmond's view, the possibilities for co-

[58] Gailey, op. cit., 69–73.
[59] Quoted in *Nationality*, 4 April 1917.
[60] Ibid.
[61] 'Ireland and the Next Session', *Nineteenth Century*, vol. XLI, January 1897, 109.

operation with non-Home Rulers was even greater, that of the agitation against Ireland's overtaxation by England.

Realignments (ii) Financial Relations

In 1893, partly to overcome Irish doubts about the financial clauses of the Home Rule bill, Gladstone had promised a royal commission on the controversial issue of Anglo-Irish financial relations. In 1894, this body was appointed and contained Irish Unionists, Parnellites, anti-Parnellites and some English financial experts. Two years later, the report appeared. It appeared to indicate clearly that Ireland had been significantly overtaxed under the Union. During the course of the evidence, Thomas Sexton, the Irish party's chief financial expert,[62] had even managed to extract an admission from Sir Edward Hamilton, assistant secretary to the Treasury, that England's interest had been 'dominant'[63] in taxation policy. Despite this, or perhaps because of it, Hamilton disputed in a cabinet paper, the Commission's results: 'consisting as it did of eight Irishmen of various shades of opinion, of six Englishmen and Scotchmen with Home Rule proclivities more or less pronounced, and of only one Unionist from Great Britain'.[64] But, as Hamilton, was forced to admit: 'The general conclusion which the finding of the Commission will be popularly said to have established is that Ireland is being annually overcharged by two or three millions.'[65] The Irish public reaction was simple: the national case had been validated by expert opinion. The Parnellites were jubilant. Parnell himself had stressed the issue, indeed had foreshadowed the results of the commission as one enthusiastic writer, C. H. Oldham, pointed out.[66] Sexton apart, the Parnellites felt they had fought the case much more systematically than the anti-Parnellites. They might expect to reap some political reward. Furthermore, here again as in the department of agriculture issue, was a basis for co-operation with non-nationalists. If Redmond had not had that thought already, it was put in his head in early 1897 by the veteran financial relations campaigner, Sir Joseph McKenna, who reminded Redmond:

---

[62] PRO Cab 37/33/7. Memorandum from the Committee of the Irish Party of Ireland on Imperial Charges 13 January 1893.

[63] *Nationality*, 12 May 1917.

[64] PRO Cab 37/42/37, 30 September 1896. Remarks on the Reports received from the Royal Commissioners who were appointed to enquire into the financial relations between Ireland and Britain.

[65] Ibid.

[66] *IWI*, 7 October 1897.

'Butt and Parnell were amazed at the case I made out *and of the hold I
had got of the intelligent Irish Tories* as represented by the *Express* and the
Irish Times.'[67] But, of course, the Parnellite leadership had viewed the
question in this way since 1893.[68]

During 1896 public meetings were held all over Ireland to protest
against overtaxation. All classes and creeds (including R. R. Kane,
Grand Master of the Belfast Orangemen)[69] happily joined in to
denounce the London Treasury. In February 1897, when John
Redmond returned from an American speaking tour, he found that the
agitation had entered a new phase. An all-Ireland Committee was
formed, which to force the government's hand, summoned a conference of Irish parliamentarians to discuss policy. The circular calling
for a conference had the names of E. J. Saunderson (Unionist),
Plunkett, Redmond and T. M. Healy. The O'Conor Don, the flower
of the Roscommon Catholic gentry, a possessor of mildly progressive
views who had become a critic of nationalism in the 1880s, also was
actively involved in the new campaign. John Dillon, now the leader of
the Irish party following Justin McCarthy's retirement, remained
aloof however. Dillon did not sign the circular though it is a sign of a
certain unease that he did attend the convention. Having been too
carping and hesitant (in Redmond's view) Dillon characteristically
was now too impetuous. Redmond had already fired a warning shot.
Speaking in Dublin in February 1897, he had said: 'I think that the
chief danger of the situation is lest men, by making extravagant
demands or by wild talk should frighten or scare away those Irishmen
who, differing from us on other questions, are willing on this one at
any rate to do their duty to their country.'[70] There is little doubt that
here Redmond had Dillon's likely interventions in mind. Against this
conception, Redmond stated his own: 'We desire that Irishmen of all
creeds and classes and parties will act as one in this financial matter;
and to that end I am personally willing to make almost any sacrifice
that can be asked from me.'[71]

But John Dillon was not willing to make similar sacrifices. He
attempted to force the conference on a collision course with the Tory

[67] McKenna to Redmond, 27 February 1897, NLI MS 15203.
[68] See *IWI* editorial, 7 November 1893.
[69] *IWI*, 15 May 1897.
[70] *IWI*, 20 February 1897. For a sympathetic account of Dillon's views, see F. S. L.
Lyons, *John Dillon*, 177–8.
[71] Ibid.

government, demanding early legislation to implement the report. The other main parties—unionists as well as Parnellites—did not see the need to be so assertive. Dillon, in response, withdrew from the united campaign; this fact, and the divisions generated by his tactics, prevented the emergence of a united Irish voice just at the moment when it had seemed most likely, thus making it easier for the government to procrastinate. John Redmond was deeply frustrated— but he remained convinced of the need to maintain his conciliatory policy.

Realignments (iii) Local Government Reform

Serious as they had been, the differences between Dillon and Redmond were soon to be put into even sharper relief. Redmond had invited the Tory government to proceed with its experiment. Reforms would be good in themselves and do nothing to weaken Irish nationalism, but by March 1897 he was declaring himself disappointed. At a meeting of the Central Branch of the Irish National League Redmond argued that it was proving 'impossible' for the government to carry out its remedial programme.[72] But shortly afterwards, in May 1897, Gerald Balfour opportunistically acted to end a parliamentary blockade by offering a genuinely far-reaching reform[73]—the establishment of a complete system of local government by elective bodies in Ireland in place of the grand jury system which still kept the country's local affairs in the control of the landowners. The government simultaneously offered the Irish landlords a massive subsidy of the rates[74]—a move which, according to Dillon's supporters, 'bought off' Irish Unionist opposition on the financial relations question.[75] Dillon was hostile, apparently fearing yet again that such a reform might undermine nationalism.[76] By the August of 1898 Dillon had modified his original hostility and was prepared to support the new legislation. But by this time he had had been outflanked by Redmond (and the

---

[72] *IWI*, 1 April 1897.

[73] For the precise nature of the Tory Government's calculations, see Andrew Gailey, 'Unionist rhetoric and Irish local government reform, 1895–9', *Irish Historical Studies*, Vol. XXIV, No. 93, May 1984, 52–84. On page 64 Gailey writes: 'Notwithstanding the gloss of statesmanship that the local government bill later acquired, it remained first and foremost the minimum compromise to resolve a particular local political confrontation.'

[74] Gailey, op. cit., 62.

[75] *Weekly Freeman*, 21 September 1907 ed.

[76] *IP*, 1 June 1907.

individualistic Tim Healy supported Redmond on this) who had been enthusiastic from the start. The Parnellite press, taking its cue from the leader, had also been jubilant. The *Irish Weekly Independent* editorial was almost delirious: 'unlike most measures meant to reform abuses venerable with age, it is as good as was expected and that is saying a good deal'.[77] This was only a specimen of the praise heaped on the bill, later described by Redmond as working a 'social revolution', smashing the remnants of ascendancy power while making the 'mass of the Irish people master of all finance and of all the local affairs of Ireland'.[78] But it was not just that the Parnellites liked the measure, they felt that it opened up the way for further important realignments in Irish politics.

In 'A hint for the landlords' the *Irish Weekly Independent* editorial at the end of May 1897 pointed out the implications of Balfour's proposed local reforms which had been announced in the House of Commons a few days before: the British government had decisively broken with the Irish landlords. One of their last privileges was now to be removed. It was time surely for the landlords to ponder on this development. Then in a remarkably generous statement, the Parnellite journal's editorial made an offer, which at the same time served to demarcate Parnellism from 'Dillonism'. Acknowledging that landlords were not likely to become political nationalists, the editorial none the less asked them to consider their children's future.

All we say is that Ireland needs their (the landlords) services as men of intelligence and culture, and if they give proof that, with the abolition of their privileges, they will cease to be "an English Garrison" . . . as they had been rightly described in the past . . . they will find that they will ultimately gain the confidence of the people, and they will fill by popular election the places which many of them occupy today through the denial of those rights which the people of England and Scotland fully enjoy. We have no sympathy for those who preach the doctrine that all that the Landlords deserve of Ireland is a single ticket to Holyhead.[79]

The editorial concluded with a plea to the landlords to play their part in freeing Ireland from 'unjust burdens' and 'developing her resources'. There is no question here that the *Independent*'s line was also Redmond's. It had also, of course, been Parnell's. One of his last

---

[77] *IWI*, 26 February 1898.
[78] Hansard, 21 March 1898 col. 450–1.
[79] *IWI*, 29 May 1897.

important parliamentary speeches before the split had called on the landlords to play a key role in the social regeneration and political leadership of Ireland.[80] Redmond was to repeat these points in Parliament himself, in a most significant speech of March 1898. He denounced the origins and history of Irish landlordism—Parnell had been right to challenge the system—but the present generation of landlords were not to blame, a fact which the 'bulk of the Irish people' appreciated.

After all, these landlords are Irishmen. They are mostly men of education and ability. While we have waged war against a system, I believe the great bulk of the Irish people never at any time desired to drive any class of their fellow countrymen from the shores of Ireland. So far from desiring to ruin them individually, I do not hestitate to say that I believe it would be a wise and blessed thing for Ireland to agree to any financial arrangement by which they could transfer their estates to the people upon such terms as would enable them to retain sufficient, at any rate, of their nominal income to enable them to remain in Ireland to take their proper place among the people. For my part, these are the views that I entertain, and have always entertained, upon this matter.[81]

The friendly attitude of the Parnellites towards the landlords was not without its risks. It attracted much sarcastic comment in the anti-Parnellite press. The *Roscommon Herald*, a paper controlled by Jasper Tully, MP for Leitrim South, duly noted that Willy Redmond and Horace Plunkett had brought in a bill to prevent the Irish postmasters sending game by post during the close season. It was easy enough for Tully to puncture Willy's aristocratic pretensions: 'Mr Redmond wants thus to pose as a great sporting character, though as everyone knows, his grouse moor would not be big enough to sod a lark.'[82] But such satire on its own would have been tolerable.

The Parnellites faced deeper problems as 1898 came to an end. Inevitably, the sheer misery of the continued disunion in Irish politics, highlighted by the 1898 centenary celebrations, had forced certain prominent Parnellites to suggest a reunion with Dillon and his forces—Timothy Harrington, a Dublin Parnellite MP, was particularly active here. Normally this was easily enough handled. The Parnellite MPs—William Field, or William Corbett,[83] perhaps

---

[80] Bew, *Parnell*, 123–4.
[81] Hansard, 21 March 1898 cols. 450–1.
[82] *Roscommon Herald*, 12 April 1898.
[83] *IWI*, 8 February 1896.

Willie Redmond[84] or if it was really necessary, as in February 1897, John Redmond[85] himself would squash such moves. But should the growing desire for nationalist unity become linked to discord on policy questions within the Parnellite party, then the whole basis of a separate Parnellite party might be undermined. In the *Black and White* interview, Redmond had claimed that 'the Irish are naturally much more conservative than the English.'[86] Such a statement was only true, if true at all, if it was presumed that the Irish tradition of agrarian radicalism was dead. Barring some local conflicts, including one that had particularly involved Parnellite forces on the Roscommon estate of diehard peer Lord De Freyne,[87] this tradition had been rather dormant since the collapse of the Plan of Campaign in 1891. But its sudden revival in the far west of Ireland in the late autumn of 1898 was to pose severe problems for John Redmond and his 'moderate' political strategy.

[84] *IWI*, 1 February 1896.
[85] *IWI*, 20 February 1897.
[86] Reprinted in *IWI*, 5 August 1893.
[87] *IWI*, 11 November 1895, 23 November 1895.

2

Unity from Below? The United Irish League 1898–1900

In certain Nationalist circles, a concerted and determined effort is
being made to treat the Irish land agitation as a thing of the past ... I do
not wish to attack their policy with any language of bitterness. But I do
propose to prove that whatever else it may be, it is not Parnellism. For
the sake of my argument I could even admit that it had a thousand
merits. But it is not Parnellism.

E. Haviland Burke, 'Parnell's Land Policy', *Weekly Freeman*,
6 January 1900.

'THE peculiar conditions of the western problem were then as little
known over three-fourths of Ireland, or even by five-sixths of the Irish
party, as the geography of mid-Africa ... The peculiar western
meaning of the shibboleth 'The Land for the People' had for a
moment blazed forth at the onset of the Land League movement; but
after the brief career of that organisation, the county of Mayo had
subsided for many years into a condition of listlessness for which the
political struggle for a Parliament in Dublin had only a distant and
somewhat ghostly interest.'[1] William O'Brien's words describing Irish
opinion in the mid-1890s provide the essential background for the
United Irish League organization launched in Mayo in 1898. For what
had been the peculiar western meaning of the shibboleth the 'land for
the people'? As early as the Land League movement of 1879–82, the
language of agrarian protest in Mayo had revealed an awareness of a
concrete fact: that the bulk of poor western peasantry, even if they
were given their land rent free, faced a life of poverty and hardship.
These people felt that they needed more land. But where were they to
get it?

In the Land League era it was easy enough to define the principal
enemy—'landlordism'. In the words of John Fitzgibbon, one of

[1] *An Olive Branch in Ireland*, London, 1910, 86.

William O'Brien's most important recruits to the UIL, the bulk of the people in 1879–82 saw that the landlords were 'a small fraction of the community differing in class, feelings and opinions from the vast majority of the nation, and what the country required was a large increase in the occupying owners'.[2]

As late as May 1898, at a Westport meeting, William O'Brien offered a description of the landlord bloc from a hostile nationalist perspective:

My friends, there is no use in shutting our eyes to the fact that as to the enormous majority of these Cromwellian strangers they are as much foreigners in Ireland today, they are as bitter enemies of our people and all their aspirations as when they first came over . . . And why are they to this day acting as a mere English garrison in Ireland? . . . Why take the county of Mayo, take the foreign garrison of gentlemen who call themselves the loyal minority . . . they are just 4000 persons out of a population of more than 200,000 and yet these 4000 persons have got the land, all the wealth, all the office, and all the power in their hands.[3]

But a major scheme of land redistribution inevitably threatened the interests not just of these 'alien' landlords—a small and isolated minority—but also of prominent local Catholic and nationalist figures, for example, James Daly, in the eyes of many the real father of the Land League,[4] or J. J. Louden,[5] chairman of the first Land League branch—men who had large grazing interests. The interests of the small men of the west also clashed with the (hesitantly defined) objectives of the Land League leadership as in 1880 when they set about attempting to build a truly national organization embracing the more prosperous farmers of the south and east.[6] When, during 1880, the League opted for an offensive war against landlordism in alliance with the strong farmers, the small western farmers were doomed to become the victims not the victors of the 'Land League revolution'.[7] Mayo, the birthplace of the Land League, was ironically the county which was to be most profoundly disappointed by its results. They voted with their

[2] Royal commission on congestion in Ireland: appendix to the fifth report, minutes of evidence and documents relating thereto, 141 (C3629), HC 1908, VI, 18439.

[3] *Connaught Telegraph*, 29 May 1898.

[4] J. Lee, *The Modernisation of Irish Society 1848—1918*, Dublin, 1973, 69–70.

[5] Don Jordon, 'Land and Politics in the West of Ireland: County Mayo 1846–82', unpublished Ph.D. thesis (University of California, Ph.D.), 160.

[6] Op. cit., 351.

[7] Ibid.

feet. In 1883, 7,831 persons emigrated—the highest number since the famine.[8]

In 1896 and 1897 the potato crop in the west was a poor one. Considerable bodies of people were forced to exist on insufficient and unwholesome food. The cabinet was told in November 1897:

The Irish government have received careful and detailed reports from the Inspectors of the Local Government Board, and also from the Constabulary on the harvest and on the condition and prospects of the poorer class as affected in particular by the partial failure of the potato crop.

The result of these reports is to show that while the cry of famine raised in the newspapers was premature and greatly exaggerated there will be an amount of distress in certain of the western parts of the island beyond the resources of the ordinary Poor Law to deal with. Speaking broadly, the year will probably be a worse one than in 1894/5, but not so bad as 1890/1.[9]

Commenting on the alleged inadequacy of the government relief efforts—which was pointedly contrasted with William O'Brien's personal generosity—the *Connaught Telegraph* made the inevitable historical allusions: 'It is the same old story of fifty years ago when the cruel and callous government of the day allowed the people to be decimated by famine; it is the same story of hundred years ago when our fathers rose against tyranny and oppression.'[10] The material and ideological conditions clearly existed to provide the basis for a movement of protest. The parliamentary attention given to western distress—though at first the government dismissed the nationalist's remedies[11]—stimulated the selfconsciousness of the area. Given the local circumstances—and the perception of them—inevitably such a movement would be organized around the explicit theme 'that the grazing industry is the curse and ruination of the west of Ireland and must, at all cost, be got rid of'.[12] This was the stated objective of William O'Brien's United Irish League, when O'Brien, three years a resident in Mayo, began to organize in early 1898. In late January of that year, O'Brien managed to tempt both John Dillon and the 'nominal' Parnellite, Timothy Harrington, down to Westport to launch

---

[8] Ibid.

[9] PRO Cab 37/45/41, Memorandum on Relief of Distress in Ireland. Gerald Balfour, 2 November 1897.

[10] *Connaught Telegraph*, 19 February 1898.

[11] F. S. L. Lyons, *Dillon*, London, 1968, 180.

[12] Jordan, 364.

the new body. This was not the first time Parnellite and anti-Parnellite had stood together on an agrarian platform—it had happened in Roscommon in 1895—but it was still a relatively good omen. Also, it is worth noting of the Westport meeting that one of the major speeches came from an important local priest, Canon Greally of Newport. It was a satisfactory start but not a brilliant one. The *Connaught Telegraph* commented with some sobriety (by nationalist press standards) that the Westport meeting 'could compare favourably in numbers and interest with any held in Mayo for years'.[13] Following the usual pious calls for self-determination and unity, the key resolution passed by the meeting was a third: 'The most effective means of preventing the frequent cries of distress and famine in this so-called congested district would be the breaking up of the large grazing estates with which the district is cursed and the pattern of them among the small landlords, who were driven on to the bog and mountains to make room for the sheep and bullocks of English and Scotch adventurers and Irish grabbers.'[14]

The United Irish League: Tactics and Strategy

If William O'Brien had expected that Dillon and Harringtons' appearance on his Westport platform signalled a firm commitment to the cause of the UIL, he was to be sorely disappointed. Dillon, apparently fearing arrest,[15] would do nothing that might endanger the increasingly demoralized parliamentary movement. O'Brien felt that the rejuvenation and reunification of Irish politics could only come from below; only the enthusiasm generated by a new grass roots struggle could dispel the torpor of the 1890s. In consequence, the United Irish League was very much one man's creation.

Part of the reason for this lay in the fact that the old Land League cadres had mostly dispersed. By 1898, Patrick Egan, the League's former treasurer, had been appointed as United States Ambassador to Chile, even though the British suspected him of complicity in the horrible Phoenix Park murders of 1882.[16] Thomas Brennan, the League's secretary, and suspected of involvement in the same crime, was a successful businessman in Omaha, Nebraska.[17] P. J. Sheridan,

---

[13] *Connaught Telegraph*, 5 February 1898.
[14] Ibid.
[15] F. S. L. Lyons, *The Irish Parliamentary Party*, London, 1951, 72.
[16] Davitt, *Fall of Feudalism*, New York, 1904, 227.
[17] *WF*, 18 January 1913.

one of the League's most famous organizers, now ran his own ranch near Denver, Colorado.[18] Malachy Michael O'Sullivan, assistant secretary, perhaps the most choleric revolutionary of all, revealed himself to a somewhat surprised John Redmond as 'a staid silver haired Dominican father' in 1896; also living in Denver.[19] Only James Lynam, aged fifty-eight, of the old Land League organizers re-appeared as a UIL organizer.[20] These 'militants' were irreplaceable: O'Brien was very much on his own. He gave a heroic performance, albeit one largely confined to the county of Mayo.

The only Irish leader of national importance who was prepared to work closely with William O'Brien was Michael Davitt. O'Brien's diaries in these early weeks pay tribute also to two local Mayo figures: one was John O'Donnell, aged twenty-five, the son of a Westport small farmer and a new recruit to politics, and the other, James Daly, aged fifty-eight, a veteran land leaguer. In his book *Recollections* published in 1905, William O'Brien described Parnell as a 'man who bore the battle on his single shield'.[21] In the early months of 1898 O'Brien felt with some justice that he was cast in a similar role. For the first six months, O'Brien did the bulk of the public speaking, organizing—and thanks to his marriage to a wealthy woman in 1890— he bore the expenses of the new movement. Yet O'Brien's isolation was not due simply to the dissolution of the old League leadership. He also faced a deeper problem; a profound evasiveness amongst even sympathetic nationalist cadres concerning the ideal of land redistribu- tion.

This is the point which may be illustrated further by looking at O'Brien and his closest aides in early 1898; for here in Mayo if anywhere was the last principled redoubt of Irish agrarian radicalism. Let us take the case of John O'Donnell. Was it pure coincidence, the police asked, that O'Donnell's cousin had been an unsuccessful applicant for that Cultrain grazing farm which had been the subject of much of O'Donnell's angry rhetoric?[22] James Daly, O'Brien's other close Mayo-based supporter, was an even more suggestive case. Although a grazier himself, Daly was a rigorous defender of Mayo's small farmers against encroachment on their lands by greedy grazing

[18] *IWI*, 20 February 1897.
[19] Ibid.
[20] PRO CO 904/10, 139–42.
[21] *Recollections*, London, 1905, 334.
[22] PRO CO 903/8, 155.

farmers. 'He shared with many subsequent Irish politicians an Arcadian vision of tillage farming in pre-famine Ireland and regularly called for grazing farms to be distributed into fifty acre tillage farms.'[23] At Keelogues in 1898, this contradiction exploded in an almost suicidal fashion, when James Daly went so far as to advocate the killing of graziers. Had Daly's advice been taken it would not have gone well for him. As the Royal Irish Constabulary report drily noted: 'He holds several large grazing farms and shows no inclination to give them up.'[24] With a genial sanity, the Mayo peasantry ignored Daly's bloodthirsty advice but they did often interrupt his speeches with reminders that his large holdings did not go unnoticed. Even much more suggestive perhaps was the case of James Daly's brother, Bernard Daly JP, who was one of the largest graziers in Ireland, holding some fourteen farms in Mayo, King's County and Westmeath. Of these at least four were in the Ballinrobe area, including Captain Boycott's farm at Lough Mask which had been the centre of one of the great Land League fights.[24] To complicate the case, part of Bernard Daly's land had been rented by the O'Hara family of Shrule—the O'Haras had been evicted in August 1881 in the course of the Land League crisis with which, of course, Michael Davitt had been so intimately associated. In most instances—as, for example, in a Maryborough speech of August 1902[25]—Davitt stressed the importance of those 'historic holdings' of evicted tenants which were still vacant after two decades. In 1900 the O'Haras were still seeking reinstatement and naturally enough regarded Bernard Daly as the worst sort of land grabber. Davitt might have been expected to follow suit—instead, he denounced Bernard's local critics and enjoyed openly friendly relations with him.[26] All this occurred on the basis of the insubstantial[27] promise from Bernard Daly to surrender his grazing lands!

Such reservation and ambiguity applied even more strongly to the clerical leadership. Formally, once again the clergy were hostile to the grazing system. It was this system which allegedly had banished the Irish to the corrupt and irreligious environments of the cities of

[23] Jordan, op. cit., 270.
[24] PRO CO 903/9, 157. For the definitive account of the Boycott affair, see Jordan, 'Land and Politics', 315–25.
[25] *IP*, 23 August 1902.
[26] *Ballinrobe Chronicle*, 22 October 1898. See also O'Brien's *An Olive Branch*, 115, and his diary 21 October 1898, reprinted in the *Irish People*, 23 March 1907.
[27] PRO CO 903/8, 68; SPO Crimes Branch Special 1904, 29357/S.

America and England. But despite this formal stance, it was very noticeable that the Catholic clergy 'on the ground' were rather reserved in their attitude towards the UIL programme—certainly as compared with their attitudes during the heady days of the Land League. As before, where the League established itself as a force the clergy felt it necessary to come to the front.[28] As before, some young curates actually made the running. But this time many prominent and nationalist clergy took a cool line. Most obviously, Archbishop Croke of Cashel who had effectively ushered the Land League into Tipperary,[29] notwithstanding an early subscription to his personal friend William O'Brien's United Irish League, refused to do the same thing for the new movement.[30]

There was a genuine uncertainty as to who exactly were the legitimate targets of popular disapproval. Why even Catholic priests held grazing land and found themselves boycotted![31] (In the Newport area, efforts were made by Canon Greally to circumvent this problem—he explicitly diverted agitation away from Catholic and towards Protestant graziers).[32] Many priests could see little reason why the ambitious Catholic family having at last gained a comfortable farm should be attacked by their fellow Irishmen. The agitation against the graziers explicitly opened the door to the politics of envy in particular and socialism in general. There were many who felt as did Father O'Connell at Carnacon, who 'condemned the practice of demanding graziers farms which they had procured by their own industry. He mentioned the fact that he himself had a farm, and said that it might any day be argued that as he was a priest, and had other means of living besides his farm, he ought to give it up. He told them however that he had a legal right to keep it and that he meant to do so.'[33] As the RIC sardonically noted: 'the peculiar part of this matter is that Father O'Connell was president of two branches of the League'.[34]

Apart from this ambiguity about the League's ultimate objective there was also a widespread uncertainty about its methods of operation. It is often assumed that the United Irish League merely

[28] PRO CO 903/8, 20, 114.
[29] Bew, *Land*, 137.
[30] *Irish People*, 22 February 1907.
[31] For example, Father Keaveney of Englishtown, Glenamaddy, PRO CO 902/8, 107.
[32] PRO CO 903/8, 22.
[33] PRO CO 903/8, 59 i, 11 December 1898.
[34] Ibid.

followed Land League methods. As P A McHugh, MP, one of
William O'Brien's few close allies in 1898, declared: 'The United Irish
League might be considered a new league, but it was not a new league,
it was the Land League come to life again.'[35] But McHugh had missed
the original Land League experience—he had been a student in Paris
at the time[36]—and his words must be taken with a pinch of salt. In fact,
the idea is profoundly misleading. Both in its objective and methods
the United Irish League was constructed on an entirely different
principle from that of the Land League. As Roscommon UIL activist,
John Fitzgibbon, put it: 'The large grazier was in the Land League, as
he was anxious to get a reduction of rent, as well as the small farmer,
but now the large grazier, along with the landlord and the grabber was
the enemy of the present movement.'[37]

The Land League in its offensive phase had been characterised by
highly expensive rather legalistic forms of resistance to the payment of
full rents. The 'boycott' and the whole apparatus of Irish rural
intimidation remained essentially subordinate to this policy. The
initial target of the United Irish League was the grazing system and
therefore resistance to rent payment—however operated—played an
inessential role. There was anyway no massive supply of Irish
American dollars available to finance a Land League type strategy.

As that experienced Irish American agrarian radical, Patrick Ford—
whose newspaper, the *Irish World* of New York, had been and still was
the main channel for Irish American funds—commented in a letter to
William O'Brien:

'Irishmen in America cannot be said to be enthusiastic over it (the UIL) . . . A
vague idea prevails that it is a mere moral force agitation which has for its aim
the buying back of the lands of Ireland from the landlords; and some
persons—some really intelligent persons—seem to imagine that these contri-
butions are, in some way, to help the tenants buy out the landlord.'[38]

Without American dollars, the UIL was thrown back on more
'popular' methods—boycotting and community pressure. Yet these
methods had revealed their limitations against determined landlords
in earlier struggles and they were now to reveal their limitation against
the grazier. Those who were outside the Irish peasant 'community', or

[35] *FJ*, 1 March 1899, PRO CO 903/8, 72.
[36] *Sligo Champion*, 5 June 1908:
[37] Speech to UIL Convention, *WF*, 23 June 1900.
[38] Patrick Ford to William O'Brien, 19 March 1900, UCC, O'Brien MS, AKA/505.

at any rate had a certain distance from it, as for example, was the case with both landlords and graziers—felt themselves well able to resist its pressures provided they stopped short of murder. And, partly thanks to the clerical pressure, [39] it was a defining and original feature of the UIL that it did stop short of murder. As William O'Brien boasted at a 'proclaimed meeting' in Sligo in January 1900: 'The League has been more than two years in active vigorous existence. There has not been a single agrarian murder in the whole province of Connaught throughout that period. Was there ever such a thing heard of before in Ireland in a great popular movement?'[40] The typical UIL branch had a clear cut method of operation. A group of sturdy young members would form a 'deputation' which would visit prominent local graziers with the suggestion that they might give up their land in order that it might be divided up for the people. This *modus operandi* was first suggested by Timothy Harrington and seems to have been put into effect as early as February 1898.[41] In most cases the grazier (and his sons) would tactfully temporise, sometimes openly reject the demand; on very rare occasions they would give in to the deputation.

Apart from the grazing interest, the UIL had, of course, to reckon with the forces of the state. O'Brien undoubtedly exaggerated in his constant polemics against 'police terrorism'. Nevertheless, the police were liable to proclaim potentially explosive meetings or prosecute when speeches passed from vague criticisms to the mention of specific graziers. Of course, it was precisely this naming of names which O'Brien felt was necessary to give the agitation some bite. In other ways too the state had the capacity to harass the new movement. In March Gerald Balfour claimed that the Congested Districts Board (which had one important nationalist clerical representative) regarded O'Brien's agitation as unhelpful.[42] O'Brien responded bitterly that this had not been the case in 1896, when he had pledged his own credit to allow the Clare Island tenantry to buy their land. O'Brien was also sharply critical of the official agents of the Congested Districts Board. These men were quick to spread the word in Mayo that they would not purchase estates—for subsequent redistribution to the peasantry—in

---

[39] *Irish Catholic*, 7 October 1899.

[40] *Sligo Champion*, 27 January 1900; see too the cogent discussion in Charles Townshend, *Political Violence in Ireland*, Oxford, 1983, 230.

[41] *CT*, February 1898.

[42] S. Warwick-Haller, 'William O'Brien', 300; P. Bull, 'The Reconstruction of the Irish Parliamentary Movement 1895–1903' (University of Cambridge, Ph.D., 1973), 163.

any locality where the UIL was established. Naturally O'Brien exploded with indignation but it had been a useful ploy. There is clear evidence that Catholic clergy, who may well have had other reasons for opposing the spread of the UIL, were exploiting a 'practical' reason for keeping it out of the parishes.[43] O'Brien was more exercised by this problem than the police: 'Balfour having failed to strike terror, has now evidently determined to fall back on boycotting as a means of vengeance for the sucess of the League.'[44]

Nevertheless, between February and June 1898 the UIL continued to make good progress in west Mayo. In March, O'Brien won a dangerous game of bluff with the Chief Secretary; by apparently openly courting arrest for illegal language, he, in fact, forced the authorities—fearful of giving the league a propaganda coup—to appear weak and indecisive. As Philip Bull has argued, this was an important moment: 'Prosecution may have given the aura of martyrdom to O'Brien but failure to prosecute not only saved the UIL from the serious setback that his imprisonment would have given but also caused public humiliation to the government and to the police by showing up their apparent weakness.'[45] Significantly, between the end of February and the end of March there was a massive increase in the number of people receiving police protection from 13 to 122.[46]

But despite such signs of UIL success, O'Brien was subject to moments of despair. O'Brien felt his isolation deeply. On 23 July he recorded: 'But I look around in vain anywhere for a helping hand.' The general tone of O'Brien's diary in July suggests that he was finding it difficult to maintain momentum. There had been one ray of hope. Dr O'Donnell, Bishop of Raphoe, the only nationalist member of the Congested Districts Board, had sent O'Brien an interesting letter which arrived on 25 July: 'He hints on high authority that the programme of our League is about to be realized, and that the debate on Davitt's motion (about emigration) will bring some remarkable announcement.'[47] But O'Brien had little confidence in O'Donnell; he felt that the Bishop of Raphoe failed to wield 'popular' influence decisively enough within the Congested Districts Board. His diary entry conceded that something might be in the wind but he continued to fear attempts to crush the UIL. There had, however, been a kernel

[43] Diary, 20 July 1898; 23 July 1898; *IP*, 5 January 1907. Also William O'Brien to Davitt, DPA 37.36.
[44] Diary, 23 July 1898, ibid.   [45] Bull, 'Reconstruction', 175.
[46] Ibid., 178.   [47] *IP*, 121 January 1907.

of truth in the Bishop of Raphoe's letter, for in under a month came just the sort of breakthrough O'Brien was looking for. On 9 August, A. J. Balfour, under pressure in the House from Michael Davitt, gave his answer to the problem of western distress, 'it is to the increase of the size of the holdings, and to that chiefly, that we must look'.[48] O'Brien was delighted:

Dt has just wired me that Balfour made a sympathetic speech tonight on the question of a permanent remedy for the West. This may mean much or little—probably little—but is bound to give a mighty fillip to our movement. All will now depend upon the amount of pressure brought to bear on the government before next session. Every parish in Mayo will feel that if it wants to share in the redistribution of the grasslands, it will have to look alive, and not boycott the League but instantly join in.[49]

A day later he added:

B's speech was a complete confession that the League is right in insisting that more land is the remedy. It is an historic admission. Three months ago he laughed the idea to scorn. He did not go into particulars and spoke of the necessary changes as 'gradual'; but an active League can soon settle the pace.[50]

The sharper side of O'Brien's (not always reliable) political intelligence is fully revealed in these pages. He knew that the first question any Irish agrarian movement had to settle was the question of credibility. The quickest and most effective way to obtain this credibility—in the eyes of the mass of the peasantry—was for the British government to take the claims of the new movement seriously. It did not matter if the government's proposed remedy was ineffective or non-existent. Indeed, it might be all to the good, for it was made that much easier to argue that a vacillating government required to be forced into action by the vigour of the Irish mass movement. Furthermore, the government, having in a sense conceded the moral case to their opponents, was inevitably hampered in carrying out any acts of repression. He judged that there was a new mood: 'Every parish of Mayo will feel that if it wants to share in the redistribution of the grasslands, it will have to look alive.'[51]

---

[48] HC debates, series 4, Vol. 64, col. 687.
[49] *IP*, 19 January 1907.
[50] Ibid.
[51] Ibid.

The UIL and Parnellism

Some controversy exists among historians to whether in its original
impulse the United Irish League may be said to have been non-
political, that is, a purely agrarian movement.[52] Was O'Brien motivated simply by the need for land redistribution in the west? Or was he
always concerned to use the League as a means of ending the 'split'
within Irish politics? O'Brien's memoirs are cloudy on these points,
but his diaries for the period from July to December 1899, which he
published in the *Irish People* in 1907, suggest that from an early point in
the UIL's history the objective of ending the split was, at least, as
pressing as the objective of land redistribution.

In this context, it is first of all, important to realise that in the
autumn and early winter of 1898 William O'Brien made a concerted
effort to create tension between Redmond and his followers in the
west. There were four particularly important UIL meetings in this
period: Claremorris on 4 September; Elphin on 18 September;
Castlerea on 30 October and Strokestown on 27 November. They
were of particular importance because each meeting marked a definite
stage in the evolution of O'Brien's relations with prominent Parnellites.

There were to be certain frustrations and disappointments for
O'Brien. It was common enough for a leading Parnellite to offer his
allegiance to the new movement and then having considered the
matter—or been pressured—to withdraw or modify it. William Field,[53]
the Dublin Parnellite MP, for example, half promised to speak at the
Claremorris meeting on 4 September—O'Brien incautiously saw this
as signalling the adherence of 'Parnellite Dublin'—but on reflection,
Field decided not to attend. Nevertheless, the Claremorris meeting
was sufficiently successful for O'Brien to claim, reasonably enough,
that many South Mayo Parnellites—and in particular, their most
impressive young leader, Conor O'Kelly—were now committed to the
UIL. Also, one significant Dublin Parnellite, E. Haviland Burke, had
made the journey to speak at Claremorris, bringing the good news that
another Parnellite MP, Pierce Mahony, was 'breast-high' for unity.
O'Brien noted of Haviland Burke: 'He is anxious to get into Parlia-

---

[52] On this point, see above all P. Bull, 'The Reconstruction of the Irish Parliamentary
Movement 1895–1903' (University of Cambridge Ph.D., 1973), 140–3.

[53] Field spoke of the 1898 centenary meeting in Castlebar, *CT*, 3 September 1898
alongside O'Brien.

ment and has all sorts of projects for forcing R not to stand in the way of unity.'[54]

Following the advance made at Claremorris, O'Brien then attempted yet again to win John Dillon over: reprimanding Dillon for not giving the League an entrée in his own East Mayo constituency, O'Brien noted: 'It is quite clear D will run no risks and give no active help himself to the League.'[55] Dillon did promise, however, to speak to Joseph Devlin, a rising young Belfast nationalist whom O'Brien wanted to have as secretary for the League.[56] Dillon had his own reasons here: Devlin had clashed with the Catholic hierarchy in Belfast and Dillon wanted to remove his young supporter from the city for a while and at the same time see him placed in an apparently important national work. This way 'loss of face' would be minimized. But on 7 September when O'Brien met Devlin he found him in a pessimistic mood—Thomas Sexton had told him that Irish nationalism was finished for a generation—and more interested in obtaining a public house in Dublin. But despite this failure to attract an energetic and eloquent young recruit O'Brien's morale remained good. On 11 September at Labasheeda, Co. Clare, he and the Leitrim MP, P. A. McHugh, were physically attacked by a 'landgrabber' McHugh had explicitly named. O'Brien speculated: 'I daresay the incident will mean prosecution—possibly suppression of the League—but it is only by such risks [that] popular spirit can be roused out of the grave.'[57] But despite this apparently gloomy appraisal, O'Brien's intuition of August—that the government was not in the mood for outright repression—remained with him: 'Balfour is in the dilemma that he recoils from any coercion campaign that might ruin the working of his local Government act and England's chance of an American alliance.'[58] On 14 September, O'Brien was noting a 'decisive' victory: in certain parts of Mayo, some graziers were signing requisitions to the Congested District Board asking them to take over their lands.[59]

Next on the agenda was the Elphin meeting in Co. Roscommon. Elphin was a Parnellite stronghold. In the elections of 1892 and 1895 no anti-Parnellite had dared to campaign there.[60] O'Brien prepared

[54] 4 September 1898; *IP*, 16 February 1907.
[55] 7 September 1898; *IP*, 16 February 1907.
[56] Ibid.
[57] Diary, 11 September 1898; *IP*, 16 February 1907.
[58] Ibid.   [59] Ibid.
[60] Diary, 19 September 1898; *IP*, 16 February 1907.

himself in a mood of some apprehension. In the event the Elphin meeting went off satisfactorily; the crowd, though relatively small, was spirited enough. More important, the local Parnellite leadership was friendly. John Fitzgibbon supported the meeting and John Hayden MP also kept his promise—given to O'Brien at a chance encounter a few days before—to attend. Fitzgibbon even went so far as to be rather indiscreet with O'Brien: 'F. told me R. had sent for him to Dublin and put the strongest pressure on him not to attend. His reply was that the movement had taken such a hold on the country that neither he nor R. dared oppose it, if they did not wish to efface themselves.'[61] On 19 September O'Brien had another interview with Fitzgibbon during which Fitzgibbon enthusiastically planned a UIL demonstration for Castlerea. But here O'Brien's impulsiveness came into disastrous play. O'Brien pushed his luck too far and immediately cabled Patrick Ford, editor of the New York *Irish World* and by now a venerable father figure of Irish American Nationalism, that the 'split' was at an end in Connaught. It was an absurd action: an example of the restiveness that disturbed even his closest allies. Even Ford, not normally a cautious man, had his doubts about O'Brien's action.[62] The Parnellite *Independent* was at last given a potent argument against the United Irish League. On 1 October, it explicitly appealed to Fitzgibbon, Hayden and Mahony to repudiate the O'Brien telegram to the *Irish World*.[63] With the anniversary of Parnell's death (6 October) only a few days away, tensions increased. O'Brien wrote in his diary: 'It is possible that under the morbid excitement always caused by the annual commemoration in Dublin, H. may give way, but F. is more gritty, and M. (if I mistake not) grittiest of all.'[64]

In fact, William O'Brien was exceptionally lucky that he was not made to pay the full price for his mistakes. The Parnellite convention met in Dublin a few days later; there was significant pressure to pass a motion hostile towards the United Irish League. This would have obviously placed most western Parnellites who were working with O'Brien in an appalling dilemma: either they broke with John Redmond to whom they obviously felt deep loyalty or they broke with

[61] Diary, 18 September 1898; *IP*, 16 February 1907.
[62] Patrick Ford to Michael Davitt, 14 January 1899, TCD DPA 60.4735: 'I regret that I ever asked Mr O'Brien to send me any cables, although my request was complemented by the injunction that he should do so only where in his own good judgement, the cause of the UIL might be served by so doing'.
[63] *IWI*, 1 October 1898.
[64] Diary, 1 October 1898; *IP*, 3 March 1907.

a new movement which was both relevant and popular in their own political base. Redmond, in particular, despite the private pressure which he was exerting on Fitzgibbon and Hayden, had good reasons to avoid presenting them with such a stark public choice. In the end, a resolution sympathetic to the objectives of the UIL was passed. This was more than O'Brien had hoped for and he was delighted: 'The tide of popular feeling is the one force that is fighting for me against myriads of enemies, natural and unnatural.'[65] The *Freeman's Journal* reported: 'No impartial observer who attended could fail to note the anxiety of the men who were personally acquainted with the condition of affairs in the West, to which the League had so prominently and successfully drawn attention, to secure the support of the convention for that body to work.'[66]

Redmond had decided to compromise with his western friends. In part this was because—at this very moment in 1898—he required their support in a rather difficult and dangerous extension of his policy of 'toleration'. Speaking on the subject of the new county councils Redmond had predictably called for nationalist majorities to be elected to the new bodies; less predictably, however, he had continued:

Now, let me ask a question: Is there a possibility, however small, in the near future of obtaining through the instrumentality of the County Councils a return to the ranks of Ireland of any men whose forefathers stood with Grattan 100 years ago, but who since that day for one reason or another, stood aloof from the National Movement.[67]

Redmond argued that if such possibility existed, no matter how slight—then nationalists must take account of it. Redmond then continued in a remarkable passage:

What has been the real stumbling block in the way of the English people in granting us Home Rule? It has been the fact that Ireland herself has been divided upon this question of Home Rule into two camps, and that many thousands and tens of thousands of the Irish people have held aloof from the national movement or a movement in favour of an Irish nation, which I desire to see, and which if it once came into existence would mean the obtaining of Home Rule within six months—in a movement in which all classes and creeds of Irishmen could unite (applause)![68]

[65] Diary, 12 October 1898; *IP*, 16 March 1907.
[66] *FJ*, 11 October 1898.
[67] Ibid.   [68] Ibid.

Redmond explained that this had been the conception of Thomas Davis. It had been also the conception of Isaac Butt: 'but the land question intervened . . . and drove from the Home Rule party many men who, apart from the land question, would have been willing to see Ireland self-governed'.[69] Above all, it had been Parnell's conception. Parnell had pointedly refused to reply to landlord vilification in kind and had always retained the hope of eventual reconciliation. Redmond's discourse, like so much of Parnell's until the last, did not really address the problem of plebeian Ulster Unionism. Redmond did in a more general way acknowledge the importance of Ireland's internal divisions. The attempted reconstruction of Grattan's eighteenth-century bloc may not have been an entirely adequate response. But his Parnellite followers vastly preferred it to what was commonly described as the 'narrow stiff-necked parochialism of Mr Dillon and the *Freeman*.'

To expand this policy, Redmond then argued that there were a few men, and 'he admitted there were only a few',[70] who 'from the administrative ability which they possessed and the public spirit upon many questions of great importance to the country which they had shown—were deserving of special consideration at the hands of the electors'.[71] The *Independent* gave the policy an enthusiastic gloss: 'By selecting the new boards in a liberal and business-like way, all the time never losing sight of the main object, working fairly and squarely, we will interest many an opponent of Home Rule, gradually absorb him in the public life of our country, and by and by make him a fellow worker in the movement for our National Independence'.[73] But who precisely deserved such toleration? Redmond committed himself here by mentioning a name: Charles Owen O'Conor, better known by the courtesy title of the O'Conor Don.

The O'Conor Don was in fact one of the holders of the ancient Irish titles still claimed in the nineteenth century by representatives of the original chiefs. Born in 1838, the O'Conor Don had in his early political career enjoyed an easy political success in Connaught. From 1858 to 1880 he represented North Roscommon as a Liberal MP; in 1873 he attended Butt's Home Rule Conference but failed to 'come up to the mark' as an Irish Nationalist. But 'through love of the

[69] Ibid.
[70] *IWI*, 6 May 1899.
[71] *Roscommon Messenger*, 25 March 1899.
[72] *IWI*, 67 May 1899.
[73] *IWI*, 18 February 1899.

old stock'[74] the electorate tolerated him until the Land League in 1880 generated a sharper feeling on agrarian and national matters.[75] Ironically, Parnell, the Land League President, was notably reluctant to push the O'Conor Don out of his parliamentary seat. (Anti-Parnellites made this allegation in 1891[76] and the Parnellite MP, Luke Hayden, fully admitted it three years later.)[77] The O'Conor Don was the very type of public-spirited landlord Parnell was anxious to keep in politics[78]—despite the rising tide of agrarian class conflict. In this case, however, notwithstanding considerable misgivings, Parnell was unable to follow out his own wishes—instead, he was forced to lead the campaign against the O'Conor Don. In a bitter and rhetorically violent campaign reflecting the tension of the time, the O'Conor Don was defeated by J. J. O'Kelly, the Land League candidate. In 1896 the O'Conor Don returned to a more public prominence, when as Chairman of the Financial Relations Commission (after the death of Hugh Childers) he impressed many people by his obvious competence. Among those impressed, of course, was John Redmond. Hence Redmond's action at the Parnellite convention in October 1898, when he gave it as his view that the O'Conor Don was precisely the sort of local figure who deserved the 'toleration' of nationalists at the ballot box in the forthcoming local government elections.[79] Redmond must have known, however, that he was asking a particular favour from the Roscommon Parnellites; they were being asked to expend their own political capital to ensure the continued local influence of a man who— though he possessed a residual popularity—had a rather 'weak' stance on the key questions of the day.

Redmond was in effect offering Fitzgibbon and Hayden a compromise. They could continue to support the United Irish League provided that they supported also the Redmondite policy of 'toleration' in the forthcoming local government elections. John Fitzgibbon may well have had his doubts about Redmond's policy—which cut across his own personal interests, as it had done in the case of Haviland Burke—but he accepted the compromise. John Hayden had been feeling the strain—'for God's sake, let there be no further talk of

[74] *RM*, 7 July 1906.
[75] Ibid.
[76] Bew, *Parnell*, 36; *RH*, 17 January 1891.
[77] *IWI*, 6 October 1894.
[78] Bew, *Parnell, passim*.
[79] *RM*, 25 March 1899.

unity',[80] he had said in a phrase which was reported back to O'Brien—
and grasped at the compromise more enthusiastically. He became a
committed and eloquent supporter of the policy of 'toleration'.

In the first issue of Hayden's newspaper, the *Roscommon Messenger*,
to be published after the Parnellite convention, the editorial proclaimed:

The (anti Parnellites) would hunt from public life every man who in political
matters do not think the same way as themselves, whilst the Parnellites are
desirous first, to recruit the new councils for the National cause and next to
admit to them such Unionists as have shown capacity for public business and
broadmindedness and toleration in their intercourse with their countrymen . . . its (this policy's) adoption upon a considerable scale in all probability
would destroy the most formidable obstacle to the attainment of National self-
government, and that is the opposition to the realisation of this demand which
comes from so many born and living in Ireland.[81]

This was generous language indeed; it may be also that such a fervent
endorsement eased somewhat Hayden's conscience. But at the very
least the Parnellites were again performing the service of reminding
nationalists that it was the opposition of Irishmen—not Englishmen—
which was the most decisive barrier to Home Rule. This was a point of
fundamental importance which the majority of nationalists traditionally seemed somewhat reluctant to acknowledge.

Much clearly depended on the Castlerea meeting. On 12 October
O'Brien received a friendly note from Fitzgibbon. It seemed that
Fitzgibbon was still prepared to organize the demonstration: 'He only
requests me to strengthen his hand by a letter making it clear that the
Parnellites who came on our platforms must not be regarded as
penitents or renegades.'[82] O'Brien was not more hopeful—'it will be
the end of trouble in Connaught if Castlerea comes right'.[83]

Significantly, John Redmond had considered it necessary to ask
Willie Redmond to make the journey to Castlerea. O'Brien, Willie
Redmond and John Fitzgibbon spent some very 'tense' and 'con-
strained' moments together before the meeting started. Pierce
Mahony was the only Parnellite to display any warmth towards
O'Brien. But once the meeting got under way, the feeling of the local

[80] Diary, 8 October 1898; *IP*, 3 March 1907.
[81] *RM*, 15 October 1898.
[82] Diary, 12 October 1898; *IP*, 16 March 1907.
[83] Ibid.

Roscommon Parnellites soon revealed itself. O'Brien recorded: 'When I came forward at the close to speak again there was no longer the smallest doubt that the Parnellites of Roscommon were won over wholly and forever.'[84] Interestingly, John Redmond sent a letter of support[85] to the meeting acknowledging that the UIL's call for land redistribution had been a theme of Parnell's political life also.[86]

Then O'Brien once again foolishly endangered all his own good work: on 5 November 'at Dillon's entreaty' he announced that he was to make a personal subscription to the party—that is, the anti-Parnellite—party funds. In consequence, the sky seemed clouded again when on 27 November O'Brien arrived in Strokestown for another joint meeting with Fitzgibbon. Fitzgibbon was in an agitated mood. Furthermore, as O'Brien wrote to Davitt, at first sight, it seemed as if Parnellite and anti-Parnellite in Strokestown were united against the League; there was, he reported, a 'diabolical combination'[87] of both sections who were involved in grazing. His diary records that:

He (Fitzgibbon) was greatly alarmed at the hostile feeling of the most influential Parnellites in town, who are in the grazing interest. Both the Redmondite papers contained attacks on the meeting and F intimated that his position would be made impossible if there was any reference to the council elections, as the Redmondites had a policy of their own on that question. The policy, it is almost certain, is to sell the county council to the landlords and graziers and make the O'Conor Don its chairman without stipulating any conditions whatever as to the new Land Bill or Home Rule.[88]

But, in a significant concession, Fitzgibbon agreed to refer the question of the chairmanship of the new Roscommon county council to a county convention of all sections of nationalist opinion. Such a convention was bound to insist on a nationalist chairman—as indeed it did. The actual meeting again passed off satisfactorily: 'One more unambiguous proof how much sounder the people are than their leaders.' The next day, Fitzgibbon had softened appreciably, O'Brien noted that:

He quite agreed that pending the abolition of landlordism, it would be madness not to man the county councils, with the most uncompromising

[84] Diary, 30 October 1898, *IP*, 16 April 1907.
[85] *RM*, 5 November 1898.
[86] *WF*, 20 July 1901.
[87] O'Brien to Davitt, 30 November 1898; TCD DPA 37.
[88] O'Brien's Diary, 30 November 1898, 20 April 1907.

nationalists to be found, and did not seem at all angered when I suggested he would himself make a more appropriate chairman than the O'Conor Don.[89]

Fitzgibbon, however, remained vulnerable to pressure. On 10 December O'Brien found that he was again wavering. O'Brien gloomily noted:

It is even to be feared R will capture him for his policy of betraying the county councils to the O'Conor Dons without an atom of compensation or of national object.[90]

Not surprisingly, the county council problem continued to obsess O'Brien. This was particularly evident in his last speech of the year given at Ballylongford in North Kerry. His speech contained much typical UIL fare: a great deal was made of the appearance on the same platform of the local MP, M. J. Flavin, and his Parnellite opponent of 1892, Edmund Haviland Burke. But it also contained a novel theme. O'Brien caught many people—in particular the police—by surprise, with these words:

Somebody may say the question of breaking up the grass ranches, upon which you lay so much emphasis, in the West, has no application in the South. Of course, it has not. It is solely and wholly a question for the congested districts of the West. Nobody dreams of extending it to the South, where the circumstances are totally different. This question of breaking up the grass ranches is not even mentioned in the constitution of the United Irish League. That constitution goes upon the principle that the people of each Parliamentary division must govern themselves through an executive formed by six delegates from every branch in the division, and that executive must decide for themselves in what way or as to what particular question this organisation may be made most useful for the people's protection or the advancement of the National cause (cheers). For instance, if you had your branches formed in every parish around, and if you had your executive sitting every fortnight in Listowel, it would be wholly for themselves to decide to what particular question they should apply themselves. But does anyone doubt they would have plenty of work on their hands, whether they turn to the Council Council elections, or to a campaign against the landgrabbers, or to the compulsory expropriation of the landlords, or the movement for securing to the labourers their full acre of land and the eventual ownership of their allotments.[91]

---

[89] Diary, 31 November; *IP*, 24 April 1907.
[90] Diary, 10 December 1898; 18 May 1907.
[91] *FJ*, 19 December 1898; *Kerry Sentinel*, 21 December 1898.

The bulk of O'Brien's speech concentrated on the county council question: yet again he emphasized the importance of electing good nationalists. At the end of the day, thoroughly satisfied, O'Brien recorded in his diary: 'I think the South has now thoroughly grasped the idea that the County Councils must be made nationalist fortresses.'[92]

O'Brien had enunciated doctrines which were to be of the utmost importance for the subsequent history of the UIL. He had clearly decided that the theme of land redistribution was pertinent only in Connaught. (The UIL constitution—*pace* William O'Brien in this instance—eventually did, in fact, call for 'the suppression of famine . . . by compulsory purchase of the grazing lands of Connaught'[93] but made no mention of any other region). To be sure, William O'Brien might have replied that his remarks in Munster implied no modification of his movement's objectives in Connaught. But there is no doubt that it did imply that the demand for land redistribution, previously the essence of the UIL's appeal, was not in itself sufficiently popular as to be the basis of an expanding movement. It also implied no less significantly that in O'Brien's view there was no case for land redistribution outside the 'west'. This was in many ways a reasonable proposition: Kerry, for example, was a county dominated by medium-sized farms. But there were many nationalists who disagreed profoundly with the notion that an anti-ranching agitation was only relevant in the west. This was, in fact, to be one of the most controversial points in Irish nationalist debate in the first decade of the twentieth century. O'Brien, at this early juncture, was marking himself out as one of those who believed that the west was a 'special' case. He was thus able to open the door to those nationalists in other provinces who may have been worried by the UIL's identification with the poorest farmers. They were invited to join the League and to mould it according to their own priorities. O'Brien was desperately keen to win further support and he was prepared to pay almost any price including that of allowing untrammelled local initiative. O'Brien's characterization of the UIL constitution entered into the consciousness of political elites. Even the police noted that O'Brien's remarks showed that the agrarian radical themes of the original Westport meeting were being

[92] Diary, December 1898; *IP*, 1 June 1907.
[93] *CT*, 4 February 1899.

moderated. Their conclusion was suggestive: '(William O'Brien) has implied that the real object of the League was a political one.'[94]

Timothy Harrington, speaking on the same day on the UIL platform at Ballinasloe, had presented the UIL objectives in a similar way. (In this instance, J. P. Hayden, also finding the line of 'toleration' under fire, was forced yet again to make a protest and to recall that the League's original objective had been that of land redistribution).[95] O'Brien was later to complain bitterly when Harrington intrigued against his leadership of the UIL. But when Harrington did so he used precisely the conceptions O'Brien had given him: the notion that the UIL was above all a broad based nationalist movement, that it should allow great room for 'local' sentiment and that land redistribution was a slogan applicable only in the west.

This shift in emphasis was to be confirmed by the 'great' UIL convention at Claremorris in late January: the objectives of the organization was given out as firstly, national self-government; secondly, abolition of landlordism, and only thirdly, western land redistribution. But the same convention made claims for the success of the UIL's campaign against the graziers which required close examination. John O'Donnell read out a list of 110 graziers who had expressed their willingness to give up land provided the terms were right.[96] This sounds remarkable; but as agrarian militant Laurence Ginnell was later to observe 'such pretended willingness' to concede was a deceit unless followed by prompt and decisive action by the graziers. The London *Times*, swallowing enthusiastic O'Brienite propaganda, spoke of a 'general surrender of grazing lands',[97] but the police somewhat more accurately spoke of 'almost total failure'[98] after a year of agitation. This does not indicate an absence of significant popular support for the UIL's objectives[99]—simply the existence of major obstacles which stood in the way of making it tell against obstinate graziers. The strength of popular feeling is well indicated by the fact that the UIL achieved considerably more success in an area where the small farmers' initiative was decisive. Even the police acknowledged that many small farmers refused to send their stock out to graziers in the normal way. The UIL was, therefore, doing enough

---

[94] PRO CO 903/8, 58.
[95] *FT*, 19 December 1898. [96] *CT*, 4 February 1899.
[97] Quoted ibid. [98] PRO CO 903/8, 111.
[99] BL Add MS 49802, f.170 (A. J. Balfour papers). Copy of a RIC memo (unsigned) sent to the Lord Lieutenant of Ireland, 23 July 1901, f.170.

to maintain its momentum but it was falling far short of a dramatic breakthrough. Mayo was its only really solid county but expansion might well be expected in other parts of Connaught. It is important to keep matters in perspective: at the end of 1898 the UIL had 94 branches in operation embracing a total membership of only 8,853.[100] In the first few months of 1899, however, the UIL began to expand into the rest of Connaught; in particular it soon developed some 40 branches in Roscommon.[101]

The policy of 'toleration' in Roscommon

The advance of the UIL in Roscommon inevitably made political relationships in the county even more complex. In one sense, Fitzgibbon and Hayden were bound to rejoice in the advance of the movement for land redistribution with which they were so heavily identified. But, at the same time, such an advance made the policy of toleration even more difficult to apply. In particular, the 'toleration' of the O'Conor Don proved to be a fraught and difficult process. William O'Brien angrily kept up his denunciation of the project. In early 1899 he was joined by a prominent Parnellite recruit J. J. O'Kelly: O'Kelly's accession was of special significance. He was just about conceivable as a leader of a reunited party—everyone accepted that a member of the Parnellite minority had to have the job as part of the healing process. Furthermore, his relationship with Redmond was traditionally poor. The open defection of the North Roscommon MP to 'O'Brienism' was a heavy blow against the Redmondite forces in the county. O'Kelly's themes were rudimentary, impassioned but also rather coarse. On 22 January he commented:

He was old enough to remember the famine graves of '47 and '48 and every time he thought of landlords—the stench of the famine dead rose in his nostrils . . .

When the South Carolina niggers were set free they had sense enough to elect men of their own class. He did not want to insult them by comparing them with niggers, but he would say that if the men of Roscommon were going to cast their votes for landlordism in the coming elections they would be worse than the South Carolina niggers (cheers).[102]

---

[100] BL Add MS 49802, f.172.
[101] CO 903/8, 144.
[102] *Roscommon Journal*, 28 January 1899.

On 30 January, at a Strokestown meeting for the purpose of selecting a Parnellite for the county district in the Councy Council, O'Kelly repeated this argument, adding: 'They would send a message to England that so long as the confiscation of Cromwell and William existed there could be no peace in Ireland.'[103]

Those loyal to Redmond clearly had their work cut out. Luckily at this moment the O'Conor Don made a powerful plea to the Home Rule electorate: 'Surely you cannot think you will make converts to the cause of home rule or self-government by refusing to admit any but Home Rulers to the administration of your local affairs?'[104] The implicit logic here, that the policy of toleration strengthened the case for Home Rule, would have heartened Redmond but some of his supporters were less confident. For already there were signs of a crack in the local Redmondite resolve. At the same Castlerea meeting, John Fitzgibbon committed himself to vote for a Nationalist chairman of the county council.[105] The editorial of the *Roscommon Messenger* explained that 'without any display of narrow mindedness or intolerance the people of Roscommon wanted to work the new system for the advancement of the national cause.'[106]

Further tensions between the O'Conor Don and Fitzgibbon emerged at a well-attended meeting in Ballinagare in March 1899. Here, five of the candidates for the district council debated in a frank but orderly fashion thus 'giving a piquancy to the proceedings', which the *Roscommon Messenger* admitted was 'not usual at these meetings.'[107] Of particular interest was the way in which the O'Conor Don's suggestive appeal was none the less queried by John Fitzgibbon. Pointing out that the district council would not be able to deal with political questions anyway, the O'Conor Don launched into a characteristic theme:

He was not a stranger nor an outsider, he lived amongst them, was known to them all and knew everyone of them. His family had been for many centuries connected with them and anyone that had read the history of Ireland had read the history of his family, which had been so long identified with the people and which had in other days been leaders in Ireland.[108]

---

[103] *Roscommon Herald*, 4 February 1899.
[104] *Roscommon Messenger*, 11 February 1899.
[105] Ibid.   [106] Ibid.
[107] Ibid., 15 March 1899.
[108] Ibid.

At this point, John Fitzgibbon felt compelled to interrupt. He asked the O'Conor Don for his answer to the burning question of the hour: was he in favour of dividing the grass lands of Roscommon on fair and equitable terms amongst the people?

Mr O'Conor said that this was a difficult matter to give an opinion upon and before doing so he would like that Mr Fitzgibbon and others who favoured his proposal, would put forward the terms of some feasible plan which he would be prepared to consider. There were many obstacles in the way which should be overcome before it could be carried out. Let them take the case of a grazing farm at Rathcroghan and divide it up, fence it and do other necessary work to start the men on the smaller holdings, and he wanted to know where would the money come from for such a purpose. He would like to see a feasible plan to remove these obstacles before he could say anything on the subject. Mr Fitzgibbon asked, supposing these obstacles were removed, would Mr O'Conor assist in removing these obstacles.

Mr O'Conor said he was greatly afraid that the matter was not at all feasible, however, when he saw the plan he would give it his consideration and until then he was not in favour of it (a voice 'you're done then') (cheers and laughter). However this was a political matter and outside the scope of the District Council.[109]

The O'Conor Don's answer had perhaps inevitably been far from satisfactory. All this was acutely embarrassing to the Parnellite leaders in Roscommon. On the one hand, they were engaged in a struggle to force land redistribution, and on the other, they were attempting to prop up the local influence of a man who declared that this project was unrealistic. The O'Conor Don's frankness and refusal to equivocate in 1880 had divided him from a friendly Parnell; in 1899 his explicit words were again tending to split him off from equally sympathetic Parnellites. Somewhat desperately Fitzgibbon responded by appealing to O'Conor to reconsider his position, reminding him of the success of the work of land redistribution at Clare Island and the French estate near Ballygar. John P. Hayden decided to make the best of a bad job: he commended the O'Conor Don's openness—perhaps, in his heart, feeling that a little evasion might have been more politic. But again, like John Fitzgibbon, he felt it necessary to insist that land redistribution could be made to work.

Some days later on 19 March O'Brien inevitably returned to the attack at Lisacull. Sharing a platform with two Parnellites, Haviland

[109] Ibid.

Burke and James Lynam, the old Land League organizer, who had recently been appointed to the same post in the UIL, O'Brien denounced the current Parnellite policy. O'Brien attempted to strip away the mythology surrounding the O'Conor Don: 'There was rubbish talked about these old Irish Catholic families', he declared. In O'Brien's opinion, 'the old families that deserve honour in Ireland are not the gentlemen who held on to their estates and castles by proving false to faith and fatherland in some hour when the fate of Ireland was hanging in the balance.'[110] O'Brien then urged the electorate to reject the O'Conor Don in favour of his opponent, R. A. Corr, a UIL activist drawn from Parnellite ranks.

Despite these difficulties, the Roscommon Parnellites refused to abandon their position. Increasingly, however, they started to play down the O'Conor Don's special virtues. Instead, they played up the case for loyalty to John Redmond. William O'Brien made such a fetish of attacking the O'Conor Don, the *Roscommon Messenger* editorial[111] claimed, not because of that gentleman's qualities or defects but as a means of weakening Redmond. At a lively meeting on 26 March at Furness, near Ballinglough, John Fitzgibbon put it pithily: 'It was not the O'Conor Don that was aimed at now. The man they sought to be bowled over was John Redmond because he mentioned the name of O'Conor Don at the convention in October.'[112] By the end of April a kind of compromise emerged. The O'Conor Don was elected to the Roscommon County Council against R. A. Corr, but he was not elected Chairman.[113] That honour fell to Farrell McDonnell with John Fitzgibbon as vice-chairman.[114] However, Hayden and Fitzgibbon paid some recompense to O'Conor Don by sponsoring him for the chairmanship of the smaller Castlerea District Council. More generally, the results were good for the UIL—despite some notable setbacks even in Mayo.[115]

At first, and for some months, it appeared as if the strategy of toleration had worked in Roscommon. The first meeting of the new Castlerea District Council near the end of April was a benign and amiable affair. Fitzgibbon and the O'Conor Don began by ensuring that there would

[110] *RH*, 25 March 1899.
[111] *RM*, 25 March 1899.
[112] *RM*, 1 April 1899.
[113] *RH*, 25 April 1899.
[114] *RM*, 6 May 1899.
[115] *CT*, 11 March 1899; *IWI*, 15 April 1899.

be a good Protestant representation on the Board of Guardians. Then, although he was proposed for the chairmanship of the council, Fitzgibbon declined the honour. In his stead, the O'Conor Don was unanimously elected. The O'Conor Don then recalled the recent election campaign. In particular, he explicitly justified Fitzgibbon's trust.

... it would be quite contrary to the truth to represent his success as a Unionist success, because he never represented himself as a Unionist, and never approached the subject from a political side ... it was quite a mistake to suggest that in this election there was any intention to say that those who supported him had changed their political views.[116]

The O'Conor Don's remarks were well taken, as he was reminded a few days later 'no man had been returned by such a large majority of Home Rule sympathies as he had'.[117] But the outbreak of the Boer War disrupted everything. The sight of the Boers taking on the British army stirred some deep chord in nationalist Ireland. Parnellite speakers, in particular, roared their support for the Boers and the methods of war. The O'Conor Don observed this development with increasing discomfort.

On 30 October 1899 Hugh Carberry, an Armagh nationalist, fell fighting for the Boers at the battle of Modderspruit. Carberry became posthumously a national hero memoralized by a Celtic cross in his home town. Michael Davitt hailed him as a 'soldier of liberty' as against those 'hirelings of the king'[118] (including, of course, many Irishmen) on the British side. The Parnellites refused to be outdone in the matter of pro-Boer rhetoric. William Redmond MP expostulated: 'We cannot fight today in Ireland as the Boers are fighting ... I wish to God we could.'[119] Patrick O'Brien MP, responded to a heckler calling out Kruger's name with the riposte that if he had Kruger's rifles 'it is not talking constitutionalism I would be'.[120]

The O'Conor Don watched all this somewhat balefully. Matters came to a head when the O'Conor Don, in his capacity as chairman of the Castlerea Board of Guardians, refused to sign a resolution of sympathy with the Boers in their warfare against the British Empire.

[116] *RM*, 22 April 1899.
[117] Ibid., 29 April 1899.
[118] *WF*, 4 June 1902.
[119] CO 903/9, 1 January 1902, Corofin speech.
[120] *Kilkenny People*, 27 September 1900, Callan speech; D. G. Boyce, *Nationalism in Ireland*, London, 1982, 268.

He made two pointed comments: firstly, it was hardly politic if the Irish wanted the English to vote for Home Rule. Secondly, and this was even more irritating, it was entirely consistent, even honourable, for openly disloyal subjects—for example Fenians—to take such a stand.[121] But here was an apparently constitutional movement delighting in attacks on the Empire. As it was clearly impossible to deny these inconsistencies the O'Conor Don's niggling (if apposite) remarks could only be dealt with by an explosion of righteous indignation. That such an explosion should come is in no way suprising. Nevertheless, it is interesting to note that it came from his recent ally, John Fitzgibbon. At first Fitzgibbon dealt merely with the general aspect of the case, 'Ireland in the first place owes very little to the English government (hear, hear). There is no gentleman in Ireland knows better perhaps than the O'Conor Don of this fact.'[122] Fitzgibbon then went further and offered up one of these comments which were meat and drink to those Unionist pamphleteers who argued that the Irish would never be satisfied with Home Rule. His precise words were:

They did not accept the Home Rule Bill of last year or the year before, or any other year as a final settlement of the Irish question, and in the words of Mr Parnell, they never put a stop to the march of a nation. They merely accepted the Home Rule Bill for the time being and was there a man in Ireland or any Nationalist in Ireland dared to say that they took it as a final settlement of the Irish question (applause).[123]

Fitzgibbon's speech was of particular significance. Roscommon Parnellites were as enthusiastically pro-Boer as anyone. The Roscommon County Council's resolution of sympathy with the Boers was praised in the Hayden press.[124] When at the same meeting Jasper Tully proposed a resolution pledging the Council to hoist the green flag over the Courthouse, J. P. Hayden's *Roscommon Messenger* — forgetting old and bitter enmities with Tully[125] asked: 'And why not? The Courthouse is the property of the people and Green Flag symbolic of the passions and the hope of a nation.'[126] By the end of

[121] *RM*, 18 November 1899. The O'Conor Don and the Boer War.
[122] *RM*, 9 December 1899.
[123] Ibid.
[124] *RM*, 18 November 1899.
[125] J. Lee, *The Modernisation of Irish Society 1848—1918*, Dublin, 1973, 137.
[126] *RM*, 9 December 1899.

1899 then the *rapprochement* between the O'Conor Don and Ros-common Parnellism was effectively over.

By the end of 1899 also Redmond knew too well that the United Irish League had disrupted the unity of Parnellite forces. Redmond could afford to dispense with the services of the frequently drunken Richard Corr or even James Lynam—to name two Parnellites who had been appointed as paid UIL organizers—for they were essentially figures of the second rank. But Timothy Harrington's defection was undeniably a serious matter. Nor could Redmond afford to lose Parnellite leaders of the stature of Pierce Mahoney. Still less could he lose young Turks of the type of Haviland Burke or Conor O'Kelly. Yet all four were now openly more committed to the UIL than they were to the 'independent' cause. Redmond had done exceptionally well in difficult circumstances to retain the personal loyalty of John Hayden, MP for South Roscommon, and John Fitzgibbon, who was clearly now a rising force in western politics. But both these men were at the same time active United Irish League leaders. It was apparent that Redmond had asked Hayden and Fitzgibbon to expend political resources in defence of a relatively unpopular cause—'toleration' of the O'Conor Don. The O'Conor Don's entirely principled refusal in November 1899 to ride with the tide of pro-Boer sentiment raised new doubts about the wisdom of the toleration policy. For years Redmond had maintained his optimism; at any rate, he had always hoped for an 'independent' breakthrough to greater popular support which would have paved the way for reunification on acceptable terms. By the end of 1899, he had to acknowledge the failure of his attempt to break the mould of Irish politics set by the massive anti-Parnellite electoral triumph of 1892. Redmond's own efforts to accommodate non-nationalists were crumbling in the wake of the Boer war recrimina-tions. O'Brien's United Irish League had not done enough to break the mould either—but it had siphoned off a significant amount of rural Parnellism at the grass roots and at leadership level. Redmond was forced to take a cool look at the political prospects. The United Irish League had not as yet really hurt the grazing system but it had hurt Parnellism. Redmond faced a future in which urban, and therefore radical, artisan and neo-Fenian Parnellism would dominate the diminished coalition he led. It is perhaps not therefore surprising that in late 1899 Redmond's interest in the reunification of the Irish party sharpened considerably.

The 'Independent' and Haviland Burke

But before reunification was achieved, Redmond's politics were to be subjected to a major critical examination by an erstwhile follower, E. Haviland Burke, former editor of the *Parnellite*. The Redmondite *Daily Independent* had declared in mid-November:

That the land laws are not what they should be is notorious, but that a land agitation in its full sense is possible at the present time is a mere dream. The vast majority of Irish farmers will only join in an agitation, which is confined to Sundays when they have nothing else to do.[127]

The *Independent* went to argue that 'compulsory purchase' was anyway a misleading and unattractive slogan. Government officials would inevitably set the price of the land too high and thus favour the landlord against the tenant. Implicit in this argument is the view that with rents in real terms steadily falling it was in the farmers' interest to employ a gradualist approach to the settlement of the land question. It was better for the time being to pay a low rent rather than a high purchase price. All this was sober enough; it reflected much of the common sense wisdom—as opposed to rhetoric—of the Irish country-side. But then the editorial shifted gear and came up with a remarkable attack on William O'Brien and Michael Davitt: 'They are reversing the true order of things. Instead of Home Rule depending upon agrarian reform, agrarian reform depends on Home Rule.'[128]

In reply, Haviland Burke was to give a full exposition of his views in a two-part article, 'Parnell's Land Policy', which was published in the *Weekly Freeman* in January 1900. The essence of Burke's case lay in the claim that the Redmondites were propounding an erroneous conception of Parnellism. He said of Redmond and his followers:

They regard the new movement for obtaining for tenants the statutory right to compel landlords to sell out on equitable terms as a mere chimera—a hopeless and mischievous delusion. And they concentrate their energies on the advocacy of reforms for which a certain amount of Unionist support may be secured. I do not wish to attack their policy with any language of bitterness. But I do propose to prove that whatever else it may be, it is not Parnellism.[129]

Haviland Burke went on to insist that Parnell had been an unmistakeable advocate of compulsory purchase or expropriation of the land-

---

[127] *Irish Daily Independent*, 14 November 1899.
[128] Ibid.   [129] *WF*, 6 January 1900.

lords. To make his case, he quoted extensively from Parnell's speeches and public statements. For example, he cited Parnell's advocacy of peasant proprietorship at New Ross on 25 September 1880. Parnell had explained: 'Now then is the time for the Irish peasantry to show their determination—to show the government of England that they will be satisfied with nothing less than the ownership of the land of Ireland.' Parnell's position of September 1880 had been somewhat more flexible than Haviland Burke implied; nevertheless, Haviland Burke's case was, broadly speaking, a convincing one. In thus emphasizing Parnell's radical side—his willingness at a certain point to support agrarian class conflict—Burke did not deny Parnell's conservatism. It would have been impossible to do so. The very New Ross speech which Haviland Burke quoted at length contained much evidence of this conservatism. Parnell at New Ross had been willing to accept the land war—'a struggle that would be short, sharp and decisive, once and for all'—but in the future he 'wished to avoid all elements of antagonism between classes'. Any solution which fell short of peasant proprietorship would inevitably lead to further tensions between landlords and tenants. Hence Parnell's advocacy of compulsory purchase on generous terms as a means of settling the land question. As Haviland Burke explicitly acknowledged, this was in good part because he saw compulsory purchase as the way that 'class feuds' would be 'assuaged'.[130] There is an obvious tension between the radical and conservative aspects of Parnell's analysis. In a sense Haviland Burke's argument was that the Redmondites had extracted only the conservative aspects of the Parnellite legacy: the conception of ultimate social harmony and toleration. But they had forgotten that Parnell had also been prepared to engage landlords and unionists in bitter conflict. While the Redmondites espoused Parnell's long-term ideal, they were not willing to support the steps which he had claimed it necessary to take in order to achieve that ideal. The Redmondites hoped to achieve by soft words that which Parnell had declared could only be achieved by struggle. In particular, their claim that O'Brien and Davitt had reversed the 'order of things' was revealing. The *Independent* had said: 'Instead of Home Rule depending upon agrarian reform, agrarian reform depends on Home Rule.' This was precisely the charge which conservative nationalists MPs—men like P. J. Smyth and F. H. O'Donnell—had made against Parnell in 1880. For these

[130] Ibid.

leaders, the promotion of agrarian reform had little to do with advancing the cause of Home Rule. In effect, such arguments had rendered Smyth and O'Donnell politically irrelevant in 1880, yet eighteen years later this 'heresy' had revived and indeed was to be found in a surprising quarter—the Parnellite press. Significantly, Patrick White, a prominent radical Parnellite, had already complained to Redmond about the 'political complexion' of the 'independent' newspapers.[131] Haviland Burke considered that Redmond had bent the stick too far to the right and was now as vulnerable as Smyth and O'Donnell had been. What Haviland Burke did not grasp—though he may have feared it—was that John Redmond also perceived this. He was preparing to abandon a policy which had turned out to be unworkable.

As F. S. L. Lyons has observed in an acute passage:

The reunion it (the party) painfully achieved between 1898 and 1900 was less spontaneous than imposed from without. Reunion came partly because even the most purblind politicians could not but be aware that their internal struggles looked cheap and trivial in the context of the centenary of the 1798 rebellion. It came partly because the outbreak of the South African war offered a chance for nationalists of different persuasions to combine in opposition to a British policy which all of them deeply and instinctively abhorred; the contrast between the undignified squabbles of the Irish and the spectacle of the Boers fighting for their independence was painfully apparent to the parliamentarians, as to others, and a powerful incentive to unity. But most of all . . . reunion occurred because if it had not done so there was a real threat that the United Irish League would supplant the divided party in the public esteem and might even in a short time obliterate it altogether.[132]

While this passage accurately defines the context of Irish party politics in 1898–1900 it should be added that two of the three developments stressed by Lyons—the Boer War and the UIL—had had a far more corrosive effect on Redmond's standing than Dillon's. Thus besieged, Redmond could, at least, comfort himself with the observation that the old divisive issue of the Liberal 'alliance' was losing its relevance. With the Conservatives in solid possession of power and the Liberals increasingly uncertain in their advocacy of Home Rule, few nationalists wished to quarrel about it. As Richard Barrett has laconically noted, the reunification of the party 'simply reflected the fact that many of the apparent or surface causes of the split were redundant given the

---

[131] P. White to Redmond, NLI MS 15,232.18 Sept. 1899
[132] *Ireland since the Famine*, London, 1971, 256.

relative irrelevance of the Liberal alliance question around 1900'.[133] Indeed, Dillon's supporters in February 1899 had found little difficulty in committing to the principle of 'independent' opposition as defined by the Parnellite manifesto of 1892.[134] Redmond had one other resource, the generous willingness of the anti-Parnellite majority to accept a Parnellite leader.

Redmond's Election

Even so Redmond's path was a difficult one and required considerable luck. At Ballaghadereen on 14 January, Dillon made a belated conversion to O'Brienism. The *Freeman* editorialized: 'The League is establishing a real unity in the country, with, as Mr Dillon said in the course of his speech, a united party as the direct and inevitable consequence.'[135] Davitt and O'Brien were reported as being of the same mind. They were also worried by Redmond's *rapprochement* with Tim Healy and his band of followers. Partly inspired by their common vulnerability and weakness the Redmond-Healy bloc was not by the standards of the time especially opportunistic—both Redmond and Healy were sympathetic to 'constructive Unionism' and both men were also relatively unenthusiastic about further agrarian agitation. Inevitably, the co-operation between Redmondites and Healyites was the subject of much outraged but also nervous comment in the Dillonite press. The *Freeman* asked if the Parnellite Dr. Kenny had given up his celebrated pre-condition for union—'that all the Bishops should walk with white sheets and candles in penitential procession round the grave of Mr Parnell'[136]—or did he now look to an alliance with the pro-clerical Tim Healy to achieve that end? But such sallies had no effect.

Inevitably the circumstances surrounding Redmond's election were exceptionally confused. John Dillon still hoped that either J. J. O'Kelly or Timothy Harrington would emerge as leader from the Parnellite section. Harrington, despite his poor health, was rather the more likely choice. Redmond regarded O'Kelly's recent disloyalty in Roscommon with some disgust and was therefore unwilling to serve under him. Redmond's relations with Harrington on the other hand,

[133] R. Barrett, 'The Policies and Political Character of the Parnellite Party' (University College, Dublin, MA, 1983), 192–3.
[134] Boyce, *Nationalism*, 267.
[135] *FJ*, 20 January 1900.
[136] Ibid.

although strained, had never broken down absolutely. Indeed, both men shared a suspicion of the pretensions of the UIL. But although Redmond might just have lived with Harrington's leadership, he decided first of all to make a bid for the chairmanship himself. He hoped to achieve success through his recent alliance with Tim Healy and his followers. Even so Redmond's bid seemed likely to fail through lack of support.

But as the decisive meeting approached, a sudden and rather unexpected development occurred. At the last minute, William O'Brien—with Michael Davitt's assent—urged Dillon and indeed his other friends to support Redmond.[137] Healy felt sure that O'Brien did so because he was unware of the Healy/Redmond *rapprochement*.[138] But, in fact, O'Brien appears to have known—it was after all a matter of public comment—that Redmond could count on Healy's support.[139] O'Brien's intervention was quite decisive. Up to the last minute, many anti-Parnellites were keen to support anybody other than Redmond. As a last desperate throw, J. J. Clancy and Edmund Leamy were suddenly suggested as suitable candidates. Both men had their good points but neither had claims remotely comparable to those of Redmond. Edward Blake, a former leader of the Liberal party in the Canadian House of Commons and an Irish MP since 1892, weary of all this tedious squabbling, finally called a halt and proposed Redmond for the chair. Even then the conflict did not end. P. A. McHugh, the North Leitrim MP and militant UIL activist spoke in the strongest terms against Blake's motion. William O'Malley, MP for Connemara, was appalled. He quickly intervened to say the obvious, as he later recalled: 'as it was agreed to have a chairman from the Parnellite section, it was most desirable that the best man should be selected and there was no question but Redmond was the best man.'[140] Whether because O'Malley's speech had a sobering effect—or perhaps because P. A. McHugh was brought up to date with the implications of William O'Brien's latest position—'the opposition to the nomination ceased and Redmond became our chairman'.[141]

[137] For good discussions of reunion, see F. S. L. Lyons, *Irish Parliamentary Party*, 67–89; *Dillon*, 205, and also, notably, Philip Bull, op. cit., 333–43.

[138] Healy, *Letters and Leaders*, vol. 1, 444.

[139] Lyons, *Irish Parliamentary Party*, 88.

[140] 'The John Redmond I knew', *Connaught Tribune*, 16 March 1918. This is a fuller account than the one given in William O'Malley's memoir *Glancing Back*, London, 1933.

[141] Ibid.

O'Brien's move had obviously been vital. Yet his motivation
remains unclear. Why should it after all be a blow to Healy to give him
what he wanted? O'Brien's actions only make sense in the light of two
considerations. One was entirely honorable: Redmond had achieved a
genuine stature. To substitute an inferior Parnellite would have been
insulting not just to Redmond but to an increasingly disillusioned
Irish public opinion. But there was another consideration and it was a
rather more devious one.

For over a year O'Brien had successfully sapped Redmond's
political strength. He had won over important militants. He had
played havoc with Redmond's support base in the west. O'Brien must
have reasoned that Redmond had been taught a fairly rough political
lesson by the UIL. The new leader would surely grant the new
organization a certain wary respect. Dillon had been keen to ensure
that a pliable Parnellite got the chair. O'Brien's priorities were the
same—or apparently so. But there was a crucial difference: Dillon
wanted a chairman who could be manipulated by Dillon, O'Brien
wanted a candidate who could be manipulated by O'Brien. In
O'Brien's eyes Redmond was that candidate: in the first few months of
1900 he was to put this theory to the test. The *New York Times*
(traditionally sympathetic to Healy) noted that the new leadership will
be in the hands of a 'commission'[142] but who now was going to
dominate that commision?

---

[142] *New York Times*, 4 February 1900.

3

'Virile' Agitation 1900–1902

If there were absolutely free transit in Ireland the Irish tillage farmers could never compete with any hope of success against America, and against the new competitor that is appearing over the Eastern horizon, so long as he has to pay rack rent. What the then member for Meath (Parnell) said in 1879 of landlords and tenants is true today: 'One must go'; and his question remains: 'Which shall it be?'

Weekly Freeman, 28 June 1902.

Nothing more remarkable has been seen of late in Ireland than the manner in which here and there throughout the country the electors have taken their courage in both hands and refused to accept the nominees of the United Irish League at the local Government elections, returning in some cases independent Nationalists, and in some cases even landlords and Unionists. The new spirit has even crept into some of the Nationalist newspapers.

Irish Times, quoted in *Weekly Freeman*, 14 June 1902.

IN the early months of 1900 the new leader of the Irish party, John Redmond, faced one absolutely overriding problem: What was his relationship to be with William O'Brien and his United Irish League? P. A. McHugh, whose opposition had been evident up to the last, was quick to issue a public warning: 'Mr Redmond repudiated any intention of hostility to the United Irish League. Of course, the United Irish League does not depend, in the very least degree for its continued extension upon Mr Redmond . . . or indeed upon the reunited Irish Party.'[1] McHugh, particularly irritated by a new Healyite venture, the *Sligo Star*, which threatened his own *Sligo Champion*, also called for an unrelenting campaign against Healy and his friends.

William O'Brien's *Irish People*, which he had established in September 1899 to support the UIL, had already outlined the movement's agrarian programme for those areas outside the west—

---

[1] *Sligo Champion*, 3 February 1900.

where the appeal of land redistribution was less obvious—in a blunt editorial: 'It is simply "Delenda est Carthago". Landlords will have to go.'[2] Redmond's response to this programme in mid-February was reasonably satisfactory to O'Brien. In his address to 'the people of Ireland' he acknowledged:

The land question is still unresolved. It can never be solved until the industry of agriculture—the main industry of our country—is freed, by the universal establishment by compulsory purchase of an occupying proprietorship, from the burden which still weighs it down and by some great scheme for replacing the land, in the poverty-stricken districts of the west in the hands of the people.[3]

But beneath the surface all was not well. From March to June 1900 Redmond was locked in a conflict with O'Brien: at stake was the whole question of the future development of Irish nationalism. For Redmond it was to be a battering and bruising experience which left him with a lifelong distrust of O'Brien.

Redmond's main adviser during this stormy period was Timothy Harrington. Harrington had been happy to use the UIL as a means of bringing about the unity of the Irish party. But, once this step had been achieved, Harrington wanted to strengthen this unity rather more than he wanted to see the expanded influence of the UIL. In particular, both Redmond and Harrington wanted to create the conditions for Healy and his followers to return to the fold. For this objective to be achieved, it was necessary to weaken O'Brien's hold over the UIL. On 10 March Redmond acknowledged: 'The United Irish League though not yet extended over every province, is now the strongest of existing national organisations.'[4] But this oblique reference to the UIL's cool reception in Leinster—'where they look with suspicion upon the grazing agitation'[5]—combined with a call for an immediate national convention aroused ire in the O'Brienite camp. O'Brienite anger was intensified by an editorial (penned by Timothy Harrington) in the *Irish Independent*[6] five days later, which developed similar themes. O'Brien's close supporters—for example E. Haviland Burke[7]—feared that Redmond hoped to exploit his personal support

[2] *Irish People*, 7 October 1899.
[3] *Weekly Freeman*, 17 February 1900.
[4] *WF*, 17 March 1900.
[5] Harrington to Redmond, 3 March 1900, NLI MS 15194.
[6] *Irish Independent*, 15 March 1900.
[7] E. Haviland Burke to William O'Brien, 16 February 1900, UCC MS AKA 100/13.

in the capital to 'boss' any convention held in Dublin. But such an analysis of Redmond's strategy cannot excuse another instance of amazing tactical ineptness on O'Brien's part.

With Redmond only just installed in the chair—and the country glutted on statements professing unity and *bonhomie* all around—O'Brien attempted to remove him. On 16 March, Redmond addressed an Irish banquet in London. He was still prepared to offer O'Brien some comfort: he rejoiced 'at the work' of the UIL and called for its 'completion'.[8] But within hours his mood towards O'Brien had changed. The reason is not hard to find: Redmond had learnt of O'Brien's intrigue against his leadership. Not surprisingly, Redmond's speech in Liverpool the next day was not to O'Brien's liking. With Healy at his side,[9] he declared: 'Ireland for the moment was quiet. There was not at the moment any great and powerful organisation at work. There was no great national agitation on foot.'[10] Under the circumstances, it was the least that might have been said. O'Brien's ill-timed and unplanned attempt to get rid of Redmond deserved no better.

Naturally, however, O'Brien did not see things this way. The O'Brienite press exploded with indignation. 'The time has come for testing Mr Redmond's capacity to lead a united country. The fact that he has already been more than a month in the chair, and nobody can tell with any certainty what is the attitude of his Party towards the only Nationalist Organisation of the people has become a matter too serious to be dealt with by simply ignoring it.' The *Irish People* continued: 'Mr Redmond must know well that there is no disposition on the part of the League to trick him up.'[11] But Redmond knew no such thing—somewhat demoralized, he soon wilted under this barrage. Harrington wrote to him and desperately urged him to stand firm. Harrington argued: 'I tell you frankly in my judgement you will have to make a stand against it instead of appeasing this insane savagery any further.'[12] In particular, Harrington insisted that the Healyites deserved toleration. 'The history of the party for you and all of us commences with January 31, 1900.'[13]

[8] *Irish People*, 31 March 1900.
[9] *Letters and Leaders*, vol. i, 448.
[10] *IP*, 31 March 1900.
[11] Ibid.
[12] Harrington to Redmond, 30 March 1900.
[13] Ibid.

But Redmond clearly felt unsure of his ground. O'Brien after all did have the support of the one vibrant mass nationalist organization in the country. He began to make conciliatory noises in O'Brien's direction. In particular, in early April Redmond sent an open letter to the veteran Henry O'Shea, the Limerick portrait painter who had been on Butt's election committee in the 1870s, which signalled his acceptance of the need to strengthen the UIL's mass base.[14] Sunday, 8 April, saw a series of UIL meetings bringing together Parnellites and anti-Parnellites on platforms in Kerry, in Waterford, Cork, Meath, Longford, and Belfast. Commending the 'sage' and 'conciliatory' attitude of Redmond, the *Irish People* commented with typical disingenuousness that the meetings had 'disposed of the last despairing hope of faction—that some sort of conflict could be engineered between the UIL and Mr Redmond and his parliamentary colleagues'.[15] But the tensions did not evaporate overnight. Redmond's ideas still seemed to be close to those of Healy. On 21 April Healy addressed an open letter to a Waterford meeting: 'the landlords' convention is advertised to meet shortly, and a speedy meeting of the national convention has been authorised by the Irish Party. Between these two bodies is it impossible to do business?'[16] Such a conciliatory tone was deeply unpopular with O'Brien—but not it appeared with Redmond. Speaking at this same Waterford meeting Redmond presented this same policy as authentically Parnellite. Redmond recalled the views of Andrew Kettle and identified himself with them:

The way the matter stands is very simple. There is a difference of perhaps, a couple of years purchase, perhaps a little more between the sum at which the tenants can afford to buy and at which the poorer landlords can afford to sell. I for my part, and I am only throwing this out as a suggestion, and I speak on this matter for myself—I for one would be glad to see that margin bridged over by money obtained from what is due to us under the financial relations (cheers). I believe this is a possible policy. I do not know what view the landlords will take of it, they have always been their own worst enemies. They were offered 20 years purchase at higher rents in '86 by Gladstone as a price of their support for Home Rule, that the people would willingly have given.[17]

Inevitably Redmond concluded by invoking Parnell's name in this context:

[14] *IP*, 7 April 1900.   [15] *IP*, 14 April 1900.
[16] *IP*, 28 April 1900.   [17] *WF*, 28 April 1900.

Fellow countrymen, I believe in conciliation, that in every sense of politics—in the spirit as was once said by Parnell (cheers) of compromise; and if these men will join with us and let us settle this question here and now, I for one would not regret that they got terms a great deal better than they deserve from their past history (hear, hear).[18]

These themes were close enough to the O'Brien speech at Dromore of November 1896 but not to O'Brien's mood in the spring of 1900. However, Redmond did at least call for support of the UIL. Some of the old Parnellites were less than enthusiastic. The police noted: 'Mr Redmond called for support of the UIL, this being practically the first time he had done so. Some of Mr Redmond's firm supporters were not pleased with his action and a drunken mêlée occurred during the evening when the meeting was over.'[19] A few days later Redmond joined William O'Brien at the Munster Convention of the UIL. Here he insisted that the settling of the land question would remove the last 'formidable' obstacles to Home Rule.[20] O'Brien welcomed Redmond's remarks warmly. It seemed that a further disastrous split had been averted. Redmond even won a minor victory—he successfully called a convention of the UIL for mid-June. This was much earlier than, for example, John Dillon wanted:[21] Dillon was a supporter of a school of thought within the UIL which wanted to have the country properly organized before any convention. That way it was felt it would be particularly difficult for Redmond with his 'Parnellite' strength in Dublin to manipulate the gathering. But even in June the convention was a lively affair and it proved to be impossible for Redmond to 'boss' it. Indeed, his ally Timothy Harrington was given a particularly rough time for daring to suggest that the people as well as the party bore some of the responsibility for 'ten wasted years'. O'Brien was delighted; he declared with all the usual hyperbole: 'This convention represents a mighty, even a sacred National power, before which any man with Irish blood in his veins need have no difficulty in bowing down and submitting himself.'[22] As yet the manœuvres of Harrington and Redmond had come to little. O'Brien was confident that he retained the initiative. The UIL's subsequent loss of momentum had very little to do with the intrigues of some of the more reluctant 'leaders'; it had everything to do with its inconsistencies as a mass movement.

[18] Ibid.
[19] CO 903/8, 73.
[20] WF, 5 May 1900.
[21] WF, 16 June 1900.
[22] WF, 22 June 1900.

The League in Leinster and Munster

Since the beginning of 1899 William O'Brien had clearly seen the need to promote the UIL's expansion outside Connaught. Connaught was the traditional centre of small farmer agrarian militancy—but the more prosperous farmers in Leinster and Munster were required to swell the ranks of any truly national movement. Munster had some tradition of militancy and was rallied soon enough. Somewhat grandly, the *Irish People* in mid-April 1900 was speaking of the 'absolute' and 'unquestioned'[23] triumph of the UIL in Munster. Even this enthusiastic editorial admitted that traditionally sluggish Leinster had not yet shaken off its apathy. The October general election gave an impetus to organization but it also gave it a particular cast. Membership grew in the year following October 1899 to 76,500 from a figure of 36,000. But this did not as yet imply any major escalation of agrarian radicalism. As the RIC acutely observed: 'In this connection, however, it might be pointed out that a large number of branches, especially in the provinces of Munster and Leinster were purely electoral.'[24] Because of his obsession with Healy, it seemed to be a price O'Brien was willing to pay—indeed, challenged by the new UIL organization, the Healyites suffered electoral eclipse. Healy was returned to Parliament almost without friends—though not without his accustomed wit and sharpness. The 'Healy question' was to all intents and purposes settled and both Redmond and O'Brien turned to face the more fundamental problems of Irish politics.

For if land redistribution was an especially controversial subject outside Connaught so also was the question of the rights of agricultural labourers. Although the Irish agricultural labourers have attracted growing scholarly attention,[25] their relationship to the UIL has not been as yet seriously discussed. As early as January 1900 James Lynam, the UIL organizer, was writing to Michael Davitt from Mullingar to say that the local labourers were 'right enough' but they required careful handling—unfortunately some of the local nationalist district councillors had shown a hard face towards the labourers' demands thus creating a 'fracas'. But Lynam was sure that the event 'will have no effect after a bit'.[26] Lynam's confidence is revealing;

---

[23] *IP*, 14 April 1900.   [24] PRO CO 903/8, 123.
[25] See, notably, David Fitzpatrick, 'The disappearance of the Irish agricultural labourer, 1841–1912' in *Irish Economic and Social History*, vii, 1980, 66–82.
[26] James Lynam to Michael Davitt, 22 January 1900, T. C. D. Davitt papers. DP A 40.

whatever their resentments against local nationalist bigwigs the labourers had no alternative but to stay within the camp. On the platform of one of the more critical Munster meetings of early April 1900, when the UIL first 'rallied' that province, William O'Brien broached the problem. He was genial if a little vague:

'So far as I have been able to study the claims of the labourers' was a revealingly amateurish phrase to fall from his lips. It is inconceivable that he would ever have said 'so far as I have been able to study the claims of the farmers'. Nevertheless, O'Brien did his best to hit the right note: 'They (the labourers) are the *backbone of every fight for Ireland* and I for one will never be a party to seeing them beaten down (cheers).'[27]

Some observers were indeed rather less optimistic about the League's ability to deal with the problem thus presented. As the *Irish People* recalled of the summer of 1900: 'We were met with all sorts of dismal arguments that the division between the farmers and the labourers was incurable; that we must either freeze out the farmers by pressing forward the claims of the labourers, or antagonise the labourers in order to gratify the farmers.'[28] But the same editorial recalled: 'We did not allow ourselves to be terrified by these forbodings.' Instead William O'Brien called for the labourers to continue to be 'the backbone' of Irish agitation. This had been their role in the past—so it should be in the future. But there were new and difficult problems to resolve. The farmers had been slow indeed to give their labourers the cottages and small plots of land as provided for in land legislation since the 1880s. As early as 1888 this was the subject of much bitter comment. In some notorious cases, local farmers had enough clout to engage in profiteering out of the provisions of labourers' cottages. The friends of the labourers—from J. Casey[29] in the 1880s to D. D. Sheehan[30] in the 1900s—recorded these abuses with a considerable sense of moral outrage. A 'Mere Irishman' noted angrily in this context in the *Irish People*: 'And today the labourers are once again asked to take a part in the fray, to throw in their lot with the farmers and strike the last and final blow against the crumbling fortress of landlordism. And what return will be their reward? What

[27] *WF*, 14 April 1900.
[28] *IP*, 10 August 1901.
[29] *Justice*, 8 December 1888.
[30] *Ireland Since Parnell*, 117.

return will they get for services so ungrudgingly rendered? The answer is coldness and contempt.'[31]

While being careful to give space to the expression of such opinions the *Irish People* sought to play down such sectional tensions: 'The farmers and the labourers are not in reality separate classes at all; they are simply the poor and the less poor among the hapless children of the soil.'[32] This editorial added: 'more than half the manual labourers of Ireland are farmers and at least a third of the farmers are manual labourers.' The conclusion was felt to be unavoidable: 'The difference between the vast bulk of the farmers and the labourers is therefore the difference between neighbours almost equally poverty-stricken struggling for the bare necessities of life within a crowded corner of the superficial area of the country, while the 10,000 landlords and their 32,000 more than a hundred acres men monopolise the fat of the land and the silk of the kine.'[33]

Yet despite this supposed unity, there is little evidence in Leinster at any rate of anyone—farmers or labourers—sharing a sentiment of 'neighbourliness'. The labourers in the end were won over. Not so much because there was an unproblematical community of interest which united the rural 'have nots' as the *Irish People* supposed, but largely for a more negative reason. The tensions with the farmers were real and never evaporated. But in a vague way, labourers might hope to gain something in the long term from the defeat of landlords and big graziers—they stood to gain nothing from their continued predominance. Much was summed up by an exchange at a UIL meeting at Portroe, Co. Tipperary. During UIL organizer David Sheehy's speech, a voice interrupted: 'What about the labourers?' Sheehy's reply was typical: 'If we get into the harbour they are safe.'[34] The labourers for the most part supported the UIL but they did so without any noticeable passion or particular enthusiasm.

But while the League with one voice somewhat casually reassured the labourers, with another voice, local strong farmers in Leinster and Munster were reassured also that no unwanted bouts of agrarian radicalism were to be foisted upon them. John Redmond, in a Wexford

[31] *IP*, 23 March 1901.
[32] *IP*, 10 August 1901.   [33] Ibid.
[34] *Nenagh Guardian*, 13 September 1902. On the absence of 'neighbourliness' in Leinster, see David S. Jones, 'Agrarian Capitalism', notably 2–10, 106–14, 291–4, also his 'The Cleavage between Graziers and Peasants in the Land Struggle, 1890–1910', in Clark and Donnelly, *Irish Peasants*, 386.

speech of February 1901, insisted on this point with particular firmness.[35] Indeed, with Michael Davitt absent in America and O'Brien prostrate through nervous tension much of the year, the UIL's agrarian militancy in 1901 seemed to be either on the wane,[36] or else rather spurious. Symbolically, the 'Parnellstown' or Kilcolooney estate in Galway—the great 'proof' of the nationalist leadership's opposition to ranching—remained in the hands of graziers rather than the small holders and labourers who they wished to help. (Parnell's Irish Land Purchase and Settlement Company had acquired this land in the 1880s; following the failure of Parnell's company, the Land Commission had rented the bulk of the estate to graziers to whom in the summer of 1901, it resolved—despite all the UIL's argument—to sell the estate.)[37] In April 1901 the *Irish People* had to point out that one western journal—apparently fully committed to the aims of the UIL— was publishing seductive advertisements for grazing farms in both Sligo and Roscommon.[38] Whilst outside the west the *Freeman* grumbled as late as September 1901 that it was 'discreditable to Leinster to have rendered such comparatively little assistance to the national cause'.[39] In March 1902 James McCann, MP for St Stephen's Green, Ireland's 'premier man of affairs',[40] published a pamphlet 'The Irish Problem: People versus Bullocks'[41] which was so enthusiastic in its advocacy of the economic benefits of tillage that even the *Freeman* regarded it as unrealistic.[42] But there was perhaps an even more profound objection to McCann's advocacy—his own extensive grazing interests. James Connolly's *Workers' Republic* commented sourly on McCann who was the promoter of the Society for the Preservation of the Irish Peasant and one of the founders of the *Irish Peasant* newspaper: 'He (McCann) grazes most of Meath and Westmeath. He is going to root the peasantry somewhere perhaps but it won't be Meath or Westmeath'.[43]

The police reports convey much of the character of the UIL 'advance'. Noting in October 1901 that the number of branches had

[35] *WF*, 27 February 1901.
[36] J. V. O'Brien, *William O'Brien*, 129.
[37] *WF*, 20 July 1901.
[38] *IP*, 6 April 1901.
[39] *WF*, 13 September 1901.
[40] *Irish People*, 5 July 1902.
[41] Reprinted in *CT*, 29 March 1902.
[42] *WF*, 24 May 1902.
[43] *Workers' Republic*, 6 October 1902.

increased by a further 330 and that membership now stood at 144,700, the police concluded: 'The League as an agrarian and intimidatory organisation has been almost confined to the provinces of Connaught and Munster, and two or three counties on the fringe of those provinces. The League in both Leinster and Munster may be practically described as a political body organised for the purpose of furthering nationalist aims generally.'[44] It is clear that as the UIL expanded across the country it made its way as an electoral and political organization. It ceased to have any pretensions as an organization of grass roots agrarian radicalism. The police reports harp on this point time and time again. It was a pressure group for land reform and national independence. It was *not* a semi-revolutionary challenge to the British state in Ireland; it was not, in other words, the Irish Land League re-born. 'The explanation of the discrepancy between the extension of the League and the extension of agrarian crime is that the east and south of Ireland are not concerned with a problem which is serious only in the west and that the UIL, founded for agrarian purposes is over the great part of Ireland a political organisation.'[45] This fact helps to explain a rather bizarre exchange between the chief secretary George Wyndham and John Redmond in January 1902. Redmond had claimed that there were 1200 branches of the UIL in existence: George Wyndham, in an Exeter speech, challenged his figure and offered his own—a mere forty branches. Wyndham, of course, meant that only forty branches gave trouble to the police. Commenting on this exchange,[46] David Sheehy, claimed at Silvermines, Co. Tipperary: 'Everybody knew there were between 1000 and 1200 branches but there were only 74 which were having a prejudicial effect. There were 17 in Clare, 15 in Mayo, 9 in East Galway, 8 in Sligo, 7 in Leitrim, 4 in Roscommon, 3 in East Cork, and 1 each in Tipperary, Waterford, Fermanagh and Cavan.'[47] Sheehy then went on to comment on the one branch, Templemore, in Tipperary; in truth, this was a particularly interesting case. It revealed much about the struggle for land redistribution, for it was one of those rare instances

---

[44] PRO CO 903/8, 123.
[45] BL Add. MS 44802. A. J. Balfour papers f.174. Copy of unsigned RIC memo sent to Lord Lieutenant, 23 July 1901 cf. G. Wyndham to A. Balfour, 2 November 1902, 'Nine tenths of the people are holding back from the agitation'. Quoted in Catherine Shannon, 'Arthur Balfour and the Irish Question' (University of Massachussetts, Ph.D., 1974), 142.
[46] *Northern Whig*, 9 January 1902.
[47] *Nenagh Guardian*, 1 February 1902.

when such a struggle was seriously launched outside Connaught. Indeed, by May 1902 the local government election threw a particularly revealing and harsh light on this subject—both in Munster and Connaught. For despite generally good results—the League won 114 out of 136 seats in Connaught, 148 out of 200 in Munster, and 158 out of 280 in Leinster—the UIL suffered also some unpleasant set-backs.[48]

Local Government Electoral Set-back (i) Tipperary

The agitation against the grazing system about Templemore appears to have commenced with a meeting of the United Irish League at Templemore on 24 November 1901, at which Kendal O'Brien, MP for mid-Tipperary, and David Sheehy, ex-MP but still a member of the UIL executive, denounced the grazing system and advocated the boycotting of grazier/shopkeepers. As a result six Templemore shopkeepers agreed to surrender their farms.[49] But this was merely a preliminary strike by the UIL. The real core of the 'grazing question' around Templemore was the notorious Barnane estate, which included 'some of the most fertile land in Munster.'[50] At the very end of 1901, the English born grazier John Thompson of Barnane received the letter which officially opened up what came to be billed as a righteous war against the 'Saxon' in Templemore. It went as follows:

To Mr J. Thompson   29.12.1901

Sir

I am directed by the Committee at Drom to communicate with you in regard to 'grazing system' now so prevalent. The system is deemed by this Committee and the Divisional Executive of mid-Tipperary to be totally at variance with the rights of the people. Your name and others have been taken at Thurles, and forwarded to all branches of the League as one who is hostile to the interests of the people. The Committee wishes you to communicate your standing and intention relative to the above system.

Joseph F. Fanning, Sec.
UIL Drom.[51]

The recipient, John Thompson, along with his brother George, held over 1000 acres of land from Captain Cardan and H. J. Butler. About 200 acres of the land were held on the eleven months system, and the

[48] Ibid.
[49] CO 903/9, 380.
[50] WF, 12 April 1902. Oral evidence to the *Freeman* of John Ryan, 85 years old.
[51] IP, 18 January 1902, PRO CO 903/9, 134.

remainder from year to year. They and their father before them had held the land for over forty years. The receipt of this letter was the opening of a vivid and unpleasant chapter in their lives.

The strategy of the militant section of the local UIL was quite clear. The object was to make life intolerable for the owners and holders of the grass land. They would then, it was hoped, be more willing to sell and the lower the price accepted, the smaller would be the instalments payable by those active agents of the League among whom the spoils would be distributed. At first, showing some resolve, the Thompsons duly ignored the letter. The UIL's reply was swift; led by R. A. Corr, who had been drafted into the county, a turbulent assembly was held at the gates of George Thompson's farm on the night of 21 January 1902, with the clear purpose of intimidation. It was the first of a sequence of such meetings, legal and illegal demonstrations and court hearings of men like Corr who were charged with unlawful assembly. R. A. Corr's speeches frequently referred to Thompson as a 'Saxon grazier'. 'I may tell you', Corr told his antagonist face to face, 'Mr Thompson, to put it all into a nutshell, that nothing but a complete surrender of every piece of these lands will satisfy the Nationalists of Mid Tipperary.'[52] The Templemore conflict was soon to be validated on (more or less) the highest authority. On 16 July 1902, at the Tipperary county convention of the UIL, which was held at Templemore, John Dillon told an audience which included the four Tipperary MPs that the evil of the grazing system around Templemore was not one whit less than that of Connaught. He concluded by investing the Templemore struggle with major significance: 'If they succeed in forcing the grazing lands around Templemore to be divided amongst the people, the rest of Ireland would follow suit in the same direction.'[53] On the surface then the Templemore fight was a resounding conflict of principle and national interests. Beneath the surface, however, motives were very much more complex; for here it is possible to reveal a world of machination and considerable personal opportunism. For R. A. Corr's efforts to exclude the Saxon graziers from the Celtic peasantry were less than fully successful. So much was publicly acknowledged in a UIL placard shown at Borrisoleigh held on 16 February 1902. 'The cloven foot has appeared in our midst,' it read, 'the Saxon grazier, that feeds on the plundered homes of your

[52] PRO CO 903/9, 132–42, for the whole incident.
[53] *Nenagh Guardian*, 19 July 1902.

kith and kin,' had found a more effective ally than the British government. 'We can fight coercion easily enough but local intrigues require the most vigorous action within our power.'[54]

The divisions in Templemore UIL circles were in fact painfully evident. Kendal O'Brien and David Sheehy stood on the same platform in November 1901, but they were soon to drift apart. Kendal O'Brien fled to 'parliamentary work' in London rather than fight with the Thompsons—to whom he was connected through his wife's family. In some embarrassment, he excused himself to Redmond by claiming that he 'lacked organizing ability' was 'not a ready speaker' and found the whole business 'disagreeable'.[55] Sheehy in anger told Redmond that if the full facts were known publicly, 'he (O'Brien) would not get ten nationalist votes in Tipperary'.[56] The more 'respectable' members of Borrisoleigh UIL branch—J. Ryan, D. O'Shea and M. O'Shea—appeared, however, to sympathize with O'Brien. Michael O'Shea, in particular, had extensive dealings with the Thompsons. They attempted to purge the militants and by February 1902 there were, in fact, two Borrisoleigh UIL branches who more than once came to blows with each other.

Even this catalogue does not exhaust the local complications. The boycotting of the Thompsons was intense: in February a Catholic lady, Mrs Bohan of Drom, who had offered the police the use of her home, had her funeral boycotted. Not surprisingly then a local hotelier named Hickey who continued to do business with the Thompsons also found himself boycotted. The police confidently insisted that the 'jealousy' of another hotelier, E. Mullally, had played the key role here. Hickey, however, had much local support, including clerical support, and the police surmised that the UIL's relatively weak showing (see Table 1) in the area's local government elections of May 1902 was due to the opposition of Hickey's following. (The Tipperary results, especially north Tipperary, were the worst in Munster: the UIL won only 30 out of 57 seats.)[57] Mullally, Hickey's opponent, was a suggestive character—over a year later, his ranching activities brought him under local pressure.

On 27 October 1903 Mullally had to appear (with several other members of the Templemore branch) before the standing committee

---

[54] PRO CO 903/9, 132–42.
[55] Kendal O'Brien to Redmond, 3 July 1902. NLI MS 15228.
[56] Sheehy to Redmond, NLI 15228 10 May 1902.
[57] PRO CO 903/9, 380.

Table 1. Percentage of Members of United Irish League Elected
(Munster)

Counties etc.	Percentage of Leaguers in County Council	Percentage of Leaguers in Rural District Councils
Clare	86.3	70.0
Cork, East Riding	78.1	78.3
Kerry	76.0	65.2
Limerick	93.3	84.0
Tipperary, North Riding	46.1	39.8
Tipperary, South Riding	58.0	61.1
Waterford	68.0	68.9

Source: PRO Co90c/9/381

of the UIL in Dublin. The police were informed that the case was
settled by Mullally undertaking (1) to build a residence for himself and
(2) to allow a portion of the farm to his herd. This settlement was
widely regarded as a victory for Mullally.[58] In this 'crisis' he had been
greatly comforted by his friend David Sheehy—the same Sheehy who
had been so tough on Kendal O'Brien—who had provided him with a
signed note exempting him from a UIL boycott and assuring him that
the agitation would soon blow over. Such matters were common
enough knowledge in Mid Tipperary; when the *Nationalist* newspaper
of Clonmel published the story of Sheehy's note to Mullally, Sheehy
threatened to sue: but in the end he backed down. One indignant local
militant felt that John Redmond himself had protected Sheehy from
the full consequences of his actions.[59] This incident must have given
the 'Saxon' Thompsons food for thought; they held on to their lands
but three years later still required police protection. By 1908 the
UIL's victory was complete, the Barnane lands were sold and
redistributed locally.

Local Government Electoral Set-back (ii) Mayo

In May 1902, the *malaise* in Mayo was to be revealed in a most
suggestive way. William O'Brien had been embarrassed by the

[58] PRO CO 903/10, 25.
[59] For this affair, see *IP*, 8 January 1908.

landlord Colonel Maurice Blake's election in March 1899 for the division of Port Royal in the Mayo Council. Locally popular with Healyite connections,[60] Colonal Blake was, like the O'Conor Don, a remnant of the old Irish Catholic gentry—indeed, he was related to the O'Conor Don by marriage ties. Parnellites then had alleged that O'Brien had been somewhat hypocritical in allowing Blake to slip in unopposed in Mayo, whilst opposing similar candidates in Roscommon. O'Brien's friends had replied implausibly[61] that Colonel Blake slipped in by an accidental failure to lodge a nomination paper to oppose him. But, three years having passed, it was clearly essential for O'Brien to prove his own good faith and to maintain the momentum of the movement by displacing Blake.

On 18 May, O'Brien spoke at Tourmakeady on the question. He vigorously urged his audience to support the UIL candidate, Patrick Tuohy, against the 'landlord' candidate, Maurice Blake. The *Freeman* comment in an editorial 'Leaguer or Landlord' was supremely confident of victory. 'It hardly needed the irresistible speech that Mr O'Brien delivered to secure the defeat of landlordism in the county which is the birthplace of the Land League and the united Irish League.'[62] There were more authoritative pronouncements to come. The following week, on the 25th May, Michael Davitt, billed as 'the most distinguished Mayo man of his generation', addressed the topic of the Blake affair at Partry, in Co. Mayo. Davitt castigated the short-sightedness of Irish landlords. They had refused the 'golden bridge' offered by Parnell in 1880; they were now forced to accept even from Tories a much diminished price for their land. It was essential for the Mayo peasantry to register their continued hostility to the landlord system: otherwise they would be spurning O'Brien's sacrifices on their behalf:

If, therefore, you electors of Partry and Port Royal, cast your votes for Mr Blake, you will do the best day's work for the landlords, the evictor, and for Dublin Castle that the worst enemies of your homes and country could wish to be struck against this cause of ours at this time. Don't misunderstand me in saying this. I know that the present contest is only a petty fight in a corner of an Irish county. Under other circumstances it would be considered and treated in its proper proportions. But the county in question is Mayo, and Mr Tuohy

[60] Lyons, *Irish Parliamentary Party*, 46.
[61] *CT*, 11 March 1899.
[62] *WF*, 24 May 1902.

has been backed in his candidature by Mr O'Brien. The contest therefore assumes an importance altogether disproportionate to this actual area and to the individual candidates. In other words, the fight is now a political one between Mayo landlordism and the League and that is why I am here to ask you not to play the game of the deadly enemies of your homes and country by supporting Blake.[63]

William O'Brien and Michael Davitt had therefore spared no effort to clarify the issues before the electorate. 'Of course, Blake has no chance' the *Freeman* had editorialized. But Blake was a popular local figure who was after all a Catholic. The Revd Michael O'Connell, parish priest of Carnacon, and the Revd James Corbett, parish priest of Partry, were determined to see that he was elected. In the end, such powerful local support proved decisive. Colonel Blake was elected for Port Royal with 599 votes against 257 for P. J. Tuohy. As the police report noted, it was a stunning (albeit local) setback, mainly because the UIL leadership had invested the result with such significance.[64] The *Irish Times* was jubilant: 'we deduce that in one portion at least of Mayo the people are tiring of the United Irish League.'[65] The *Freeman*[66] along with the local *Mayo News* attacked the anti-nationalist role of the Catholic clergy. It was pointed out that Father O'Connell had professed to be a staunch supporter of the UIL, and in the old days, Father Corbett had been an ardent supporter of the Land League. The *Mayo News* asked in anguish: 'What has wrought the change?' It provided its own answer: 'if it is to be attributed to the fact that Colonel Blake was a Catholic what a blessing in disguise . . . that the great body of Irish landlords are not Catholics.'[67] Undoubtedly Blake's Catholicism had helped him. But it is important to note that the two priests had always been critics of the UIL. Father O'Connell may have been president of two UIL branches, but as the police noted as early as 1898, he combined this with a public disapproval of the UIL's land redistribution programme.[68] Father Corbett had been a supporter of the old Land League, but his June 1898 correspondence with Michael Davitt explicitly acknowledged his disagreement with Davitt's new agitation.[69] Davitt described Corbett as a 'old time Land

[63] *Mayo News*, 31 May 1902.
[64] PRO CO 904/7S, Co. Insp. Bourke's report on Mayo in May 1902.
[65] Quoted in *Mayo News*, 31 May 1902.
[66] Ibid.   [67] *Mayo News*, 31 May 1902.
[68] See above, Chapter 2.
[69] Fr. Corbett to M. Davitt, 29 June 1898, TCD, DPA 58, 4624.

Leaguer but an active enemy of the present movement.'[70] The *Mayo News* took some comfort from the fact, that, at least, public attitudes were now more clearly defined. 'During the past year the people in more parts of Mayo than Port Royal have shown very lamentable lethargy in the national struggle.' The *Connaught Telegraph*[71] expanded the point: it noted that the UIL had contested twelve seats in the county council elections but had been defeated in no less than four contests. It acknowledged that the result was the best gauge of Mayo sentiment and reflected a substantial decline in nationalist morale. Recording set-backs in such strongholds as Claremorris, Castlebar and Westport the local county inspector rated the UIL's performance as even worse than the Mayo home rule press admitted. Pointing to the return of Lord Oranmore, Colonel Simpson Burke and a number of local graziers, County Inspector Bourke concluded: 'it has been abundantly demonstrated that the League has not that hold upon the people it was supposed to have and that its best or worst days are over.'[72] Mayo had been the original birthplace of the Land League movement in 1879; by 1881 in a context of much political division, chaos and disappointment, it had quietly drifted out of that movement. Except for scattered remarks before the Special Commission in 1888 by William O'Brien and Parnell, this fact received little attention outside the county itself. Apparently now in the 1898–1902 period a similar process was repeating itself: but this time the matter achieved national prominence. Most observers now realized that the League's stronghold was, in reality, no such thing. The *Connaught Telegraph* left its readers with an uncomfortable question to ponder:

Three years ago the United Irish League was little more than in its infancy, yet it was strong enough to make a successful fight against all the mighty powers directed against it, and gained many victories for the men who elected to wage war against the enemies of our country from under the shelter of its protecting banner. Three years have now passed away and the League has become a power throughout Ireland. What has become of it in its birth place?[73]

The advent of T. W. Russell

But despite these problems in its traditional citadel, Irish agrarian radicalism gained at this point a new and perhaps rather unexpected

[70] *Melbourne Advocate*, 15 May 1902.
[71] *CT*, 31 May 1902.
[72] PRO CO 904/7S, Bourke's report.
[73] *CT*, 31 May 1902.

ally in T. W. Russell, Ulster Unionist MP for Tyrone South. Even by Unionist standards, Russell was in many respects a rather unlikely friend for the UIL. He had been acrid in his anti-nationalist rhetoric: 'All over the south and west the story is the same. Protestantism is simply being squeezed out, all the three Protestant denominations are feeling it . . . here in Ulster we have made up our mind. We shall not have these men with their infamous record to reign over us.'[74] As late as 1900 Russell gave an indication of his debt to vigorous Ulster Protestant sentiment: he proffered his constituency supporters in South Tyrone an undertaking that he would resign from any conservative government which conceded a Catholic university to Ireland. Some feeling of his constituency party's mood can be gained from the fact that at the Aughnacloy meeting where he made this concession, Russell was criticized for having had the audacity to pay visits to the local Catholic clergy in his constituency! William O'Brien's *Irish People* (21 July 1900) commented bitterly on 'an extraordinary and unprecedented bargain with the bigots of South Tyrone . . . We have had traitors, factionists, and renegades galore. But we search in vain for the name of anyone who made such a bargain as that clinched at Aughnacloy last Saturday by Mr T. W. Russell.' But William O'Brien and his newspaper were soon to take a kinder interest in Russell; for as F. S. L. Lyons has written of Russell: 'his position was anomalous, for although he was a Unionist , that is to say a member of a party which confessedly represented the landlord interest, he held . . . that the only solution of the land question lay in the direction of compulsory sale.'[75] As early as 1894 Russell had made himself deeply unpopular with the more conservative and pro-landlord leaders in the unionist camp: 'I was warned not to attack T. W. Russell but the warning indicates the slough we are in,' wrote the Duke of Argyll to the Marquis of Dufferin and Ava, adding for good measure, 'The Ulster Unionists are as unprincipled as the Connaught nationalists when robbing the landlords.'[76]

Despite such opponents, Russell had the patronage of Joseph Chamberlain and was thus appointed to a junior post in Salisbury's administration in 1895.[77] Partly as a result of 'imprudent'[78] direct

[74] *IWI*, 18 May 1912.
[75] *Irish Parliamentary Party*, 135.
[76] PRONI D1041/HBF, Argyll to Dufferin, 5 December 1894.
[77] Gailey, 'Unionist government policy', 23/4, 94/5.
[78] PRONI D1041/HBF 156, Argyll to Dufferin, 28 April 1897.

appeals to Salisbury on the land question in 1897, however, senior conservatives felt less and less inclined to humour Russell. Russell responded by trying to whip up grass roots support.

In March 1900, under Russell's influence, a North Antrim Land Association was formed. Russell's appeal was to a substantial tenantry as opposed to the impoverished small holders of the west. It was obvious to all that this increase in activity coincided with high rather than low agricultural prices in Ulster. The *Ballymoney Free Press*, a key supporter of Ulster land reform, observed: 'The philosophy of it is that an improved financial position puts backbone in men to struggle more strenuously for what they consider essential to their assured prosperity.'[79]

On the eve of the general election of 1900, Russell was approached by J. R. Fisher, the editor of the *Northern Whig*, the main liberal unionist journal in the province, and advised to step up his land purchase campaign.[80] The result was Russell's famous Clogher speech of 20 September 1900 which called for £120 million pounds worth of financial assistance from the British Treasury to resolve the Irish land question: 'The central proposition is that the fee simple of the agricultural land in the country not in the use and occupation of the landlord himself should as speedily as possible be transferred to the occupier at a fair valuation, the state advancing the purchase money to the purchaser, and, in certain cases, adding a bonus to the agreed sum as a compensation for compulsion.'[81] For the *Whig*, this amounted to a 'great speech',[82] Salisbury was less impressed. He decided not to re-appoint Russell to his post as parliamentary secretary to the Local Government Board. Russell reacted to his sacking with vigour: on 7 January 1901 he opened the first of a series of meetings on the land question at Coleraine.[83] Russell's tone was decidedly Unionist. Redmond believed, he pointed out at Glendermott, that compulsory sale would breed Nationalists: Russell, on the other hand, believed it would strengthen support for the union.[84] The *Whig*, which supported Russell solidly throughout 1901, argued an even more Unionist case: only Unionists, it claimed, were sincere land reformers; nationalists always had ulterior motives. On 5 June Russell

[79] Quoted in J. R. B. McMinn, 'The Revd J. B. Armour and liberal politics in North Antrim 1869–1914' (Queen's University, Belfast, Ph.D., 1979), 336–90.

[80] *Northern Whig*, 7 February 1902.

[81] *NW*, 21 September 1900. [82] *NW*, 21 September 1900.

[83] *NW*, 8 January 1901. [84] *NW*, 18 April 1901.

called some 8000 delegates to a conference at the Ulster Hall: the
largest gathering at that venue since the great Unionist convention of
1892. The *Whig* hailed the 'stolid seriousness', the 'stern decorum',
and the 'attentive, dead serious'[85] *mien* of the meeting—as opposed, of
course, to the allegedly frivolous and excitable mood of nationalist
gatherings. A new body was formed: the Ulster Farmers' and
Labourers' Union and Compulsory Purchase Association, 'a rather
cumbrous but sufficiently definite title'. In November, when Russell
'wound up'[86] his campaign at Finaghy, 'no corner of north-east Ulster'
had been spared his message.

Russell's sense of political direction began, however, to waver. He
started to identify himself with the UIL struggle on the Catholic Lord
De Freyne's estate in Roscommon in late 1901.[87] This was bound to be
a controversial move—especially as the UIL's campaign, led in this
instance by John Fitzgibbon, had been bitterly condemned as
foolhardy adventurism by prominent nationalists such as Jasper Tully.
Russell himself had described the plan of campaign of the late 1880s as
a 'fraudulent conspiracy'—to most Unionists the De Freyne struggle
was merely a later variant of the same conspiracy. Even the *Whig*,
previously so favourable to Russell, declared the De Freyne affair was
'simply a case such as that boasted of by Mr John Dillon when he
offered to produce men who "can't pay and won't pay because I tell
them not to pay"'.[88]

Russell refused to step back from such controversies, however; in
January, his new movement backed James Wood against Colonel
Robert Wallace, a prominent Orangeman helped by the legendary
William Johnston of Ballykilbeg, in the East Down by-election. To
win the seat, Russell needed the votes of the 2500 Nationalists in the
constituency plus at least a thousand Unionists. Before the end of
January Redmond had decided to throw the nationalist vote Russell's
way. Russell did not yet cease to be a Unionist. Speaking in
Downpatrick during the Wood campaign, T. W. Russell explained his
position:

He made an earnest appeal that day for help for Mr Wood—an appeal for
support in the formation of Ulster of reinforcements for the rest of Ireland on

[85] *NW*, 6 June 1901.
[86] *NW*, 14 November 1901.
[87] *NW*, 19 December 1901.
[88] *NW*, 3 July 1902.

that (agrarian) question. Let them differ on home rule—that could be fought
out again. (A voice—we won't get it now anyway.) I quite agree, replied Mr
Russell, and they know it.[89]

In short Russell argued that with a strong conservative government in
power there was no possibility of Home Rule. Unionist tenant farming
voters could afford to vote therefore on their class rather than their
'national' interests. But it was his effective dependence on nationalist
support which appalled his erstwhile supporter, the *Northern Whig*.
Russell was quoted as having said that he had in the past 'wholly
misjudged the Irish leader',[90] the day after Redmond gave instructions
to the nationalist electorate to support the tenant right candidate. The
Whig commented bitterly: 'the Unionists of the North have convinced
themselves, as Sharman Crawford convinced himself long ago, that
Ulstermen cannot ally themselves in political action with rabid
repealers and haters of England and those principles of religious and
political liberty with which the name of England is identified with all
the world over.'[91] The *Whig* published a number of historical articles
on earlier tenant right agitations to 'prove' the point. The lesson was
clear: 'Then as now there were those in the South who joined in the
cry (for land reform) . . . because they wanted their money and votes to
use for their seditious and treasonable ends.'[92] Nothing that Russell's
supporters said could allay these suspicions: Wood declared himself a
'convinced Unionist' pointing out that the 'Union was not in the
slightest danger in the present parliament'; but the *Whig* preferred to
promote the recollections of William Bryson, a Co. Down Liberal
Unionist, who remembered Wood as having sided initially with
Gladstone in 1886.[93] The *Whig* asked bitterly: 'We wonder whether he
(Russell) has yet done penance for the Belfast speech in which he
explained the real cause of the intolerable hardships of Ireland.
Ireland lacked prosperity he said, because they the Nationalists had
chased it away by their blackguardism and crime. They cursed the
British government when they ought to have cursed their own leaders
and themselves.'[94] The *Whig* was not alone among the Unionist
and Orange forces in insisting that Wood could not be seen 'as
anything but a Nationalist'.[95]

[89] *NW*, 24 January 1902.   [90] *NW*, 28 January 1902.
[91] *NW*, 22 January 1902.   [92] *NW*, 20 January 1902.
[93] *NW*, 21 January 1902.   [94] *NW*, 3 July 1902.
[95] *NW*, 5 February 1902.

The same newspaper did not fail to remind its readers of the attitude of certain nationalists towards the Irish Presbyterian community. Patrick Ford, editor of the New York *Irish World* was quoted: 'Their fathers went to Ireland to plunder and exterminate the native race, and they inherit and retain the spirit of their fathers. They are an alien element in the Irish population . . . Ireland will have independence in spite of these Presbyterian foreigners, and theirs will be the shameful record of having cast their votes against the freedom of the country in which they have found comfortable homes.'[96] All such attempts to taint Wood by association could not prevent the Russellites' narrow victory. Following Wood's triumph by 147 votes the *Whig* logically admitted 'a severe blow to Unionism in one of its strongholds.'[97] It condemned the thousand or so Unionists who had voted with 2500 Nationalists to give the Russellite victory. The only comfort lay in exploitation of Russell's incautious campaign remark that a majority of less than 2000 would be a defeat. In truth, Russell's victory had been a precarious and narrow one: during the course of the campaign he had decisively broken with the main liberal Unionist organ, the *Northern Whig*. It was only to be expected that Russell's dependence on nationalist votes would create suspicions among his remaining Unionist support. As the *Pall Mall Gazette* declared: 'He has prepared a very tasty dish for the Presbyterian farmers. It is rather more spicy than we expected and we rather think it will upset the stomachs of those who Mr Russell professes to speak for who are, after all, Unionists.'[98]

It is arguable that Russell's narrow majority in East Down, presaged his gradual slide—via acceptance of financial support from Herbert Gladstone[99]—to the point where in 1910 he 'was the official (Irish) party candidate in all but name.'[100] But in the short term Russell's victory, close run thing though it had been, merely served to enhance his prestige.

The accession of strength which Russell represented was all the more important, because there were those in the government whose mind was running towards repression. Lord Cadogan, in a cabinet

[96] *NW*, 22 January 1902.
[97] *NW*, 7 February 1902.
[98] *Pall Mall Gazette* quoted in *NW*, 1 October 1902.
[99] T. W. Russell to Herbert Gladstone, 17 February 1904, Herbert Gladstone papers, BL Add. MS 46061.
[100] Murphy, *Derry, Donegal and Modern Ulster*, 205.

minute 'Condition of Ireland' of 10 March 1902, acknowledged that Lord Clonbrock had made in the previous summer a powerful case against the full utilization of the Crimes Act powers. However, since then there had been a sustained movement against rent payments on the De Freyne, Murphy, O'Grady, Willis-Sandford estates as well as the more usual opposition to graziers. Cadogan's 'precis of official opinion' argues:

While it cannot be said that the UIL have been the instrument through which serious crime has been committed, it is at the same time far from being true that the League has been a crimeless organisation. Since the 1 January 1901, the League has been responsible for 52 cases of recorded outrage, i.e. serious crime. Though these offences consist in the main of intimidation by threatening letters and notices, they include several cases of malicious burning, maiming cattle and firing into or outside dwellings. The criminal action of the League is not, however, to be measured by the actual overt crime in which its operations have resulted, but rather by the boycotting and overt intimidation which it had practised and to which in many cases its victims have readily succumbed. A resort indeed to serious crime may be said to be unnecessary from the League point of view, seeing that as a rule, it can enforce its behest by the less violent, though equally unlawful means of boycotting and intimidation.[101]

Particular mention was made here of the UIL's activities in Templemore. In response, the cabinet agreed to the proclamation under the Crimes Act of Cavan, Cork, Leitrim, Roscommon and Sligo on 16 April 1902. Wyndham, at the same time, dropped his first rather ill-considered proposals for land reform introduced to parliament on 25 March. The *Freeman* bitterly claimed: 'Agrarian legislation is lightly abandoned; agrarian agitation is bitterly assailed.'[102] But such a comment was much too pessimistic; the anti-reform lobby was not dominant in the cabinet.[103] Two weeks later the *Freeman* editorial itself pointed out that the Congested Districts Board had given up any attempt to discriminate against the United Irish League.[104] It was possible for O'Brien to argue with conviction that the government required just one more summer of agitation in Ireland before producing the major and far reaching reform which was required.

But Redmond had his reservations about such an analysis. By the

---

[101] PRO *Cab* 37/61/58; Shannon, 'Balfour', 143.
[102] *WF*, 14 April 1902.
[103] *WF*, 19 April 1902.
[104] *WF*, 28 June 1900.

end of summer the government had placed two-thirds of the country under the Crimes Act and had gaoled a total of eleven members of Parliament as well as two former members.[105] In Mayo and Tipperary, the UIL had tried to force the pace of agrarian radicalism; the results had been less than impressive. Within eighteen months of taking the chairmanship of the party, Redmond had rediscovered his optimism about the prospects for Home Rule.[106] More generally, Redmond seemed anxious to switch the focus of action to Westminster. But he was still unwilling to distance himself in public from O'Brien. On 5 July Redmond and O'Brien *in tandem* addressed a meeting at Limerick. Redmond still seemed to be full of fight.

Let every upholder of the Government, and every upholder of unjust and intolerable landlordism, in the future feel the effect of this movement in one shade or another in every parish in Ireland (cheers). This is a serious matter in which we are engaged . . . I say, let the people, as far as it is in their power— and with union and determination their power will be enormous—let them enter on the path of coercion against their enemies (loud cheers).[107]

Following Redmond's speech, in a phrase which Redmond must have found irritating and which was to be repeated in the O'Brienite press, O'Brien proceeded to 'dot the i's of the eloquent and resolute appeal and warning' of Redmond. He called for a vigorous system of universal boycotting. Revealingly, however, O'Brien felt it necessary to lament the 'apathy' of the 'young men' and the 'selfishness' of the fathers, and declared that in certain districts there had been a decided relaxation. The number of branches was all right but they suffered from a want of purpose.[108] Later that month, O'Brien and Redmond again shared a platform at a convention of the Cork UIL. Redmond was once again rhetorically militant. He spoke of wanting to see a 'formidable' and 'dangerous' organization in every parish.[109] But once again it was O'Brien who—in the words of his own newspaper's editorial—'pointed out the way to give practical effect to Mr Redmond's eloquent and impassioned appeal.'[110]

At the end of August, however, Tim Healy moved to puncture the talk of 'universal boycotting'. The *Wexford Free Press*—the paper's keen interest reflected the fact that Wexford was the 'premier county' in

[105] Shannon, 'Balfour', 144.
[106] See especially his article, 'The Liberal Party and Home Rule', *Weekly Freeman*, 4 May 1901.   [107] *IP*, 12 July 1902.
[108] *NW*, 8 July 1902.   [109] *IP*, 26 July 1902.
[110] Ibid.

Ireland for land purchase—asked a number of key public figures to comment on the current agitation. Healy's reply of 27 August was characteristically percipient. He had heard much talk of social ostracism, he noted:

But I ask if the landlord to be paid on the gale day, and if he is not to be shot, what terror can any threat of 'social ostracism' have for him? His tenants do not give garden parties. Oh, but it may be urged that his horses won't be shod, and his grass lands can not be taken. Very irritating no doubt to the small gentry of the west: but what effect will such pinpricks have on Mr Wyndham's bill or on those who really control legislation? Who are these? They are Lord Lansdowne, the Duke of Devonshire, Lord Londonderry, Lord Clanricarde, the Duke of Abercorn, the Marquis of Waterford, the Marquis of Ormonde, Lord Barrymore, Lord Cloncurry, Lord Fitzwilliam, Lord McNaughten.

How could I tell poor mountainy men that we can win them free land by a slight turn of the wrist? Unless men are prepared to adopt the methods of Nihilism or Dacoity, and go to the gallows instead of to Galway gaol, we know they need not hope to disturb the serenity of the Gilded chamber. A procession of ragged match girls has more effect on the British Parliament than of half Ireland on the plank bed.[111]

At this point Tim Healy's views were untypical of the rest of the nationalist leadership only in so far as they were publicly expressed. In a brutal process of private re-education, the party leadership finally succeeded in making it clear to O'Brien that they did not want him to give effect to their appeals, however eloquent and impassioned.[112] In a series of painfully frank exchanges T. P. O'Connor and John Redmond made this point to O'Brien. In the north too there was a similar 'very amazing change of tone':[113] T. W. Russell, who, during the East Down campaign, had appeared to dismiss voluntary purchase as opposed to compulsion, now rediscovered the merits of the voluntary principle. Nevertheless, it is the cynicism of the nationalist politicians which is most striking: as late as 5 July, Redmond had called for 'the people . . . to enter on the path of coercion against their enemies.'[114] But such a double standard, in which a public militancy was in sharp contrast to the private moderation, was possibly only because the UIL as a mass

[111] NW, 1 September 1902.
[112] See the excellent accounts in J. V. O'Brien, William O'Brien, 135–6; P. Bull, 'The Reconstruction', 354–5.
[113] NW, 1 September 1902.
[114] IP, 12 July 1902.

movement lived by just such a double standard. William O'Brien, humiliated on account of his agrarian radicalism, assessed the implications savagely: when the opportunity to play the moderate statesman was unexpectedly presented to him within a few months he seized it.

4

The Swinford Revolt

It would be easy to speak for others, I might pile up declarations of Mr Parnell at every stage of the Land League movement—from the League's original offer to the landlords of twenty years purchase of Griffith valuation down to the support of Gladstone's land bill which would have forced the Irish tenants to pay twenty two years purchase of first term rents, or 27 years of purchase of second term rents, and to his pleas for conciliation throughout the entire home rule cycle, which are in every particular in agreement with our present attitude towards the loyal minority.

William O'Brien, *Irish People*, 7 November 1903.

(O'Brien's) policy has broken down absolutely, not because it was in conflict with 'Tom Sexton the Bastard' but because it was in conflict with the country and with commonsense. The country looks to you and properly so, to save our situation . . .

Laurence Ginnell to John Redmond, 29 November 1903, NLI MS 15191.

B Y the summer of 1902 there were clearly many indications of war-weariness on the tenants' side. Yet, interestingly, it was precisely at this moment that some landlord representatives attempted to launch a conciliatory initiative. At the request of the editor of the *Irish Independent* (now Healyite) and the *Irish Times*, L. Talbot-Crosbie, a Kerry landlord, wrote a letter to the *Freeman's Journal* in mid-June calling for a conference of moderate men 'representative of the several parties' to work out an agreement on the land question. O'Brien in particular spurned this advance but by September even he had 'moderated' his position. On 3 September, another rather obscure landlord, Captain John Shawe-Taylor, made a similar proposal but this time he actually suggested the names of both the landlord and the tenant representatives. O'Brien found himself named alongside Redmond, Harrington and T. W. Russell. The chief secretary's support for the proposal dispelled early cynicism; by 19 September both O'Brien and Redmond were enrolled as supporters of the new politics of conciliation. By

12 December T. W. Russell assured Redmond that he was in 'substantial agreement'[1] on agrarian matters. The four tenants' representatives met the four landlords—the Earl of Dunraven, the Earl of Mayo, Colonel William Hutcheson-Poe and Colonel Nugent-Everard—in conference in Dublin on 20 December. These landlords were unrepresentative in their moderation, a fact which was in the medium term to tell against the conciliation process.[2]

It is clear that Wyndham's good graces and promises of government credit were the decisive element in this development. He explained his thinking to the cabinet:

The Land Bill introduced on the 25th March of this year has stimulated the desire on the part of both landlords and tenants for a comprehensive settlement of the land question on the basis of voluntary sale. Both parties realise that revisions of rent by judicial procedure recurring every fifteen years impose a handicap on agriculture, the main industry of Ireland, which it cannot bear in an age of keen international competition. A premium is placed on bad farming, and the interests of both parties are subjected to the costly and uncertain lottery of litigation.

The following Table illustrates the further aggravation of these evils since the Bill was introduced on the 25th March.

	25 March	1 October
Total rents brought into court	336,000	365,000
Total rents fixed by Sub-Commission	240,708	247,924
Appeals	73,756	77,386
Appeals outstanding	13,000	13,446
Second-term rents fixed	45,000	50,441
Appeals	22,000	24,940
Percentage of appeals	49 per cent	49.4 per cent

There is a sincere and widespread desire for a settlement. Landlords realize that they are being ruined, not by agitation but by the automatic action of recurring litigation. Tenants realize that a probable though uncertain reduction of rent every fifteen years is dear at that price. The vast majority would now prefer to compound for a moderate reduction effected by purchase, which would free them from litigation and secure to them absolutely the fruits of their industry and enterprise.[3]

[1] T. W. Russell to John Redmond, 10 December 1902, NLI MS 15223.
[2] For discussions of the conference, see S. Warwick-Haller, 'William O'Brien', 378–83, and P. Bull, 'Reconstruction', 359–64.
[3] PRO Cab 37/62/139 Irish Land Bill. Cabinet memorandum by George Wyndham, 6 October 1902.

It is evident also that Wyndham's hand was not forced by the UIL—
the agitation was visibly losing momentum. Wyndham was probably
just as worried by the northern tenants movement led by T. W.
Russell.[4] On 8 December 1902, the chief secretary was able to
publicize figures—probably 'fed' to him by the discontented agrarian
radical Jasper Tully—to the effect that 184 officials (presidents, vice-
presidents and committee men) of the UIL either held the land of
evicted tenants or held land on the 'eleven months system' favoured by
graziers.[5] Laurence Ginnell, one of the UIL's most militant officials,
admitted in a letter to Redmond that, while the figures were exaggerated, there was some truth in them.[6] In reaction, the UIL
expelled Jasper Tully: the socialist republican James Connolly commented sardonically from outside the circle of 'official' nationalism:
'No wonder he was expelled. To give the game away on his fellow
criminals was disgusting.'[7] Indeed, it was precisely because of his
awareness of these divisions in the UIL, that Wyndham felt able to
write to his mother: 'Ireland is more interesting than at any time since
'87. There is more to win and lose in the next six months than ever
before. A certain amount of fighting is necessary to prevent them from
bullying each other. But with that there are better hopes of a longer
peace than I have seen.'[8] An extravagant and ambitious personality—
not without a tendency to grandiose delusion[9]—Wyndham could not
resist the opportunity to give constructive unionism a more radical
tinge; the objective was to settle the 'Irish land problem—in Unionist
eyes—*the* Irish question—for all time'.[10] At first, Wyndham's endeavours were remarkably successful: in his work at this time, Wyndham
was greatly assisted by the appointment of Sir Antony MacDonnell to
the post of under-secretary at Dublin Castle. A scion of a Catholic
landowning family in Mayo, MacDonnell had enjoyed a highly
successful career of some forty years in the Indian Civil Service.
MacDonnell's politics were ambiguous; he was happy to describe

[4] S. Warwick-Haller, 'William O'Brien', 365; A. Gailey, 'Unionist Government
Policy', 162, 212, 300.
[5] *Notes from Ireland* January 1903; *Workers Republic* vol. 3, no. 5, January 1903. John
Dillon suspected Tully of such activity, see Healy, *Letters and Leaders of my Day*,
vol. 11, 459.
[6] Ginnell to John Redmond, 1 December 1902, NLI MS 15191.
[7] *Workers Republic*, ibid.
[8] Gailey, *Unionist Government Policy*, 177.
[9] Ibid., 196; H. Robinson, *Further Memories of Irish Life*, London, 1924, 138–9.
[10] Ibid., 189.

himself as a 'liberal with nationalist leanings' though he could not accept that the Irish were fit for Home Rule. MacDonnell's appointment was a further sign of Wyndham's reformist zeal.[11]

Wyndham and MacDonnell were delighted to find that their views of William O'Brien and those of Dunraven were surprisingly close. They both sought to gain an equitable price for the landlord who wished to sell his land—the government was asked to supply the funds to bridge the gap between what the tenant could afford to pay and what the landlord would accept. Again, both O'Brien and Dunraven agreed on the need for special treatment for the west, though they did not call for compulsory sale in that region. A meeting of 39 Irish MPs—not including John Dillon or Joe Devlin—praised the conference report embodying these views which was published on 4 January.[12] Finally on 25 March Wyndham who had been such a friend to the whole conference process, introduced his own bill. Wyndham's bill embodied many of the recommendations of the Land Conference, and compared with previous legislation was 'a real and generous attempt to provide a lasting solution to the land question.'[13] Land purchase on a large scale was the aim, and if three-quarters of the tenants on any estate consented (in some cases, a bare majority was sufficient), proceedings for sale could commence. The principle that O'Brien had often emphasized, that the tenants' annuity should be less than his present rent, was recognized. Prices to be paid by the tenants would range from twenty-one-and-a-half to twenty-seven-and-a-third years' purchase on second term rents, and eighteen-and-a-half to twenty-four-and-a-half years' purchase on first term rents. The state would advance the money to the tenants, who were to repay it over sixty-eight-and-a-half years at an annuity rate of $3\frac{1}{4}$ per cent. To induce the landlords to sell a bonus of £12 million was provided. The most revolutionary aspect of the 1903 Act[14] lay in the fact that the new body of commissioners—set up to administer its working—were given the power to buy untenanted land from the landlord for redistribution to tenants or other deserving persons, provided a price could be agreed and the landlord was ready to sell.

The act of 1903 contained a controversial 'zone' proposal. If, in the case of agreed direct sales between landlord and tenant, the agreed

[11] Ibid., 178–83.
[12] Lyons, *Irish Parliamentary Policy*, 100–3.
[13] S. Warwick-Haller, 'William O'Brien', 400.
[14] C. F. Kolbert and T. O'Brien, *Land Reform in Ireland*, Cambridge, 1975, 41.

price fell within a zone which secured the tenant's annuity at between
10 and 30 per cent reduction of the previous rent, the estates
commissioners accepted that the price was based on sufficient
security and did not themselves inspect the land; thus the act was
intended to encourage friendly voluntary agreements between landlords and tenants. As government inspection had traditionally led to a
lowering of the price,[15] it was perhaps inevitable that nationalists came
to resent this 'zone' proposal arguing that it led to an inflated price for
Irish land. These same critics also attacked the 'bonus' proposal in the
1903 legislation. Nationalist critics also claimed that the act failed to
address itself to the need for land redistribution—most especially in
the western area of the country. William O'Brien acknowledged
(though he claimed it was partly a result of Dillon's inept tactics) that
the 'Congested Districts clauses, which were among the very latest in
the Bill, had to be hurried through without any adequate attempt by
amendment to develop the sound principles in the Bill which
undoubtedly might have been led to germinate in a great and blessed
settlement of the western problem.'[16] Yet in reality matters were more
complex: Wyndham did not simply leave the problem of land
redistribution to one side, he tampered with it both rhetorically and
administratively and thus raised hopes which subsequent governments found it hard to satisfy. Wyndham's speech introducing his
measure had been of considerable importance because it gave a
special significance to the problems of the west of Ireland. In parts of
the west, Wyndham had recently seen that:

The tenants were living in conditions which you would not find amongst the
kaffirs in S. Africa . . . We ought to build up the agrarian situation in Ireland
from the bottom. The system of village communities seems in the west of
Ireland to have decayed, and at some stage in this decay to have become
fossilised. So if it were not a contradiction in terms you might say it was at
once rotten and rigid.[17]

Twice[18] in the course of his speech, Wyndham argued that landlords
would have to be willing to sell their untenanted land if, as was
desirable, the problem of congestion was to be tackled. It was not

[15] H. Brougham Leech, *The Continuity of the Irish Revolutionary Movement*, London,
1913, 143.
[16] *An Olive Branch*, 246.
[17] Hansard 4th series, vol. 120, col. 190 (25 March 1903).
[18] Ibid., cols. 197 and 207.

unreasonable to argue as the *Freeman* did, that Wyndham had put forward the salvaging of the 'rotten' and 'rigid' communities as the first object of the policy that was to be facilitated by the bonus.[19] The *Freeman* also claimed that Wyndham had insisted that landlords would not be allowed to sell their estates without their untenanted land.[20] This was an understandable 'misreading'—Wyndham's pious hope that landlords would sell their untenanted land did not have the force of a compulsory law. Wyndham had been opposed to compulsion in principle and anyway, as he told Redmond, 'to introduce compulsion now would be to throw the ball in the Lords to those who are not too friendly to the Bill and to myself'.[21] Nevertheless, Wyndham's language *had* raised the expectations of the land hungry, and indeed, one rather important provision of his legislation was to have special significance in this respect. This provision seemed to imply that in the eyes of the state that while western congests had a claim to the fruits of land redistribution, other groups might also be considered. With the intention mainly of allaying the hostility which had greeted some migrating congests, section 75 acknowledged that in the distribution of estates, the claims of farmers' sons, landless men, labourers and even local mechanics who lived near the estate might be recognized.[22] H. Brougham Leech sourly observed that this provision would 'have worked well in any other country but in Ireland was used as a stimulant for disorder.'[23] Despite a promise to the contrary given to cabinet colleagues, Wyndham *had* consulted Irish party leaders on these questions.[24] For this reason in part, Redmond warmly praised Wyndham's sincerity.[25] It was, of course, in the interest of nationalists to underline and even exaggerate Wyndham's generosity. There were instances when Wyndham struck a more cautious note—as, for example, on 24 June when he warned that there was simply not enough land to go round.[26] By November he was openly warning against attacks on the grazing system.[27] John Dillon for one never believed

[19] *Weekly Freeman*, 26 November 1907.
[20] Ibid.
[21] George Wyndham to John Redmond, 5 July 1903, NLI MS 1447.
[22] Royal Commission on congestion in Ireland, final report (Cd 4097) HC 1908, xliii, 14–15 (Dudley Commission).
[23] H. Brougham Leech, *Revolutionary Movement*, 76–7.
[24] Gailey, 'Unionist Government Policy', 139, NLI MS 11447, G. Wyndham to J. Redmond, 5 July 1903.
[25] Hansard, 4th series, vol. 120, cols. 208–48.
[26] Hansard, 4th series, vol. 124, cols. 466–7.
[27] *Weekly Freeman*, 26 November 1907.

that Wyndham's schemes would lead to significant land redistribution.[28] But taken in the round, it does seem reasonable to argue that Wyndham's rhetoric and proposals did serve to arouse the hopes of the rural poor. In a more particular sense, Wyndham certainly miscalculated. Within six years, ten millions out of the twelve millions Wyndham had allotted for the bonus had been used up[29]—as 253,625 tenants (as against 75,858 previously)[30] moved to purchase under the act—but the western question remained largely unresolved.

On 16 April, Irish nationalists held a popular convention in Dublin which—dominated, some were later to say manipulated, by O'Brien—applauded the bill, which passed in August. Some nationalists were delighted and few were openly critical. 'When I was a young man this would have been thought a marvellous Bill;' wrote Sam Young, the Cavan MP to Redmond, adding, 'I think it even now.'[31] But beneath the surface, there were signs of discontent and unease on the nationalist side. John Dillon, who had returned to Ireland from an Egyptian trip at the end of April, was particularly worried.[32] Dillon's fear that Home Rule might indeed by killed by kindness had not entirely left him.[33] He confided in Wilfred Scawen Blunt on 5 May 1903; Blunt noted in his diary:

John Dillon came to see me early and gave me his views of the situation very frankly. *He spoke last night in support of the Bill*, but he tells me that but for loyalty to the party he should be inclined to oppose it in Committee and vote against it on the third reading. His view is that it is useless trying to get the landlord class on the side of nationalism, that they would always betray it when the pinch came, *that the land trouble is a weapon in nationalist hands and that to settle it finally would be to risk Home Rule, which otherwise must come.*[34]

Criticism of the Land Act's shortcomings increased in the fortnight after it became law in August. The *Freeman's Journal*, under ex-MP and financial expert Tom Sexton's direction, suggested that the landlords were getting an inflated price for their land. Dillon too, at Swinford on 25 August, made a sharp public attack on the 'doctrine of

---

[28] Hansard, 4th series, vol. 128, col. 628 (15 June 1903).
[29] PRO Cab 37/100/113 A. Birrell memorandum, 18 August 1909.
[30] Leech, *Revolutionary Movement*, 143.
[31] Sam Young to John Redmond, 10 April 1903, NLI MS 15242.
[32] F. S. L. Lyons, *Dillon*, 230.
[33] Ibid., 232.
[34] Ibid., 233–4. For similar views amongst Dillon's friends see Joe Devlin's letter to Dillon (7 September 1903), TCD Dillon papers 6729/96 and John Roche also (14 October 1903), 6750/49.

conciliation'.[35] O'Brien was furious and urged Redmond to act decisively against Dillon's revolt. Redmond's reply was both sanguine and cautious. He feared above all for the loss of party unity. Nevertheless, Redmond felt sure that the country would rally to the party's official policy. On 7 September 1903 Redmond wrote to O'Brien:

the more I think of it the more I am inclined to disagree with the policy of openly attacking *at this moment* ... I feel quite certain from what Dillon has said to me that he would feel bound in honour to come out openly to defend Sexton ... this I would regard as a most disastrous thing. It would be taken by the whole country—friend and foes alike—as an end of the unity in the party as it would really be ... when we take the platform, all misunderstanding of the situation will speedily disappear in the country and if the *Freeman* attacks us— a most unlikely thing—we can deal with it then. *If we had a daily paper we could rely on, the situation would be different* though even then I would be against this resolution.[36]

O'Brien later commented: 'While Redmond hesitated (and it is only too certain because he hesitated) Mr Dillon acted, and before another month placed himself at the head of the 'determined campaign' against the policy of the party.'[37] But Redmond retained his optimism. On 21 September he happily contemplated the possibility of a shooting party at Augavanagh—Parnell's old place which he had acquired—with some of the leaders of landlord opinion. Above all, he told Parnell's biographer, R. Barry O'Brien, he 'wanted to lead the Irish people to understand how great a change had come to Ireland.'[38] O'Brien replied in like vein with news of friendly interviews with George Wyndham and Lord Rossmore.[39] But even Redmond, with his remarkable capacity for looking on the bright side of things, must have been worried by the *Freeman's* continued truculence. On 23 September, the *Freeman* moved from vagueness about those who were the object of its sallies to make explicit mention of William O'Brien from whom it 'respectfully differed.'[40] On 26 September the *Freeman* published a letter from Michael Davitt which described the Dunraven group as having achieved a 'counter revolution' in the value of landed

[35] Lyons, *Irish Parliamentary Party*, 101–3.
[36] O'Brien, *Evening Memories*, London, 1920, 486.
[37] Ibid.
[38] John Redmond to Barry O'Brien, 21 September 1903, NLI MS 15211.
[39] R. Barry O'Brien to John Redmond, 22 September 1903, NLI MS 15211.
[40] *FJ*, 23 September 1903.

property which was without parallel in the history of agrarian or political reform.[41]

In early October, moreover, Redmond faced a new and distracting assault. His candidate for a by-election in South Meath, David Sheehy, was challenged by John Howard Parnell. Parnell, who felt he had been eased out of the seat by means of skulduggery in 1900, was prepared to make an alliance with—of all people—Tim Healy and Jasper Tully, his brother's arch-opponents in 1891. For Healy and Tully it was a last desperate attempt to strike a real blow against the Irish party. With a remarkable lack of scruple, Tully, in particular, was prepared to use the Parnell name against Sheehy and Redmond. Perhaps this shameless operation was too much for the voters who on 9 October elected Sheehy with 2,245 votes against Parnell's 1,031. The low poll was widely attributed to the fact that a significant number of South Meath electors could not bring themselves to vote against a Parnell.[42] His Parnellite colleague of the 1890s, Edmund Leamy wrote in some relief to Redmond: 'They (Tully's supporters) would never have written in so open and brazen a fashion unless they thought the game was in their hands.'[43]

Having survived the challenge in Meath, Redmond made an important visit to the west. Fifteen years later Redmond's response to the 1903 act was caustically described as 'effusive':[44] but such comments only serve to obscure the precise nature of his reaction. For Redmond knew well that there were flaws in the act, particularly as regards the west and that this was already the subject of controversy. He promised a major statement on the western question. The occasion chosen was a meeting held under the auspices of the north and south Roscommon executives of the UIL on 11 October. On the day before the speech, the *Freeman* made an unusually sharp personal attack on O'Brien;[45] Redmond's response was obviously of considerable importance. He did not conceal his pride in the new legislation. He 'spoke of the possibility—given goodwill on all sides—that a few short years will see the end of the Irish land question.'[46] But he acknowledged to the full the special grievances of the west:

[41] *FJ*, 26 September 1903.
[42] *FJ*, 10 October 1903.
[43] E. Leamy to John Redmond, 11 October 1903, NLI MS 15242.
[44] *Waterford News*, 8 March 1918.
[45] *FJ*, 10 October 1903.
[46] *Roscommon Messenger*, 17 October 1903.

The place on which I am speaking today reminds me there are two land questions in Ireland entirely distinct and different. There is the land question in the west of Ireland and they are in their very essence, entirely different . . . (in Connaught) the land is, as in this district, congregated in the hands of a small ring of graziers . . . The problem therefore, in Connaught, is the breaking up of these grass ranches, the enlargement of the holdings, the redistribution of the land and the population.[47]

While Redmond argued that it would 'be absurd and untrue to say that the new land act does not make great improvements in the possibility and prospects of a land settlement in Connaught'[48] he also admitted that major obstacles to the solution of the problem remained. The Act gave the Congested Districts Board new financial resources. It was now possible—as it had not been before—for the Board to buy up enough land necessary for the working of a substantial land redistribution policy. Nevertheless, the Congested Districts Board had not been given powers of compulsory purchase as the Irish party had demanded. Wyndham had taken the view that the advantages held out to landlords (in the congested districts in particular) by the Act were sufficient as to make compulsion unnecessary. Redmond registered his disagreement with Wyndham's thesis on this point: 'I must say that candidly my opinion is that until compulsory powers are given to the Board *that it will be found impossible to have a real settlement of the question in the province of Connaught*.'[49] He also added that he objected to the 'insufficiently strong',[50] (that is to say insufficiently nationalist), constitution of the Congested Districts Board. (John Fitzgibbon had already commented suggestively privately to Joe Devlin: 'I mentioned that should there be a good position in connection with the Congested Districts Board, I would be open for such . . . I may be a little premature in giving the hint but I wish to give you timely intimation.')[51] Redmond in effect had said enough to indicate that he doubted if the Wyndham measures were sufficiently far-reaching as to resolve the problems of Connaught. Redmond insisted: 'The success or failure of this land act will depend absolutely upon its success or failure in Connaught, and when I see the great bodies of well-to-do tenants of some of the richest land in Ireland buying their farms in the province of Leinster, I am glad of it, of course . . . but what I say today is that—no number of sales of that kind throughout Ireland can settle

---

[47] Ibid.
[48] Ibid.
[49] Ibid. Emphasis added.
[50] Ibid.
[51] John Fitzgibbon to Joe Devlin, 15 February 1903, NLI MS 15242.

the land question (cheers).'[52] Redmond's acknowledgement of the
act's deficiencies in the west worried O'Brien. O'Brien must have
asked himself if Redmond was weakening in the face of criticism,
especially as the main nationalist newspaper the *Freeman's Journal*,
guided by Sexton, was now openly chiding him whilst on 12 October
hailing Redmond's Tulsk speech, as, quite simply, 'great'.[53] Then on
19 October came the decisive break when John Dillon addressed his
Swinford constituents again. Dillon made it clear that he supported
Sexton's views as expressed in *Freeman* editorials—'I agree with nearly
every word that has appeared in the editorials of the *Freeman*.'[54] Much
of the speech was a deliberate assault on the good faith of prominent
conciliationists. In particular, Dillon concentrated on a conference
which Talbot Crosbie, the Kerry landlord, had held with his tenantry,
local priest, and MP M. J. Flavin. Speaking of Talbot Crosbie, Dillon
did not manage to avoid a gratuitous sectarianism: 'his (Crosbie's)
speech was a long one; it was full of conciliation, he commenced by
indicating an extraordinary interest in the roof of the chapel
(laughter), though I don't think he belongs to our faith.'[55] Dillon
attacked Talbot Crosbie's notion that Chamberlain's tariff reform
proposals would ever gain a popular majority in Britain; Britain, he
was sure, would remain a cheap food economy and Irish farmers
should not be tempted to fantasize about change: 'All the Chamber-
lains that ever were born won't make the working people of England
submit to having the price of their food raised by taxation and if they
don't where does the profit come to you?'[56] Rather Dillon foresaw
moves in the opposite direction of greater free trade; in particular, he
discussed the likelihood of free importation of Canadian cattle leading
to a slump in the price of young cattle in Ireland. In conclusion, Dillon
argued that the talk of conciliation—like the talk of tariff reform—was
designed to lull the farmers into an uncritical frame of mind. Dillon
noted firmly: 'I believe that all the talk of conciliation which we hear so
frequently now from Shawe-Taylor, Lord Dunraven, Lord Mayo and
company is simply in the nature of soft sawder to divert the minds of
the Irish people from the question of the number of years' purchase
they are going to give for their farms.'[57] Dillon had, however, taken

[52] *Roscommon Messenger*, 17 October 1903.
[53] *FJ*, 12 October 1903.
[54] *Weekly Freeman*, 24 October 1903.
[55] Ibid.   [56] Ibid.
[57] Ibid.

care to avoid an open attack on Redmond. Indeed, he took the trouble to praise the Tulsk speech in which Redmond had criticized the Wyndham act's failure to deal with the western problem.

O'Brien, Dunraven, and T. W. Russell

William O'Brien meanwhile found himself moving even more firmly in a different direction. At the beginning of October he conceived a new and original project: he decided to open the pages of the *Irish People* to expressions of non-nationalist opinion. For the first time in recent history, a nationalist journal was prepared to allow space to political arguments normally dismissed as rank 'humbug'.

On 31 October T. W. Russell produced an optimistic article on 'The Future of Ulster'; the Protestant working man, he explained, was not a conservative but a 'radical' with 'a monomania about the Pope'.[58] An upsurge of democratic struggle was, however, fracturing the old reactionary Orangeism—the new democratic Orangemen were like men who had wandered from a 'dark room' into 'sunlight'. 'They are dazed and hardly know where they are.'[59]

In an even more sensitive manœuvre, O'Brien asked Lord Dunraven to contribute a statement of his own political views. The correspondence between the two men revealed much about the tensions, as well as the opportunities, of the time. O'Brien pushed Dunraven for some display of 'openness' on the subject of Home Rule. Dunraven was, however, reluctant to go so far: 'From my earliest days I was filled with purely Irish sentiment, all my inclination was to support Mr Gladstone's policy; but my commonsense forbade an independent parliament.'[60] He added: 'I look for considerable devolution of power in the United Kingdom to relieve the Imperial parliament.'[61] There were other touchy subjects; O'Brien had to thank Dunraven for his 'large minded readiness to drop the Boer passage.'[62]

On 7 November, Dunraven's much edited article 'National Good Fellowship' appeared. Despite all efforts, it was very difficult to hit the right note: 'The Irish language must be looked upon as a luxury, a very valuable luxury but not a necessity of life. Material welfare must not be sacrificed to sentiment.' More generally, Dunraven argued that

[58] *Irish People*, 31 October 1903.
[59] Ibid.
[60] Dunraven to W. O'Brien, 26 October 1903, NLI MS 8554.
[61] Ibid.
[62] W. O'Brien to Dunraven, 27 October 1903, NLI MS 8554.

Ireland 'can never become a great manufacturing country' but that as land was available in a decidedly limited quantity, a more variegated economic activity was desirable. Indeed, so great was Ireland's need for regeneration, that arguments about the form of the state should be postponed. 'Is it wise, is it patriotic to neglect to make the best use of the machinery at hand until exact plans have been drawn up of the machinery that may be preferred? The first thing to do is to put Ireland on her feet. She has got to be regenerated. The time for a merely critical negative policy has passed. The ground is clear and the time for a positive constructive policy has come.' To this end, Dunraven went beyond O'Brien's call for a 'free platform' and called for 'a council of representative men' including business and expert opinion who would guide Irish public opinion. Most nationalists could only regard this as an attempt to usurp the role of the Irish party, but to O'Brien, it was new and imaginative thinking.

For O'Brien matters had now come to a head. He pleaded with Redmond to 'discipline' Dillon and the *Freeman*. O'Brien condemned the 'Swinford revolt' as a revolt against solemn and democratic decisions of the Irish party and convention. But Redmond refused to act in the way demanded by O'Brien. Instead, he defended a policy of 'wait and see' in a long letter to O'Brien on 31 October:

I don't agree with you as to the party. With the exception of a mere handful, I consider the men quite sound. But what I fear is that if the present differences as to the best prices were to degenerate into an open and undisguised split with Dillon on the other side, the Party would be instantly rent asunder . . . Davitt does not count for much, allowance is made for him by the country. Dillon is going away on 1 December for six months. The *Freeman* is making no impression. The tenants are taking our advice not theirs. In this way I am convinced we can get along until Parliament meets, when over the Land-owners Bill and other matters there will be no chance of division of opinion. On the other hand, if I come out to declare to the country that there is a conspiracy on foot to divide the country and disorganise the Party I have not a shadow of doubt I would precipitate the very thing I wish to avoid.[63]

O'Brien later argued that Redmond's political influence and credibility at this point was greatly weakened by an alleged scandal concerning the price extracted by the sale of the Wexford estate left to the Irish leader by his uncle a year previously. As O'Brien wrote privately at the time to Dunraven: 'Mr Redmond's Wexford bargain

[63] Redmond to O'Brien, 31 October 1903, NLI MS 10496.

makes him apprehensive of attack by the *Freeman* and the more serious personages behind it.'[64] But in public, O'Brien felt it necessary rigorously to defend Redmond.[65] O'Brien's charge was that a weakened Redmond was afraid to challenge Dillon vigorously: all too obviously Redmond seemed to have had a personal reason for being soft on landlords. In consequence, he fudged the conflict with Dillon and infuriated his ally, O'Brien. O'Brienites later claimed that the *Freeman*, whilst now and then publishing the odd embarrassing detail about the sale, never published Davitt's full blast of criticism against the Redmond 'Price'. They preferred to hold this over for use against a frightened Redmond.[66] Redmond's biographer, Denis Gwynn, vigorously rebutted O'Brien's claims,[67] but there is no doubt that the sum originally mentioned for the Redmond estate was acutely embarrassing. The 'Redmond Price' was announced on the Irish leaders own authority as twenty-four and a half years' purchase. On 31 October the *Freeman's Journal* editorial had produced a most revealing verdict on this affair:

The tenants resolution sets out that their offer was based on full consideration of all the facts, the lowness of the rent, the exceptional character of family charges which may any day lapse, and the special services of Mr Redmond to the tenantry of Ireland. To tenants and landlord alike, the last consideration is most credible. It explains a very generous price, a price which includes something of a tribute for Mr Redmond's political service, a tribute that comes most appropriately from tenants who have been brought into such close and kindly relations with the chairman of the Irish party and President of the National Organisation. Are there any other landlords who can point to such exceptional circumstances?[68]

This was a faint praise indeed: rather it was a highly ambiguous recommendation of Redmond's deal with his tenantry. The use of the words 'very generous'[69] to describe the price was hardly intended to flatter the Irish leader. The notion that the price included a 'tribute'[70] to Redmond on account of his services to Ireland was likely to provoke only disbelief, coming as it did from a newspaper which had more often than not been sceptical of the value of those services. Thus battered Redmond was unprepared for the new crisis which on 4 November

[64] O'Brien to Dunraven, 8 May 1904, NLI MS 8554.
[65] *Irish People*, 8 November 1903: 'The Redmond estate: Some Wild Fallacies Dispelled'.   [66] *Irish People*, 27 April 1907.
[67] Gwynn, *Redmond*, 103–4.   [68] *FJ*, 31 October 1903.
[69] Ibid.   [70] Ibid.

O'Brien sprung on him. Redmond's problems were considerable. He had approached the sale with some care and the terms agreed were in no sense harsh. But not all the tenants were sympathetic to him and indeed some may have hoped to benefit from his public discomfort. The landlords took a delight in doing the same: all over the country they paraded their satisfaction with the 'Redmond Price'. This was not entirely fair as the rents on the Redmond estate had been exceptionally low. As another of Redmond's friends put it: 'When selling landlords take Mr Redmond as an example; they should take as the basis of purchase his rental—25 per cent under Griffith's valuation.'[71]

In fact, in the end Redmond, partly in consequence of the furore provoked by his original announcement, was to receive far short of twenty-four-and-a-half years' purchase. The majority of the tenants bought on eighteen-and-a-half years' purchase and none paid twenty-four-and-a-half years' purchase. For this reason his biographer has sought to gain him absolution and as far as it goes Gwynn was justified.[72] But, of course, the original figure struck was quoted again and again both by Unionist and Nationalist opponents of Redmond. O'Brien did his best to defend Redmond at the time but later recalled that had his advice been sought by Redmond: 'I should have implored Mr Redmond to defer all negotiations, or at least all newspaper mention of the matter, for a few months, until we should have succeeded in establishing a more moderate standard of prices in the less opulent parts of the country.'[73] Andrew Kettle put it more bluntly in 1908: 'Redmond', he said, 'was a landlord whom the fates used to give the landlords a pretence for raising the price of land.'[74]

The most painful and obvious (if unfair)[75] comparison was with the Parnell estate, which John Howard Parnell had sold at the Ashbourne price, apparently more cheaply at seventeen-and-a-one-half years' purchase. Jasper Tulley, quite mindless of his own part in destroying Parnell, snapped: 'Poor Charles Stewart Parnell was deposed as

[71] *Limerick Leader*, 22 November 1903.

[72] Gwynn, ibid.

[73] *An Olive Branch*, 282.

[74] *Irish People*, 5 May 1908. Tom O'Donnell, the Kerry MP claimed 'Mr Redmond got £16,000 too much from his tenants', *United Irishman*, 6 February 1904.

[75] 'En passant I may tell you that the tenants who fared worst were the Parnell tenants' wrote local solicitor, M. J. Connor to Redmond on 25 April 1903. 'During the late Mr Parnell's time they obtained a reduction of 20%. When he died this was taken off and they had to buy at 20 years purchase', Connor added. Redmond never employed this defence. NLI MS 15242.

leader and driven with execration to his grave for a sin he committed against the home, such as that home was, in smart English circles. Mr John Redmond has sinned against the interests of every working farmer in Ireland by this transaction.'[76] While assuring Redmond that 'the feeling is not general', Stephen O'Mara, a prominent Limerick nationalist, wrote to Redmond on 4 November 1903: 'There is no doubt that among a certain class of farmers there is a strong feeling about the sale of your Wexford property.'[77]

Redmond's tactics

Thus weakened, Redmond was 'understandably reluctant to risk a breach with the formidable trio of Davitt, Dillon and Sexton, and if a choice had to be made between O'Brien and them, it would be O'Brien who would go to the wall.'[78] Accordingly on 6 November 1903, O'Brien announced his resignation. Efforts were made to persuade him to reconsider his decision and on 24 November the party actually passed a resolution in that sense, but it was all in vain, and by the end of the month O'Brien had retired into private life. In this context it is, however, worth looking at Redmond's correspondence in November 1903. He received numerous notes from prominent nationalists bemoaning the new split.

Without exception, everyone who wrote to Redmond presumed that his heart was with the policy of conciliation. But the letters are also full of the horror of another 'civil war' in Ireland. From Kilkee, the local curate James Clancy, who in subsequent years ironically remained one of O'Brien's few close clerical supporters,[79] wrote in some anguish: 'I for one would prefer to see the *Freeman* and Dillon and Davitt playing all kinds of pranks than to go through another period like that from '90 to '99.'[80] By 27 November Father Clancy sadly reported: 'Of course the interview with William O'Brien turned out as expected. Captain Donelan will have told you all about it. I think the best thing now is to drop all references to his detriment. Keep the League going. Keep the people steady and preserve the authority of the Directory, no matter from what quarter it is challenged.'[81] On

[76] *Roscommon Herald*, 24 October 1903.
[77] S. O'Mara to John Redmond, 4 November 1903, NLI MS 15219.
[78] Lyons, *Irish Parliamentary Party*, 107.
[79] Six years later the *Irish World* (6 March 1909) reported of the UIL convention: 'There were 300 priests at the convention and only one of them voted for Mr O'Brien.'
[80] Fr. Clancy, 23 November 1903, NLI MS 15242.
[81] NLI MS 15242.

9 November J. J. O'Kelly had written to Redmond: 'I hope you will be able to persuade O'Brien to withdraw his resignation. It is much better to rely on the commonsense of the people than to abandon the field to the *Freeman*.'[82] (O'Kelly also suggested that Redmond might place the issue before the local councils which he clearly suspected were O'Brienite in sympathy.) But by 22 November O'Kelly's line had softened palpably. He was afraid that the poorest tenants would be at a disadvantage under the Wyndham act. Events however had reached the point where people had to make their own bargains. 'From this point of view the attitude of the *Freeman's Journal* is not without its advantages. By leaving everyone a free hand you defeat the secondary object which I fear was behind the *Freeman's* campaign.'[83]

Tim Healy made one dramatic effort to turn the tide. On 9 November 1903 he met with J. J. Clancy to discuss the political situation. Healy told Clancy that he and his friends had been buying up *Freeman* shares; he proposed a bloc with O'Brien and Redmond. The object would be to place four new men on the *Freeman's* editorial staff—two nominated by O'Brien and Redmond and two by Healy himself. Healy expressed himself determined 'to break Sexton's neck.'[84] It was an attempt to exploit Sexton's unpopularity in the Irish party.[85] Clancy reported, as he was clearly requested, to Redmond. Redmond's note under the heading 'Healy' 10 November 1902, merely records Clancy's opinion: 'it was all impossible'.[86] But two days later, Healy sent another emissary; this time it was Moreton Frewen. Redmond recorded: 'He said a number of *Freeman* shares had been acquired by certain people and that if O'Brien, Healy and I would join hands we could command enough shares to cashier Sexton and those who were directing the *Freeman*.'[87] Redmond's reply was certainly suggestive: 'I said I would have nothing to say to any such scheme which would mean the commencement of a new split and that my one objective was to hold things together and that I would never again take part in a civil war in Ireland.'[88] For many people—not least O'Brien and Healy—Redmond's refusal to take up the cudgels for a policy he genuinely believed in was inexcusable. Yet Redmond believed he had no other choice. Fear and loathing of the prospect of another split was deep within him, and in this respect he was entirely in tune with Irish

---

[82] 9 November, ibid.
[83] 22 November, ibid.   [84] Healy memo, ibid.
[85] *Irish Times*, 2 November 1932, Sexton's obituary touches on this point.
[86] Ibid.   [87] Ibid.   [88] Ibid.

public opinion. His letter of 7 September to O'Brien had made it clear that even *with* the support of a reliable daily newspaper, he would refrain from an open assault on Dillon and Sexton.[89] Reasonably enough Redmond must also have harboured much resentment against Healy's friends who had so embarrassed him during the recent Meath by-election.

What was particularly noticeable about all this is the way in which Redmond refused all the options which would have brought on a critical test of strength. This applied not just to Healy's strategy for dealing with the *Freeman*, but also to O'Kelly's suggestions that the UIL directory open up a debate designed to clarify once and for all the implications of the new land legislation. In his defence, Redmond might just probably have pointed to the way in which O'Kelly, for instance, came round to supporting his policy. Bitterly disappointed, O'Brien resigned from public life in early November 1903. O'Brien's sense of frustration had been great but this proved to be an utterly disastrous move. The effect of O'Brien's resignation may best be judged by looking at the provincial press. In the middle of January, and later in the middle of March 1903, William O'Brien had a specially warm relationship with a wide range of important provincial newspapers. In the province of Connaught he had support in Mayo (the *Connaught Telegraph* at Castlebar and the *Mayo News* at Wesport), in Kerry (the *Kerry People* at Tralee and the *Killarney Echo*), in Sligo, he had the *Sligo Champion* and in Roscommon the *Roscommon Messenger*, both based in the county towns. In the province of Munster, William O'Brien could count on the editorials in the formerly Parnellite *Limerick Leader*, the *Midland Tribune* from Birr and the *Southern Star* of Skibbereen. In the province of Leinster he had the *Westmeath Independent*, while in Ulster he had the *Anglo-Celt* of Cavan.[90] These newspapers covered a very wide variety of nationalist opinion, most of them either directly controlled by, or closely associated with the local nationalist MP. It was therefore an impressive list and if O'Brien had retained the support of this grouping he would have been in a very strong position in late 1903.

Let us consider first of all the case of Connaught. The remarkable fact to note is that by the end of November 1903 O'Brien did not have the full support of any of the six papers with which he had been so

---

[89] O'Brien, *Evening Memories*, 486.
[90] *Irish People*, 14 March 1903, for this list.

closely associated. He had much sympathy but no firm political
backing. The *Mayo News* at Westport was quite unambiguously hostile
to O'Brien. It declared its opinion roundly: 'We cannot share Mr
O'Brien's views that the articles published in the *Freeman's Journal*
have given any cause for offence to him or to any Irish Nationalist.'[91]
The *Kerry People* was also clearly hostile to the policy of conciliation.
Old agrarian grievances loomed large. They strongly supported their
local MP, M. J. Flavin, who called the policy of conciliation 'flum-
mery'.[92] The editor of the *Sligo Champion*, P. A. McHugh, MP,
acknowledged his strong admiration for O'Brien, but added: 'At the
present moment he felt bound to say he could not admit the validity of
the grounds on which Mr O'Brien appeared to have based his
resignation.'[93]

J. H. Gillespie, the editor of the *Connaught Telegraph* seems to have
remained loyal in a personal sense[94] to O'Brien. At least, he attended
O'Brienite meetings and gave enormous coverage to pro-O'Brien
speeches as Mayo public bodies rushed to support O'Brien. Perhaps
significantly though he refrained from strong O'Brienite editorial
comments. At any rate, even in Mayo—the cockpit of his support—
O'Brien's action had provoked a certain amount of unease. Only J. J.
Louden, son of an old opponent, openly criticized him. But one
supporter, James Daly, a former editor of the *Connaught Telegraph*,
admitted that he was 'surprised' by O'Brien's reactions to the *Freeman*
criticisms. William Dorris, chairman of the Westport Board of
Guardians, and a rising political figure in the area, observed,

of course, there were a lot of argumentative questions. Mr O'Brien said that
the *Freeman* banished him out; nothing that the *Freeman* did should banish
him out. Mr Davitt was a little too bitter, but he was built quite that way; he
could not write a line without being bitter. Mr Davitt was a little too bitter
now, but the *Freeman* could not make O'Brien retire; there must be something
under the surface that they did not quite understand.[95]

The *Killarney Echo* and the *Roscommon Messenger* were also sympathetic. The *Killarney Echo* openly agreed that demagogic attacks were
being made on conciliatory landlords—the reference here was clearly

[91] *Mayo News*, 14 November 1903.
[92] *Kerry People*, 31 October 1903.
[93] *Sligo Champion*, 14 November 1903.
[94] *Connaught Telegraph*, 21 November 1903.
[95] *Connaught Telegraph*, 14 November 1903.

to Dillon's remarks about Talbot Crosbie.[96] The *Roscommon Messenger* sympathized with O'Brien's desire to win over the landlords to nationalism: 'there probably are amongst this class some with generous impulses and a love of their country who, if the Land Question were out of the way, might be found taking their part in a National Movement.'[97] But both papers insisted that O'Brien was exaggerating his differences[98] with other nationalists and offered their support to Redmond. This survey of the Connaught press suggests that out of six erstwhile supporters, O'Brien had decisively lost three, whilst retaining only personal sympathy from the remaining three. When O'Brien's huge political investment in Connaught is recalled, this was a poor showing.

The Munster papers all formed a pattern. They each declared apparently solidly in favour of O'Brien only for their support to shift rapidly—within a matter of days—to Redmond. The *Limerick Leader* reacted sympathetically but Redmond's visit to Limerick sent it into paroxysms of relief.[99] Redmond's effort to fudge the issue was treated as statesmanship of the first rank. The *Southern Star* declared that 'Mr O'Brien's withdrawal would be nothing short of a national calamity',[100] but within a week was also calling for unity behind Redmond. The *Midland Tribune* followed in the same mode: 'If he (O'Brien) has met with criticisms and attacks at any rate they did not spring from the people.'[101] However, again within a week a shift of emphasis had occurred, as the paper began to support Redmond. The *Freeman's* policy was still 'the most insidious policy ever advanced' nevertheless, O'Brien was making too much of the affair: 'after all the opinion of the Irish people is more important than the statements of any newspaper.'[102] Four years later it described the Wyndham act as a landlord's relief bill in every respect.[103]

Leinster's reaction was similar to that of Munster, the *Westmeath Independent* declared: 'From one end of Ireland to the other a feeling of resentment has been occasioned that a policy of criticism, amounting to the hostility and bitterness of an active campaign, should have

---

[96] *Killarney Echo*, 14 November 1903.
[97] *Roscommon Messenger*, 14 November 1903.
[98] *Roscommon Messenger*, 21 November 1903; *Killarney Echo*, 21 November 1903.
[99] *Limerick Leader*, 14 and 21 November 1903.
[100] *Southern Star*, 14 November 1903.
[101] *Midland Tribune*, 14 November 1903.
[102] *Midland Tribune*, 21 November 1903.
[103] *Midland Tribune*, 2 April 1907.

driven out of public life a man who in the course of a long and splendid career, devoted his splendid services, with the most unselfish purpose to the regeneration of his country.'[104] Such enthusiasm for O'Brien was however soon tempered. This paper was above all Redmonite at this time and a week later, it too was moving away from any too close association with O'Brien and back towards the camp of Redmond and 'unity'.

> The voice of the country spoken from all sides, undoubtedly calls in trumpet tones for the return of Mr O'Brien, but the resolutions, we are glad to note, are almost invariably concluded in terms of moderation and good sense—there is no needless vituperation and no such thing as an effort to utilise the situation for the purpose of once more plunging the country into turmoil and strife.[105]

The *Nationalist and Leinster times* followed an exactly similar course.[106]
Only in Ulster did an O'Brienite sentiment express itself in uncomplicated and unmodified fashion. The *Anglo-Celt* (Cavan) said: 'the old story is repeated. Another great Irishman has been driven from public life. Not remember by the enemies of our country but by those who a month ago posed as his friends.'[107] But it can hardly have comforted O'Brien to have his most explicit support in the province where nationalism was weakest.

It is quite clear therefore that O'Brien was not facing simply the opposition of a dissident clique in the higher echelons of nationalism— Dillon, Davitt, and the *Freeman*. It was simply impossible for a weakened Redmond, whatever his personal feeling on the matter—to call the movement to order in the autumn of 1903. O'Brien's resignation was therefore a major political error. Revealingly O'Brien and his supporters were driven to compensate by taking refuge in fantasy. O'Brien refused Dunraven's suggestion of an alliance with Healy and the *Independent*; he—like Redmond—had too many recent bitter memories of the 'mischief makers'. With less substance, O'Brien added: 'It would be to desert my own party, 99% of whom are with me.'[108] A police informer was told in similar wildly optimistic vein by one of O'Brien's most prominent friends in Westport: 'You have not heard the last of William O'Brien yet; when the proper time comes he will be

---

104 *Westmeath Independent*, 14 November 1903.
105 Ibid., 21 November 1903.
106 *Nationalist and Leinster Times*, 14 and 21 November 1903.
107 *Anglo-Celt*, 7 November 1903.
108 William O'Brien to Dunraven, Christmas 1903, NLI MS 8554.

found again to the front and taking a leading part in directing the policy of the UIL and the country and with that object in view their desire is to have unity in the ranks of the UIL.'[109]

But such talk was absurd. The 'unity' of the UIL now operated in Dillon's favour while O'Brien had pushed Redmond into the Dillonite embrace. On 7 October Redmond had given a revealing reply to Dillon's attacks on conciliation: while acknowledging that he was 'pained' and 'uneasy' Redmond made no gesture to reduce Dillon's suspicions, in fact, their future relations were left in the air with the pious hope 'that by the time we have to fight a general election we may be pulling together as heartily as ever'.[110] On 6 November, shaken by O'Brien's resignation, Redmond himself reopened the communications with Dillon—which he had himself allowed to lapse—in a letter which pointed out that he had known nothing of O'Brien's action.[111] By 21 November Devlin was happily telling Dillon that Redmond was 'anxious to do the right thing'.[112]

In one of his more honest passages, O'Brien admitted to Dunraven at the end of the year:

The *rapprochement* between classes which would have been quite feasible if the Land Act were working well, is under present circumstances impossible or at least indefinitely postponed . . . The central princple of the Land Conference is still the sheet anchor of the situation and the only one. Truth to tell, I do not think the members of the Land Conference, either on your side or ours, have shown sufficient moral courage in asserting themselves against stupidity and prejudice on both sides.[113]

The sudden collapse of O'Brien's apparently strong position may require some comments. In reality Dillon's area of success had been a narrow but vital one. He was powerless to stop the Irish tenantry from exploiting beneficial legislation in 1903—just as Parnell had been powerless in 1881. But Dillon had ensured that no change in atmosphere, no abandonment of traditional mistrust, would accompany the working of the new act. Probably the majority of the Irish tenantry accepted Redmond and O'Brien's positive assessment of the Wyndham act but they had less reason to share O'Brien's enthusiasm for compromise with long standing enemies. It was this fact which

---

[109] SPO CBS 1904 29357/S.
[110] TCD Dillon MS, 6749/165.
[111] 6749/51.   [112] 6729/101.
[113] William O'Brien to Dunraven, Christmas 1903, NLI MS 8554.

Dillon exploited to his own advantage. As O'Brien glumly summed up: 'the act of course was working but the sense of "generous compromise and cooperation on either side" is wholly lost'.[114]

Redmond's personal instinct for conciliation remained as strong as ever. In an interview with the *Pall Mall Gazette* at the end of November, John Redmond again revealed himself against a supporter of the new land legislation. He insisted—against the opinion of his interviewer—that the press figures underestimated rather than over-estimated the number of sales. Furthermore, Redmond claimed that a spirit of compromise was present in most transactions. The Archdale estate in Fermanagh, a notorious early example, had been offered by the landlord at twenty-five years purchase. It now seemed that a settlement was to be reached at a figure of twenty-three years purchase.[115] However it may be explained, Redmond's capitulation to Dillon had none the less vitally important consequences. O'Brien's departure meant that it was impossible for Redmond to gain a sympathetic hearing within the party for the Dunraven devolution proposals in September 1904. Dunraven's Reform Association called for Ireland to be given more extended powers of local government. John Redmond was in America when the proposals were launched: he immediately stated 'with these men (meaning Lord Dunraven and the progressive landlords of the Irish Reform Association) with us home rule may come at any moment.'[116] The most significant aspect of all this was not Redmond's optimistic statement but the fact that the *Freeman* failed to print it. In October 1904, Dillon's withering critiques destroyed the hope of nationalist support for the proposals.[117] Ulster Unionist resentment when it was discovered that the Dublin Castle Under-Secretary, Sir Antony MacDonnell, had had a hand in drafting the proposals made it easier for Redmond to hide his embarrassment. In the end the Unionists failed to dislodge the resolute Sir Antony, but the less resilient Wyndham was driven from office on 7 March 1905.[118] During these harangues all hopes for Dunraven's schemes were

---

[114] William O'Brien to Dunraven, 6 April 1904, NLI MS 9554.

[115] Quoted in *Mayo News*, 5 December 1903.

[116] D. Gwynn, *Redmond*, 106.

[117] Lyons, *Dillon*, 274.

[118] For the devolution crisis, see F. S. L. Lyons, 'The Irish Unionist Party and the Devolution Crisis of 1904/5', in *IHS*, vol. vi, 1948–9. But see also for its effects, H. Patterson, 'Independent Orangeism and Class Conflict in Edwardian Belfast: A Reinterpretation', *Proceedings of the Royal Irish Academy*, vol. 80, C, no. 1, 1980, 212–87.

effectively destroyed.[119] The Ulster Unionists dug themselves in even deeper by the formation in March 1905 of their Ulster Unionist Council which at once became the rally point of the more intransigent Unionists.[120] Such developments further restricted Redmond's room for manœuvre. His public pronouncements increasingly reflected the sentiments of a conformist nationalism. On 4 October 1904, Redmond wrote to Patrick Ford, editor of the *Irish World* in New York, accusing Sir Horace Plunkett of 'undisguised contempt for the Irish race',[121] and declaring his opinion that the real object of the movement headed by Sir Horace Plunkett was 'to undermine the national party and divert the minds of our people from home rule.'[122] Making all due allowances for a justified irritation occasioned by the patronizing tone[123] of Plunkett's book *Ireland in the New Century* published in 1904, such a comment was a sad epitaph on the political friendship of the two men in the 1890s. In July 1905 the hapless Redmond declared the Wyndham act a 'failure' and refused to countenance Tory attempts to improve its finance.[124] Some months later, making a virtue of necessity, Redmond summed up his own position in a comment which embraced both 'Dunravenism' and the new independent Orange movement in Belfast:

Here at home in Ireland the ranks of our enemies are being split. Now I am not one of those who think it useful to decry or belittle the action either of Lord Dunraven or his friends, on the one hand, or of Mr Sloan and his more tolerant Orangemen on the other. I regard the action of these men as the greatest indication yet of the irresistible and onward tendency of the Irish National Movement (cheers) and therefore I am not in favour of one offensive word being said to them: but I say to men for God's sake let them alone (hear, hear). Do not embarrass them. Do not make the position of these men approximating our position any more difficult. Aye, do not make it perhaps impossible by falling upon their necks and attempting to join hands with them. Let them go along their own lines.[125]

---

[119] For a most impressive analysis of Wyndham's collapse see A. H. Gailey, *The Unionist Government's Policy Towards Ireland 1895–1905*, 212–87.

[120] Lyons, *Ireland since the Famine*, 217.

[121] Quoted in *Irish Times*, 25 April 1907.

[122] Ibid.

[123] F. S. L. Lyons, *Culture and Anarchy in Ireland 1890–1939*, Oxford, 1979, 74. But see *Leader*, 9 April 1932 for a surprisingly sympathetic review of Plunkett's book.

[124] R. G. Mullan, 'The Origins and Passing of the Irish Land Act of 1909' (Queen's University, Belfast, MA, 1978), 64.

[125] *Irish People*, 21 October 1905.

Redmond and O'Brien, of course, were not the only major political figures to be knocked off course by the Swinford revolt. George Wyndham, the chief secretary had been similarly disconcerted. His comment in a letter to Morton Frewen of mid-November—exaggerated and self-important though it may be—gives his perception of the damaging effects of Dillon's *demarche*:

I had convinced my colleagues, a majority of our supporters in the House, and a still larger majority in the large towns of England, that it was right in itself to foster union among Irishmen and to obliterate the vestiges of ancient feuds without troubling ourselves about the ultimate effect of social regeneration on Ireland's attitude towards the 'Home Rule' versus Union controversy . . . to put it shortly, I can not get (1) imperial credit (2) make and keep savings for Ireland if every action taken by the government by the advice, and with the assent of Irishmen, is used only to attack the fortunes and insult the feeling of those classes in Ireland whom the great majority in England feel bound to protect . . . On the other hand if the English were once assured by their safety, Parliament would, I believe, be very ready to sanction the development of Ireland on Irish lines.[126]

This is a poignant declaration. It is open to one very obvious criticism: Wyndham rather overstates the effects of his politics on English, particularly Conservative opinion. In particular as regards finance, there was growing rank and file opinion that Ireland had received more than her fair share.[127] But this is not to deny that Wyndham was attempting to open up a space for 'progressive' developments within Ireland, a space for the reduction, at least, of certain traditional animosities. It was a policy Wyndham certainly expected Redmond to favour, indeed, in another part of this letter, Wyndham stressed the need for a policy of 'toleration' in local government—the very policy for which Redmond had made such sacrifices three years earlier. Indeed, in 1899 Lord Dunraven—elected for Croom—had been one of the beneficiaries of this policy: Redmond's press had vigorously defended Dunraven against the attacks of Davitt.[128] Nevertheless, the Earl of Dunraven and his friends continued their efforts. As F. S. L. Lyons has explained: 'Lord Dunraven did not, indeed, surrender easily and he continued for several years to attempt a *modus vivendi*

---

[126] Printed in J. W. Mackail and Guy Wyndham, *Life and Letters of George Wyndham*, London, 1925, vol. ii, 472–3. See also Moreton Frewen to Redmond, NLI MS 1775.

[127] Shannon, 'Arthur Balfour', 152.

[128] Catherine B. Shannon, 'Local Government in Ireland: The Politics and Administration' (UCD, MA, 1963), 194–6. This is a most valuable thesis.

with William O'Brien.' But as Lyons has also pointed out: 'Even at the height of his expectations Dunraven had never succeeded in converting the bulk of the Ascendancy class. The Irish Reform Association attracted consistent support from only about thirty landlords.'[129] Dunraven's failure here had, of course, as its counterpart in Redmond's failure on the other side.

In later years Redmond's eventual political eclipse was to be ascribed largely to his post-1914 policies. However, it is worth noting, that one of his few prominent western supporters who remained faithful to the last, J. Duncan, argued that Redmond's failure to build on the opportunity created by Wyndham had been the truly decisive error in the Irish leader's career. 'We venture to say that his mistakes were not in the last years of his life ... if there was a mistake in his career it was that he did not more wholeheartedly co-operate with George Wyndham and Lord Dunraven after the passing of the 1903 Land Purchase Act, with a view to obtaining from a Conservative Government a measure of autonomy which, we believe, could have been secured.'[130] No personal blame attached to Redmond, observed another supporter of this view, he had been merely the victim of circumstances.[131]

---

[129] Lyons, *Ireland since the Famine*, London, 1971, 216–18.
[130] *Ballina Herald*, 4 March 1918.
[131] *Westmeath Independent*, 18 April 1908.

5

The Policy of Fight

Many people who were in no sense of the word congested tenants have shared in the division of untenanted land. Hopes have been excited; land hungry eyes have been greedily cast on the untenanted land by persons living in the district; they marked them for their own. Parochialism has prevailed over nationalism in this matter.

Augustine Birrell, Chief Secretary for Ireland, Hansard, vol. 196, col. 283 (23 November 1908).

Ginnell's invention of cattle driving had it been thought of in 1881/2 (before legislation tempered the heat of agrarian fever) would have shortened the reign of landlordism. The Wyndham Act had in his day made half the peasants owners of their farms and the rest expectants. So there was only narrow scope for his tactics.

Tim Healy, *Letters and Leaders of My Day*, vol. ii, 565.

IN keeping with his residual conciliationism, Redmond did, however, contrive to allow O'Brien and his friends a free run in the January general election, despite O'Brien's continued 'retirement' from official nationalist politics and despite the constant pressure on Redmond to break decisively with the policy of 'loyalism and water' as Davitt had stigmatized O'Brienism. On the eve of the election, O'Brien managed to make a deal with Redmond which protected both his own seat and that of his allies from a nationalist challenge: 'up to a few weeks ago they were making all kinds of secret preparations to fight everyone of my friends and dispute Cork City with myself',[1] he told Dunraven. Neither side seems to have wanted an open conflict, with the result that the O'Brienites reappeared as a minority within the majority nationalist bloc. O'Brien's support was already beginning to look suspiciously reliant on his personal popularity in Cork—where

[1] William O'Brien to Dunraven, 20 December 1905, NLI MS 8554. For Davitt's critique of O'Brien, see *The Nationist*, 26 October 1905; see also editorials 25 September and 19 October. The 1906 results are given in Brian Walker, *Parliamentary Election Results in Ireland 1801–1922*, Dublin, 1978, 165–70.

key friends like D. D. Sheehan MP and James Gilhooly MP were also to be found. Nevertheless, the fact remained that its enemies had not dared to attempt to extinguish 'O'Brienism'. 'Russellism', that other important strand of the new mood of 1903–4 was not so fortunate. A symbol: the ebullient but sectarian Unionist politician Captain James Craig (later to be Prime Minister of Northern Ireland) outpolled James Wood (Russellite), in East Down by 4011 votes to 3341. Russell's other supporters, A. H. White, Edward Mitchell and S. R. Keightley all went down to defeat leaving Russell himself, elected in Tyrone South, and R. G. Glendinning elected in North Antrim, as the sole remaining parliamentary standard bearers of his brand of 'liberal' Unionism. The most striking personal triumph of the general election was enjoyed by Joe Devlin who was returned for Kilkenny County (North) but who also, and more remarkably, defeated the Unionist John Reid Smiley in West Belfast. Devlin was an ambiguous figure—on the one hand the father figure of the Ancient Order of Hibernians—a mixture of friendly society and defender of Irish Catholic interests—and thus the *bête noire* of non-sectarian nationalists who despised its Catholic particularism. The AOH had already begun that organizational expansion which 'made it difficult or uncomfortable for Catholics of the professional and working class to prosper outside their ranks.'[2] On the other hand, in the context of Belfast's bitter divisions, Devlin was capable of adopting relatively humane and progressive stands on various issues.[3] Redmond could not, therefore, resist giving Devlin's West Belfast election victory an over-enthusiastic gloss which, none the less, revealed much about his personal predilections:

The point we ought to emphasise is that this was a victory won by Protestant votes cast for Mr Devlin. It would have been impossible for Mr Devlin to have headed the poll were it not that hundreds of so-called Orange Protestant working men of Belfast voted for him. Think for a moment what that means. It would have been easy for us to have obtained National self-government for Ireland at any time for the last 25 years if we could have presented a united front, Protestant and Catholic combined, to England. We have waited all these years, mistakes have been made upon our side as well upon the other,

---

[2] H. Robinson, *Further Memories*, 145. By about 1914 one quarter of the total insurable Catholic population was in the AOH, Boyce, *Nationalism*, 276.

[3] E. G. Phoenix, 'The Nationalist Movement in Ireland 1914–28' (Queen's University, Belfast, Ph.D., 1983), 56–8, 153–66.

and those of us who believe in Ireland a nation have been waiting all these
years for the dawn of the day when Protestant Orange working men in the
North of Ireland would begin to understand that, after all, Ireland a nation
means for them as much as for us—freedom, prosperity, and happiness—and
how many of our race, how many of our comrades and friends in the last
25 years have gone down to the grave in despair of ever seeing that day. But the
day has dawned.[4]

More generally, in the UK the Liberals swept the board in the 1906
election. They had an overwhelming majority; Redmond's confident
predictions of 1896 that this could never happen in his own lifetime
were confounded. The *Leader*, D. P. Moran's strongly national
journal, felt it necessary to carry an article under the heading 'The
danger of whiggery'. The *Leader* feared that the liberal programme of
reforms might reduce the intensity of nationalist sentiment. In the
countryside, men who hungered for land but not independence might
be satisfied. The Catholic upper middle class, too, which would
always find Church of Ireland domination irksome, might expect to
cut a finer figure in the new condition of affairs. The lower classes in
the cities were perhaps the only class likely to remain unaffected.[5]

But the majority of nationalists found little that was pleasing in the
election of the new government. 'The Liberal majority in the new
Parliament is too overwhelming',[6] declared Jasper Tully. Here (one is
tempted to say, for once) Tully was merely stating the conventional
nationalist view. Michael Davitt immediately informed a newspaper
interviewer that there would be no Home Rule bill in the new
Parliament. Davitt pinned his hopes for the future on the rise of
Labour. 'When the Labour representation in the House of Commons
is hundred and fifty strong, as probably it will be in the very next
Parliament, *then we will talk about home rule*. I am convinced that the
balance of power will rest with the Labour party in the next
Parliament.'[7] Tully grumbled: 'If it had been a majority confined
within reasonable bounds—if it had been possible to threaten it with
some combination of Irish, Labour men and Tories then something
substantial could be squeezed out of its necessities.'[8] But there was
now little likelihood of that. When, as was commonly estimated, the

---

[4] Redmond, quoted in the *Irish People*, 12 December 1906.
[5] *Leader* 3 March 1906.
[6] *Roscommon Herald*, 3 March 1906.
[7] *Irish People*, 10 February 1906.
[8] *Roscommon Herald*, ibid.

Liberals could in effect count on a majority of eighty to one hundred votes over all other parties combined, the outlook for Irish interests was far from promising.

Indeed, in certain important respects, it was possible that the Irish case might even lose ground. This was partly a matter of debate of course, but Liberal objectives in certain areas were defined by some as antagonistic to Irish interests. The more ostentatiously Catholic amongst the Irish MPs looked on liberal education policy with considerable disfavour. Perhaps, even more sensitive, however, was a directly economic question. It was difficult to see how the government could resist the demand for free importation of Canadian store cattle. It was generally believed that the removal of restrictions would mean a sudden influx of the Canadian stores and a big run on them by English and Scottish farmers for stall-feeding purposes. The cattle would fit the eastern counties of England and would be found suitable generally throughout Scotland. But these were the places where Irish store oxen were sold in quantity.[9] Many felt such a move was the apparently logical product of the free trade principle which had triumphed in the election. Such a change would, it was calculated, be disastrous for Irish farmers; reducing the price of stock £2 or £3 a head.

The Canadian cattle question led Michael Davitt to produce what was to be one of his most interesting interventions in Irish political debate. He was worried by the fact that the Irish party's position on the Canadian cattle question tended to align it with the right in British politics. Davitt wrote:

When the question of removing these restrictions comes to be debated and considered in Parliament, the Irish Party who will probably resist the proposal, will not be able to count upon much substantial support except from among the pro-landlord section of the House of Commons, and a few dozen liberals who represent rural constituencies.[10]

On the other side of the argument, however, were Michael Davitt's more natural allies, 'the Free Trade and Labour feeling and interests'. Davitt was convinced anyway that the triumph of the free traders on this issue was inevitable. He pointed out that in the long run, the case for cheap food for the labouring masses in England was likely to prove irresistible. The Irish farmers could expect little sympathy. 'The

---

[9] *Leader*, 15 August 1908.
[10] *Irish Independent*, 31 March 1906. 'Canadian cattle question. Another aspect of the matter.'

bowels of English compassion are seldom agitated by any self-denying
consideration when the privilege of English stomachs are at stake.'
But despite this thrust at British attitudes, Davitt insisted the root of
the problem lay not in England but in Ireland. He argued that the Irish
farmer had to react to the new challenge not by insisting on any God-
given right to his traditional markets but by adopting better methods
of 'growing cattle'. Following agriculture experts such as W. P.
Coyne[11] and J. R. Campbell,[12] Davitt stigmatized current methods in
Ireland as 'slovenly' and 'wasteful'.

What is required is that breeders of stores shall make every possible effort to
complete their own work, instead of handing over the half-finished article to
graziers and others, who make the major portion of the profits out of the
industry and risks of the smaller tenants. This can be done by cultivating the
necessary root and other crops for that purpose and thereby putting the land
to the natural, its legitimate, and more profitable use. It is the neglect of this
rational method, and of the true commercial principle involved in the carrying
on of the industry here in Ireland which menaces the future of the tenants
engaged in it, far more than the threatened competition from Canada. It would
be much more helpful to the tenants in any case, and infinitely better for the
country, if attention was directed to some real and effective remedy of this
kind, than by relying upon the much easier industry of passing resolutions
against the interests of Canadian cattle growers.[13]

There is much that is highly traditional in this aspect of Davitt's
argument. Post-famine Irish nationalists had always criticized over-
reliance on grazing and argued for more tillage. In one important
sense only, Davitt was to find himself adopting a novel thesis. In the
traditional case, the neglect of tillage was easily enough blamed on the
landlord conspiracy to denude Ireland of her people and replace them
by bullocks. But by 1906 matters had clearly become rather more
complex and it is to Davitt's credit that he fully acknowledged this.
The power of the landlords had been substantially reduced in Ireland.
It was increasingly up to the Irish to do with Irish land what they
willed themselves. And it was precisely in this area that, as Davitt
admitted, recent developments were so unsatisfactory:

[11] *Weekly Freeman*, 25 May 1901; for Coyne, see also the sympathetic assessment by
Irish Party, MP Tom Kettle to be found in J. B. Lyons, *The Enigma of Tom Kettle: Irish
Patriot, Essayist, Poet, British Soldier*, Dublin, 1983, 55.
[12] *Limerick Leader*, 1 October. It was 1916 before the number of cattle exported as fat
exceeded those imported as stores. The *Freeman* twice called this a revolution, *WF*,
30 December 1916, 20 January 1917.
[13] *Irish Independent*, 31 March 1906.

The present system of using every available acre of land for cattle raising, is a deadly injury to the country. Land purchase is not stopping this pernicious practice. Quite the contrary. It has increased it, so far; which means that the rights won for the peasant proprietors of the future at enormous sacrifices to the nation of our day, are in no way helping to solve the industrial problem, nor to materially lessen the disastrous effects of emigration. The tendency among large numbers of tenants who have recently bought their holdings is to turn more land into grass, and thus to narrow still more the opportunities of employment for labour. This is a most serious national concern, and cannot be ignored much longer without our conniving at the slow, but certain and inevitable, ruin of the towns and villages that can only subsist economically upon an industrial population.

It is here where this coming inrush of foreign stores—into Great Britain, if not actually into Ireland—may compel tenants to discard the present plans of growing cattle, and to adopt the only method that successfully defies foreign competition—that of feeding and finishing their animals until ready for the beef market, instead of half doing the work, as now, at a maximum risk: and seeing prices go down until all profits on the industry must entirely vanish.[14]

Davitt remarked that Irish agriculture was falling behind European competition. Indeed, Irish natural advantages of fertilty were being squandered. The fault too was not lack of capital but of intellect and application. He called for more 'persistent' and 'intelligent' liaison from the farming community: 'Every practical farmer knows, or ought to know, that an acre of land property tilled and used, can be encouraged to grow more food for cattle than an acre of grass can provide.'[15]

Davitt's assessment of the effects of land purchase was not particularly original or in itself especially controversial. Pointing to the land use on thirty-acre farms in Roscommon, the O'Conor Don had told George Wyndham, then Chief Secretary: 'Give the people more land if you like but do not think they will till if you do.'[16] The conservative and unionist *Irish Times* observed sardonically in the autumn of 1907: 'there has been no notable extension of the tillage system under which, according to popular theory, Ireland is to attain her Saturnian age.'[17] In a paper presented to the British Association meeting in Dublin in September 1908, Dr Moritz Bonn, author of *Modern Ireland and her Agrarian Problem* (1906), asked the question, has

[14] Ibid.
[15] Ibid.
[16] Hansard, vol. 180, 12 August 1907.
[17] *Irish Times*, 2 October 1907.

land reform conferred on the Irish people the benefits which, a generation ago, were so confidently predicted for it? Bonn acknowledged a slight increase in the yield of crops and a considerable improvement in the standard of living; but in a predominantly negative analysis he drew attention to the decrease in the area of crops, the failure of Irish cattle to improve in quality and above all, the failure of mixed farming and intensive culture to make real progress.[18] Acknowledging these points, the *Tuam Herald*, one of the leading nationalist journals in the west, noted heretically: 'We think there is something in what the advocates of the present large farm system say,' adding 'we are told that a number of the newly created peasant owners are not only grazing every acre of their new holdings but going about far and wide looking for grass and taking it on the eleven months system, and that they are at this very moment, the men who are really forcing up the price of land.'[19] The significance of Davitt's declaration therefore lay not in its content but its source.

Davitt's letter constituted a most explicit statement by a senior figure of Irish nationalism that somehow the old Land League programme had run into major difficulties. The realization was a comparatively recent one for Davitt; for although there are hints of it in some of his 1903 remarks[20] his major book *Fall of Feudalism in Ireland*, published in 1904, contains no acknowledgement of these fundamental problems.[21] It is a triumphal, if in places evasive, celebration of the Irish agrarian revolution. In a sense then—and despite their increasingly bitter polemics—Davitt shared with William O'Brien an awareness that the unfolding of Irish nationalist destiny was not going quite according to plan. Where they differed, of course, was in their response: O'Brien reacted by attempting to develop a new politics freed from many of the constraints of the old faith. Davitt, on the other hand, attempted to reinvigorate the old faith by calling for a 'return' to virtue. Implicit in his argument, is the view that the farmer who was coming into the fruits of his inheritance as the victor in the land war ought to bear in mind the interests of those other groupings, in particular, urban radical nationalists and also agricultural labourers who had helped in the struggle. Davitt can hardly have been optimistic that this would actually be the case. As the *Leader* later

[18] *Irish Times*, 2 September 1907.
[19] *Tuam Herald*, 15 October 1907.
[20] *Roscommon Herald*, 22 March 1903.
[21] New York, 1904.

observed of this period: 'the country called in vain for extra tillage, and the graziers, the ranchers and the eleven months men snapped their fingers as it were to all the unanimous resolutions of all the Leagues. Even the men who were getting rather small farms were we believe doing the grass trick to a great extent themselves.'[22]

Davitt's text helps to explain why the Irish party at first reacted somewhat sluggishly on the Canadian cattle question—which, after all, posed a major threat to the material interests of the Irish farmers. There was a strain of opinion which had tired of the Irish farmers and their ways—in particular, it had tired of those many thousands of farmers who bought their land under the 1903 Act or failed to turn it over to tillage. Farmers who, in short, refused to listen to the advice of John Dillon or Michael Davitt. But it would have been political suicide for the party to allow such sentiments to dictate policy: hence an uncharacteristic uncertainty. For six weeks the party was strangely reserved as the advertised parliamentary debate on the Canadian cattle issue approached; again unusually, it met only two days before and the decision to issue whips to vote against the freer importation of the Canadian beasts was taken only a day before the debate.[23] It is perhaps noteworthy, however, that John Dillon was amongst those absent on the whip for the division against the bill. One of his henchmen, John Cullinan MP, a few days later in a Tipperary speech, seemed to speak for Dillonite sentiment when he said that he personally was prepared to remove the present restrictions on Canadian cattle 'today rather than tomorrow'.[24] Some two years later, Cullinan gave a fuller account of his thinking in a Fermoy speech:

When the question of the opening of the ports was introduced, he had said he would prefer that the ports be opened today than tomorrow, and he was of the same opinion still, for it they had been opened they would knock ten or twelve years off the land of Ireland in purchase. The question put to him then, was *would he ruin the farmer who had already purchased and his answer was that he would rather see one fourth of the farmers of Ireland smashed than to see the whole of them smashed*, and it would be easier for the Irish party to deal with the government on the question of the one fourth than on the question of the whole.[25]

This was an amazingly blunt speech. It seemed to justify fully the claim of the O'Brienite press that Dillon's supporters had a basically

[22] *Leader* 2 March 1918.
[23] *Irish People*, 28 April 1908.
[24] *Irish People*, 12 April; 28 April 1906.
[25] *Irish People*, 19 September 1908.

punitive attitude towards those farmers who had bought their land under the 1903 Act. But despite all these millenarian speculations, the party did after all tamely vote against lifting the restrictive measures in force since 1896. In these circumstances though it is hardly surprising that it was William O'Brien who gave the most impressive and vigorous display of opposition. The effect of the proposed legislation, the senior member for Cork had argued, would render at least two hundred thousand Irish holdings unprofitable.[26] It is little wonder that M. J. Nagle, secretary of the South of Ireland Cattle Dealer's Association, gave O'Brien the lion's share of the credit for the defeat of the proposed change.[27] But the party's confusion over the Canadian cattle question was as nothing compared with that generated by the Liberal government's flirtation with a scheme of devolution for Ireland.

Devolution: 'Latin for Home Rule?'

Nationalist Ireland reacted unfavourably to the new Chief Secretary, Augustine Birrell, when on 8 May 1907, he offered in parliament a measure of devolution which explicitly fell far short of Home Rule. The Bill, Birrell explained: 'does not contain a touch or a trace, hint or a suggestion of any legislative power.'[28] Birrell's bill proposed to set up an Irish Council consisting of 82 elected, 24 nominated members, and the Under-Secretary for Ireland. To this Council, it proposed to transfer the control of 8 out of the 45 existing departments of government—the most important of these were the Education Boards, the Local Government Board, the Congested Districts Board, and the Department of Works, and the Department of Agriculture and Technical Instruction. The Liberal government was under the impression that the nationalist party would give this bill—timid and contaminated by the undemocratic principle of nomination as it was—their guarded support. As the *Irish Times* observed: 'Mr Birrell would never have dreamed of introducing a Bill which was not assured beforehand of the support of the Nationalist party.'[29]

Indeed, the initial omens were reasonably favourable. Even in public, the Irish party leadership—which had been engaged in private

[26] *Irish Independent*, 12 April 1906.
[27] M. J. Nagle to William O'Brien, 7 April 1906; *Irish People*, 14 April 1908.
[28] A. C. Hepburn, 'The Irish Council bill and the fall of Sir Antony MacDonnell, 1906–7', *IHS*, vol. xvii, no. 68, September 1971, 470–98, 475.
[29] *Irish Times*, 22 May 1907.

consultation with Birrell—was optimistic in tone. At Waterford on
1 February, Redmond spoke confidently of 'the early triumph of the
cause of national self-government.'[30] Speaking at Bradford on
16 March, he said that the Bill would prove to be 'no bar, but a help
and a further advance, to complete Home Rule.'[31] At Ballinasloe, on
19 February, Dillon allowed himself to describe the government's
forthcoming Bill as a 'great instrument to complete the emancipation
of the country'.[32] T. P. O'Connor even went so far as to describe
devolution as Latin for Home Rule. Perhaps even more important,
there was a certain amount of alarm on the Unionist side. Professor
A. V. Dicey, the leading Unionist academic, said simply that the
Liberal proposals went 'two thirds' of the way to Home Rule.[33] The
Ulster unionist members launched a 'clumsily organized'[34] demonstration of protest when the Bill was introduced in parliament. Even
the unpredictable O'Brienites were solidly favourable; O'Brien later
explained that he supported devolution because it would have linked
Ulster to the rest of the island in an elected national assembly. 'It is
now clear enough', O'Brien was to write with his usual dogmatism,
'that had the Irish Council Bill been allowed to pass, the partition of
Ireland would never have been heard of'.[35] But despite such arguments, Irish public opinion was mobilized against the Bill.

The reaction set in almost immediately after Birrell's presentation
of his proposed legislation on 8 May. The *Freeman's* parliamentary
correspondent noted sourly of Birrell's case: 'He was full of reasons
why no Unionist should oppose the Bill; but very bare of reason why
any Home Ruler should support it.'[36] Redmond's response was
profoundly cautious. It would be fatal to accept the Bill if they thought
it unworkable: If, on the other hand, it could be made a success in
operation, he felt sure it would help Home Rule. He carefully
abstained from commiting either himself or the Irish party. It was
Birrell's all too frank avowal which impressed Irish nationalists most
deeply: 'in not one word or line, or sentence of the bill was there even a
hint of legislative powers'.[37] A critic of Redmond's employing the *nom
de plume* 'Irish Nationalist' described the sequence of events vividly in
the *Pall Mall Gazette*:

[30] Ibid.   [31] Ibid.   [32] Ibid.
[33] *Irish Independent*, 7 May 1910.   [34] *Weekly Freeman*, 11 May 1907.
[35] *The Irish Revolution*, 36; Tim Healy, a bitter critic of the bill (*Galway Express*,
18 May 1907) later came round to O'Brien's position.
[36] *Weekly Freeman*, 11 May 1907.   [37] Hepburn, op. cit., 475.

Public bodies began to denounce the measure, most of them probably not having read a line of it or given a moments consideration to the possibility of its being made to serve the higher purpose of Home Rule. Public meetings followed suit. The bill was mentioned only to be derided. All that the people knew or cared about was that it wasn't Home Rule. That was sufficient; that was why it was denounced. On its merits the bill was never considered at all. If, as was generally believed then, and is believed to this day, the Irish leaders favoured the bill they should have said so from the very start, but their silence remained unbroken, the tide of opposition continued to rise and the situation passed beyond Mr Redmond's control.[38]

Redmond, who with John Dillon, had been sympathetic in principle to the devolution scheme—the logic of the Liberal alliance left them with little alternative—was soon knocked off course. Traditionally, an Irish convention had to decide on the nationalist attitude on such an important issue. On 18 May, Redmond of necessity made up his mind to reject the bill.[39] The convention duly met on 21 May in an excited and tense atmosphere. The mood of tension changed to one of enthusiasm when Redmond vigorously condemned the Irish Council measure as 'utterly inadequate in its scope' and urged its rejection by the Irish nation. As John Dillon, who was not present due to the tragic death of his wife, had urged, further resolutions were passed calling, in particular, for major agrarian reform.[40] Thus it was that what became known as the 'policy of fight' was decided upon.

For Redmond's biographer it was rather strange that 'the belief persisted that he had been forced against his own judgement to denounce the Council Bill'.[41] But in reality such a belief was well founded. Redmond's queasiness was apparent for all to see. The *Freeman* noted defensively of his convention speech: 'Mr Redmond laboured too long in defending himself against the charge of responsibility for the bill.'[42] But, less than a fortnight later, at a meeting in Oxford, Redmond was again, in the words, of one critic, 'dallying with devolution'.[43] At any rate, Redmond still seemed prepared to consider the possibiity of some 'half way house' on the route to Home Rule. 'I say that any proposal to confer self-

---

[38] Quoted in *Roscommon Herald*, 4 January 1908.
[39] Lyons, *Dillon*, 296–8.
[40] Ibid.; D. Gwynn, *Redmond*, 145–8.
[41] Gwynn, *Redmond*, 149.
[42] *Weekly Freeman*, 25 May 1907.
[43] *Irish People*, 8 June 1907.

government upon Ireland which is based upon liberal and democratic principles, and which offers a chance of being worked successfully may be accepted as a weapon to get more.'[44] Nevertheless, Redmond can have had few illusions about the future. In rejecting Birrell's scheme, nationalist Ireland—sent to 'the heart of things'[45] in T. M. Kettle's phrase—had opted at the convention for a policy of fight. Summarizing the effect of this 'fight' from a unionist point of view, W. Alison Phillips was to write: 'conditions were not so bad as in the days of the Land League, but they were bad enough and they had less excuse'.[46]

The Ranch War

One of the most influential analysts of the origins of the ranch war was Lord Dudley. As viceroy in Ireland, Dudley had been close to the Wyndham experiment[47] and as chairman of the royal commission on congestion he had inevitably acquired a considerable knowledge of agrarian realities. In a striking speech in mid-February 1908, Dudley insisted: 'Cattle driving was a factor which had been produced not by mere land hunger amongst one class of the population but by the old story of the national demands of the people.'[48] Following the rejection of the Council Bill—or so Dudley argued—the UIL had decided to manipulate agrarian issues in order to make it impossible to govern the country. Dudley insisted: 'He did not think that cattle driving had been carried on by those who wanted to obtain possession of the ranches for small holdings.'[49] There is little doubt that there was a substantive basis for Dudley's argument. With sharp insight he noted the contradiction in the UIL activity: 'cattle driving had been carried on by those whose ideas sharply conflicted with the ideas of the congested population.'[50] Nevertheless, Dudley may have slightly overstated his case. As viceroy he had committed himself (though not the government)[51] to the view that Ireland ought 'to be governed according to Irish ideas and not according to English ones'.[52] In accordance with this earlier assessment, Dudley may have been

---

[44] Ibid.
[45] *Weekly Freeman*, 27 September 1913.
[46] W. Alison Phillips, *The Revolution in Ireland*, London, 1923, 56.
[47] Gailey, 'Unionist government policy', 178.
[48] *Irish Times*, 14 February 1908.
[49] Ibid.   [50] Ibid.
[51] Dudley to John Redmond, 26 May 1905, NLI MS 15186(6).
[52] *Freeman's Journal*, 12 June 1903.

inclined to overestimate by a degree the purely political elements in the UIL calculation. It must be acknowledged, however, that his views find much support in the police reports. H. F. C. Price, in a report for the RIC, argued that the ranch war was not wholly due to the agrarian problem and that it had to be seen 'in relation to the rejection of the Irish council bill'.[53] To disguise their 'tactical error' in their handling of Birrell's proposal the nationalist leaders sought to launch an aggressive new movement: 'the grazing system and the agrarian   position generally, afforded material for such a movement'.[54] But as Price pointed out in another report, even before the rejection of Birrell's bill, there had been some 15 instances in which UIL MPs or organizers advocated 'breaches of the law'[55] as part of a campaign against the graziers. Even though the campaign greatly intensified after the rejection of the Irish Council Bill, significant agrarian agitation none the less pre-dated this event by some months (see Table 2). Such an assessment raises the issue of Wyndham's act's effect on the volume of agrarian grievances in Ireland.

Rural discontents

For the agrarian radical wing of the Irish party it was an article of faith to claim that the Wyndham act had been a failure. In the first place, Dillon and his friends claimed that the Irish peasantry had been tricked into paying too much of their land. Indeed, it was widely accepted by contemporary opinion that land prices under the 1903 Act were much higher than anticipated. The average price of tenanted land sold under the 1903 Act by 31 March 1909 was 22.5 years purchase. But one important point requires to be noticed here—sales under the 1903 act tended to be based on second term rents. These were usually 20 per cent lower than the first term rents—fixed before 1896—which made up the bulk of the sales under previous acts. Thus John Dillon's argument to the effect that prices had arisen from 17 to 18 years purchase before the 1903 act to 23 years purchase after it was in an important sense misleading:[56] it hid from the public the fact that

[53] SPO Crimes Branch Special, Intelligence notes 1906–14, Box no. 2. 'Present condition of the country (1907)'. A report by H. F. C. Price DI under supervision of the Inspector General, dated January 1908.

[54] Ibid.

[55] SPO Crimes Branch Special, Intelligence notes 1906–14, Box no. 2. 'Report on the general state of Ireland in 1907.' H. F. C. Price, dated 15 January 1908.

[56] *Weekly Freeman*, 24 October 1903.

Table 2 Comparative statement showing the results of the agitation against the Grazing system 1907–8.

County	May 1907		May 1908	
	Farms Unlet	Acres Unlet	Farms Unlet	Acres Unlet
Kildare	–	–	2	201
King's	5	1435	17	4051
Longford	–	–	11	2146
Meath	–	–	26	3208
Queen's	5	633	7	1668
Westmeath	1	399	4	440
Galway E.R.	9	892	19	2198
Leitrim	3	600	4	110
Mayo	3	389	5	595
Roscommon	46	4509	23	3473
Sligo	4	1358	16	1586
Clare	13	1329	39	5681
Cork E.R.	1	24	–	–
Cork W.R.	–	–	1	187
Limerick	–	–	1	176
Tipperary N.	3	244	14	2587
Tipperary S.	2	296	–	–
Total	174	20339	284	37507

[a] In May 1906, there were 67 farms of 6725 acres unlet.
[b] By 31 Dec. 1907–59 people received constant protection and 222 persons were protected by patrols.
By 30 June 1908–71 people received constant protection and 270 were protected by patrols.
Source: S.P.O., C/B/S Intelligence notes. box no. 2, 1907, 127.

after 1903 annual payments were in the main substantially lower. The *Freeman's Journal* justified the more or less constant use of such comparisons by claiming that agricultural values had fallen sharply.[57] In this form, the nationalist argument is clearly exaggerated; nevertheless, many genuine friends of the conciliation process—including William O'Brien, T. W. Russell and Sir Antony MacDonnell—felt that the landlords had been too hard-nosed.[58] William O'Brien admitted in 1908 that overall prices were at least two years too high;[59]

[57] *Freeman's Journal*, 30 September 1903.
[58] For an excellent discussion see Mullen, 'The Origins and Passing of the Irish Land Act of 1909', 14–20.
[59] For further evidence of O'Brien's disenchantment see J. V. O'Brien, *William O'Brien*, 161–2.

when it is remembered that one-third of sales by 1909 under the 1903 act were calculated on the basis of first term rents, the rise (by four-and-a-half years) in the purchase price does seem excessive.

But in a sense even O'Brien's criticism of the landlords was beside the point. Annual repayments under the 1903 Act were usually 10 per cent lower than existing rent levels. There is little doubt, that despite the controversy over prices, the 1903 Act worked successfully in many areas of the country. By the end of October 1908, 316,984 holdings had either been sold or agreed to be sold; this left some 282,888 holdings untouched.[60] It was evident, therefore, that the 'bulk' of the well-to-do tenants had purchased (or agreed to purchase) by this date.[61]

But despite this obvious area of success, the Wyndham Act's 'failure' in the west was a major theme of nationalist orators. In fact, the Congested Districts Board had moved rapidly to expand its purchase operations in the wake of the 1903 Act. In 1901, there were 180,320 holdings in the scheduled area of the congested districts and over two-thirds of these had a valuation of £10 and under. By 31 December 1907, 39,000 of these holdings had been bought from their owners and 28,000 cases were pending. But it is important to note that long before the end of 1907 the pace of the Board's work was clearly slackening off; the total volume of purchases declined from £649,559 in 1904–5 to £98,485 in the nine months leading up to the end of 1906.[62] The parsimonious attitude of the British treasury, which refused to allow the Board the necessary funds, was at the root of this unfortunate development. Privately, Birrell confessed to Redmond that he felt 'like a beaten dog'[63] because of the treasury's attitude on the congested districts. Publicly, Birrell acknowledged that it was easy to understand the popular impatience on the issue.[64]

Nationalists, of course, also liked to blame the landlords for failing to co-operate with the Board. Although some landlords were as frustrated as the tenantry by the treasury's stance, there were some remarkable instances of landlord obduracy—the unbending Marquis

[60] Return giving, by counties and provinces, the area, the Poor Law valuation and purchase-money of lands sold, and lands in respect of which proceedings have been instituted and are pending for sale under the Irish land purchase acts; also the estimated area, Poor Law valuation, and purchase money of lands in respect of which proceedings for sale have not been instituted under the said acts (Cd 4412). HC 1908, xv 1402.

[61] *Irish Independent*, 10 May 1909.

[62] Mullen, 'The Passing of the Irish Land Act 1909', 31.

[63] Redmond to Dillon, 4 March 1908, TCD Dillon papers 674/24.

[64] Hansard, vol. 183, col. 586, 3 February 1908.

of Clanricarde, who refused to recognize the 1903 Act and maintained a besieged band of 'planters'[65] on his estate in place of evicted tenants was the most famous. As John Roche, MP for East Galway, pointed out to Redmond, landlords like Clanricarde, 'our strong card',[66] were valuable aides to the UIL. But as Birrell told the cabinet: 'Everybody, except Lord Clanricarde is willing to sell and I dare say even Lord Clanricarde would accept a sum were it offered him in sovereigns and did he think it sufficient.'[67] This is the root of the matter; few were motivated by an irrational desire to hold on to Irish land in the face of economic pressure—rather, for numerous landlords, ownership of Irish land was still a paying proposition. More generally, many landlords were able to let or personally farm their best grazing land at a profit, and therefore had little incentive to sell. As T. W. Russell, a former supporter of the conciliation policy, analysed the act's 'failure' in the west to the Dudley commission on 3 September 1907:

I don't attach the importance to the money market at the present moment— the want of sufficient money to pay the landlords—that would regard it as an adequate explanation. That is very serious but it is not the real reason why the act has not worked here. The real reason is these grass lands cannot be had. There are some grass lands of the west (that) can not really be had at a price that will warrant ... purchasing and reselling them. That is the problem, a very grave problem for the government of the country, for the people were promised these lands by the mouth piece of the government.[68]

It is evident that Wyndham's presentation bedevilled the actual working of his legislation. As T. W. Russell, who in a rather unprincipled manœuvre replaced Plunkett as vice-president at the department of agriculture in the summer of 1907,[69] put it, the 1903 act had worked only sluggishly in the west: 'but the people were promised

---

[65] PRO CO 904/77/5.

[66] NLI MS 15223. John Roche to John Redmond, n.d. See Royal Commission (Judge Mathew) on Evicted Tenants in Ireland, Report, Evidence, Appendices-Index, PP 1893, vol. 6, 128, for an initial clash between Roche, a Woodford miller and farmer, and Sir Edward Carson acting in the interests of Clanricarde. Carson's task being complicated by Clanricarde's refusal to 'recognize' the Royal Commission.

[67] PRO Cab 37/95/74283. Questions raised by the Dudley Report, 22 October 1908.

[68] Royal commission on congestion in Ireland; appendix to the ninth report, minutes of evidence ... and documents relating thereto, 185 (C 3844), HC 1908, xli, 483 (hereafter cited as congestion comm. evidence, app. ninth report).

[69] Liam Kennedy, 'Farmers, Traders and Agricultural Politics in Pre-Independence Ireland', in S. Clark and J. S. Donnelly, ed. *Irish Peasants: Violence and Political Unrest 1780–1914*, 351.

these lands in the parliament by the spokesman of the government.'[70] But, Russell added glumly: 'No doubt no department has to administer Mr Wyndham's speeches, they have to administer an Act of Parliament.'[71] The same point was made even more bitterly by the *Freeman*: the *Freeman* placed the blame for subsequent outbreaks of agrarian militancy firmly at the former chief secretary's door:

Is it any wonder that they fell back upon agitation? Is it any wonder they began cattle driving? When they read Mr Wyndham's thrilling periods; when they saw their sores and tribulations placed at the very forefront of the plea for a free grant of £12,000,000; when they read that the House of Commons was thrilled to generosity by the picture of their condition they were filled with a great hope. But no sooner was the £12,000,000 procured than they saw it begin to pour into the pockets of the great landlords, while the only effect on their own miserable fortunes was to raise the price of their bogs from 14 years purchase to 24 or 27.[72]

Understandably Birrell also liked to take refuge from his difficulties by stressing this point: 'there can not be lasting peace or contentment until the hopes which the unionist promises had raised for the people's minds are realised.'[73] For these reasons, Sir Antony Mac-Donnell, who remained a supporter of the conciliation policy, and of voluntary purchase in the rest of Ireland, became convinced that compulsory powers were desirable in the exceptional case of the west—if only to convince the people there of the government's seriousness of intent.[74] But this did not satisfy a militant like Laurence Ginnell; Ginnell believed that forceful action was required over most of Ireland to bring about a more equal distribution of land. In 1906 alone, he could point out, forty-six new holdings of over 200 acres were created, the area of land used for this purpose being 49,000 acres.[75] In Ginnell's view there were no fewer than twenty-two counties in Ireland in which land redistribution was a serious issue.[76]

The first shot in the Ranch War was fired not in the traditional

---

[70] Congestion comm. evidence, ap. ninth report, 185.

[71] Ibid.

[72] *Weekly Freeman*, 16 Novemebr 1907.

[73] *Irish People*, 18 April 1908.

[74] For western protest see *Mayo News*, 11 January 1908; 7 November; 28 November 1908. See also the interesting material on the west in W. J. Johnston, 'The Land Purchase Problem' in *Journal of the Statistical and Social Inquiry Society of Ireland*, December 1906, vol. xl, pt. cxxxvi, 408–11.

[75] *Weekly Freeman*, 18 January 1908.

[76] Hansard, vol. 196, col. 1064, 17 November 1908, for Ginnell's concern.

centre of agrarian radicalism, the west, but in north Westmeath, and this in itself was significant. At a 'great gathering of young men' called to denounce the grazing system at the Downs, Co. Westmeath, on 14 October 1906, Laurence Ginnell MP moved beyond mere denunciation of ranchers and advocated a novel form of action: cattle-driving.[77] Ginnell was at this point a supporter of Dillon. He had acted as Dillon's secretary;[78] indeed on Dillon's recommendation, Lord Morley employed Ginnell as his research assistant on the *Life of Gladstone*.[79] (Ginnell always maintained that Gladstone's anti-Catholic side was carefully obscured by Morley.) Ginnell lacked charisma 'afflicted with a harsh voice he had an unsympathetic manner and was not good to look upon'[80] but he lacked nothing in industry, determination and desire for martyrdom.

The midlands venue of the first cattle-driving meeting was of some importance. The Wyndham act, or at any rate section 75, had at least raised the possibility that some landless men outside the west—as well as western congests—might benefit from land redistribution. Hence, Wyndham had created some hope at least in the hearts of those peasants Ginnell sought to lead. By autumn 1905, as Joe Devlin pointed out in a UIL circular, in a small number of cases such landless men had indeed triumphed. But as Devlin noted in the same document, for such developments to occur on a wide scale, it was necessary to make more land available by smashing the grazing system.[81]

By July 1906 this revolution of rising expectations had intensified. The Dudley Commission to enquire into congestion had been appointed. This commission was intended to investigate the western problem but would this new body give anything to the rural poor outside the west? Laurence Ginnell, in particular, liked to harp on this point: 'The Congested Districts Commission would do them no good in Westmeath if they submitted to those oiled and slipperied gentlemen who composed it nothing more than oral evidence.'[82] Ginnell also was careful to implant the idea in his audiences' mind that liberal governments would be reluctant to apply coercion in Ireland. Having taken care to explain that his policy had good

[77] *Irish Times*, 15 October 1906.
[78] Tim Healy, *Letters and Leaders of My Day*, vol. ii, 565.
[79] Ibid.   [80] Ibid.
[81] PRO CO 903/12, 138–9, see also PRO Cab 37/95/74283.
[82] *Roscommon Herald*, 20 July 1907.

prospects of success Ginnell then turned to an explanation of its 'kernel'. His 'great gathering of young men' were treated to an exposition of what became popularly known as the 'Downs policy'— cattle-driving. The peasantry were advised by Ginnell to take the cattle off the graziers land (usually at night) and 'drive' them. Usually these unfortunate beasts were simply left to wander along the country roads. The object was to harass and demoralize the graziers; eventually, it was hoped, such men would surrender their land to the surrounding peasantry, rather than have their lives made a misery. Ginnell, as he later acknowledged, was at first alone and acting on his own responsibility in this venture.

But his ideas were not ignored. In Roscommon, the 'first cattle drive in Ireland'[83] took place on the Tonlagee grazing farm of John Beirne. In mid-January, a chastened Beirne surrendered his farm publicly to John Dillon at a meeting held appropriately enough to unveil a memorial to the anti-grazier activist Matthew Harris, MP, in Ballinasloe. John Beirne explained that his action was due to his 'respect for the Irish party'.[84]

In February an even more significant development marked a change in Irish party opinion on the land question. John Dillon and John Redmond supported an aggressive private member's bill presented by the inarticulate Michael Hogan (known as 'Farmer' Hogan) MP for North Tipperary.[85] The main features of Hogan's proposed legislation were:

(1) the abolition of the zones
(2) compulsory sale and purchase
(3) alteration of the bonus to a sliding scale
(4) increase in the area of the scheduled congested districts
(5) alterations in the rent fixing in the Land Court
(6) provision for landless men

In its attack on zones, voluntary purchase and the bonus, the Bill was attacking the most salient elements of the 1903 Act, elements which had allowed mutual agreement in 1903. The proposal to alter rent fixing mechanisms had a particular resonance; here the party clearly seemed to be holding out the prospect of continued dual ownership

---

[83] Royal commission on congestion in Ireland: Appendix to the ninth report, minutes of evidence . . . and documents relating thereto, 214 (C 4006), 1098, xii, 312.
[84] *Irish Times*, 21 January 1907.
[85] *Irish Times*, 20 April 1907.

(on better financial terms, of course) as an alternative to peasant proprietorship on 'conciliatory' terms. The suggestion that new legislation should make provision for landless men was equally symptomatic; here the party officially sanctioned a thorough-going agrarian radicalism. But inevitably this involved a certain duplicity; even the radical 'Farmer' Hogan found it easy to defend landless men in London, but when necessary in Tipperary he was quite happy to ally with graziers if it was necessary to keep his seat. As M. L. Kennedy, one of Hogan's local critics was to put it: 'The eleven months man is the enemy of the people? Was Mr Michael Hogan a subscriber to this philosophy when he went crawling to a man with eleven months land for his vote?'[86] In keeping with this new militancy, in a series of hot-tempered encounters from 21 to 23 March, the UIL's officially accredited representative, John Fitzgibbon, outlined revolutionary proposals before the Dudley Commission. Fitzgibbbon went so far as to call for the expropriation of farmers who had recently bought their land under the 1903 act in order to satisfy the landless men.[87] In April the ranch war moved even more substantially out of the realm of theory and into that of practice. On 29 April some 300 men assembled in the neighbourhood of Loughrea and marched to the grazing farms at Earl's Park, Ballinlawless and Tullyhill, where they cleared the farms of all the cattle by driving them on to the public road.[88] As late as 30 April 1907, Dennis Johnstone, the UIL secretary, wrote to John Dillon: 'it is very awkward to have the League associated with the attempts now being made to drive cattle off the grazing lands.'[89] Acting in accordance with this sentiment Johnstone withdrew one particular aggressive UIL organizer (Dermot Cogan) from Elphin in Roscommon. Such reservations, however, were soon to be suppressed in the course of the next two months. On 1 May cattle drives took place at Ballinamore Bridge and Clooniskert.[90] On 21 May the convention decided on its 'policy of fight'. On 26 May a large anti-ranching demonstration was held at Elphin—with T. J. Condon, David Sheehy, and John Fitzgibbon as the principal speakers.[91] More

[86] *Midland Tribune*, 1 January 1910.
[87] Royal commission on congestion in Ireland: Appendix to the fifth report, minutes of evidence . . . and documents relating thereto, 1401 (C 3629), HC 1908, xxxvi, 439.
[88] *Galway Express*, 18 May 1907.
[89] Dennis Johnstone to John Dillon, 30 April 1907, TCD Dillon papers 6763/29.
[90] *Galway Express*, 18 May 1907.
[91] *Weekly Freeman*, 1 June 1907.

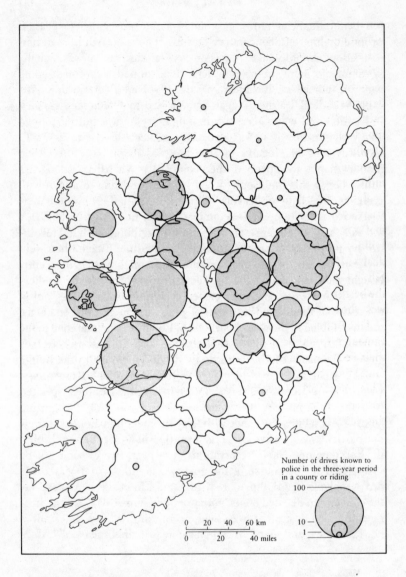

Number of drives known to
police in the three-year period
in a county or riding

100 —

10 —
1 —

0   20   40   60 km
0   20   40 miles

2. Cattle Drives 1907–1909. Number of drives known to the police in the three-year period in a county or riding

generally there was a dramatic increase in cattle drives—there were 36 in that month as against nine in April.[92] Laurence Ginnell was clearly no longer involved in an isolated struggle. The 'policy of fight' decided upon at the May convention was seen by many as the official seal of approval for Ginnell's 'new departure'. In June, Joe Devlin was openly organizing a large scale cattle-driving campaign.[93] Equally openly, Devlin urged John Redmond to apply pressure on Irish MPs to support the new movement.[94] Devlin went so far as to warn Redmond that the new Sinn Fein movement was threatening to outflank the party by its greater militancy on this question[95]—though, in truth, a more rounded analysis would have shown that even Sinn Fein was infected by the party's ambiguities.[96] A letter from Joe Devlin to John Dillon on 5 June marks the change of mood at the UIL headquarters. Devlin wrote to Dillon: 'prompt steps should be taken to give the country a lead and to deal with the situation which has arisen since the rejection of Birrell's bill.'[97] Devlin admitted 'it is rather difficult to know what precisely is the best course to adopt'[98] but of one thing he was sure: 'the fight in the west should be judiciously encouraged'.[99]

The authorities were fully aware that their initial response to this campaign would be of decisive importance. But the police found that their task was not an easy one. To their suprise and annoyance, they found that the graziers did not co-operate fully with their endeavours. This refusal to co-operate had two aspects. In the first place, the graziers—even though 'everything pointed to increased difficulties this year'[100] refused to improve the security arrangements for their

---

[92] H. F. C. Price's 'Report on the general state of Ireland in 1907'. loc. cit.

[93] Hepburn, *Liberal Policies*, 492.

[94] Ibid.

[95] Ibid.; see also Tom Garvin, *The Evolution of Irish Nationalist Politics*, Dublin, 1981, 93.

[96] See, for example, the *Longford Leaders* exposé (16 May 1908) of grass grabbing by a prominent Granard Sinn Feiner. 'Mr L. O'Reilly . . . can never during his lifetime get rid of this fact: that at a time when he was a member of the UIL, and a leading nationalist . . . when a large grazing farm was given up in the district, he stepped in and grabbed it, so did his little bit to maintain landlord ascendancy.' Even more persuasive evidence of this point is provided in Chantal Deutsch-Brady, 'The cattle drive of Tulira', *Journal of Galway Archaeological and Historical Society*, vol. 34, 1974–5, 35–9.

[97] Joe Devlin to John Dillon, 5 July 1905, TCD Dillon papers, 6729/118.

[98] Ibid.   [99] Ibid.

[100] Report compiled for the chief secretary by the deputy inspector general of the RIC in reply to Mr Lonsdale's question of 12 June 1907, with a covering note by A. P. Magill, 20 June 1907. CSORP 1907/13617.

cattle. 'Having regard to the threatened danger prudence should have suggested that a place of safe-keeping, say a strongly fenced paddock, should have been established at or near the farm or herds' house in which the cattle could be placed at night.'[101] No such measures were, in fact, taken. Secondly, and perhaps more seriously, the graziers seemed to be characterized by an ambiguous attitude towards the ranch 'warriors': 'in very many (cases) the owners and herds failed to assist the police either actively or by identifying offenders, failed subsequently to give truthful evidence, and on occasion played into the hands of the raiders'.[102] The police themselves had bitter memories of being used effectively as herdsmen by graziers in the 1880s, and this too seems to have led to a number of cases of negligence on their part.[103]

By the end of 1907, H. F. C. Price, in his report for the RIC, was compelled to admit: 'in many counties and I do not confine myself to the well-known disturbed districts, the law is *entirely inoperative* in respect of any case which involves an agrarian element and crime is widespread in certain localities.'[104] In the period from August to December 1907 there were some 292 cattle drives reported. Yet, despite the clearest possible evidence of guilt, no ordinary common jury (except in one Dublin instance) could be trusted to convict. During the course of 1907 no fewer than 28 cases of failures of justice were reported. There were also 18 cases of similar failures before the petty sessions where local magistrates were often either UIL supporters or feared the pressure of UIL intimidation. Eleven magistrates who delivered unpopular decisions were boycotted during 1907. For the police there was only one conceivable remedy: the immediate and forceful implementation of the coercive 1887 Crimes Act. It is worth noting however that H. F.C. Price also argued more positively that there was a need for 'money to buy the grazing tracts, money to secure the transfer of estates, money to supply adequate staff for all purposes'.[105] Irish Unionists nevertheless denounced the government's failure to put a stop to the cattle driving campaign. The *Irish Times* noted savagely: 'Agrarian agitations may come in "movements" but the movements, are not the result of abiogenesis. They spring from a perception of the physical and moral weakness of governments like

---

[101] Ibid.   [102] Ibid.   [103] Ibid.
[104] H. F. C. Price, 'Report on the general state of Ireland in 1907'. loc. cit.
[105] H. F. C. Price, 'Present condition of the country' (1907), loc. cit.

the present.'[106] The same journal added later: 'the West of Ireland is ripe for an agrarian outbreak owing to the scandalous laxity with which the law has been administered since the present government came to power'.[107]

As this comment of the *Irish Times* implies, the traditional centres of anti-ranching sentiment were easily enough mobilized. On 8 June 1907, the *Connaught Champion* gleefully publicized Birrell's admission that 327 grazing farms were receiving police protection. Tongue in cheek it proclaimed: 'We feel such an admission reflected no credit on Irish nationalists. There is not a grazing farm in Ireland that ought not to be in the same position today.'[108] By 22 June there were 35 cattle drives—25 in Galway East, three in Roscommon, two in Queen's County and five in King's County. The police had twelve cases pending against 143 people.[109] On 30 June 1907, with a heavy symbolism, a large demonstration was held at Straide beside the ruins of the Davitt home on the Gallagher ranch. The keynote speeches of Joe Devlin, Father Dennis O'Hara and John Fitzgibbon were all characterized by hostility towards the grazing system.[110] Perhaps inevitably direct action followed. James Gallagher, the grazier whose land embraced the holding originally held, before their eviction in 1854, by the parents of Michael Davitt, found himself the victim of a cattle drive.[111]

This activism in Ireland had its counterpart in Westminster. In July and August 1907 the Irish party did, in fact, win an important agrarian victory. Birrell managed to get through the House of Commons a bill providing for the restoration of the evicted tenants—'the wounded soldiers of the land war'. The objective of this legislation—which in its original form was strongly supported by Dillon—was to empower the estates commissioners to acquire land, if necessary by compulsion, for the resettlement of evicted tenants and to declare the land so acquired to be an estate within the meaning of the Land Purchase Acts. Those occupying tenants dispossessed were to be compensated or given as good land elsewhere.[112] In fact, one of the three estates commissioners,

---

[106] *Irish Times*, 26 July 1907.
[107] *Irish Times*, 27 August 1907.
[108] *Connaught Champion*, 8 June 1907.
[109] CSORP 1907/13770. Statement compiled and submitted by the under-secretary at Dublin Castle, 22 June 1907.
[110] *Connaught Telegraph*, 6 July 1907.
[111] Ibid., 15 February 1908.
[112] Lyons, *Dillon*, 298.

Frederick Wrench, the least 'popular' in his sympathies, profoundly doubted the wisdom of the evicted tenants' proposals. In Wrench's view, out of 5,700 evicted tenants seeking reinstatement, 'a considerable proportion were men who would be failures in any rank of life and to whom it would be dangerous to advance public funds'.[113] In the House of Commons, a sceptical Walter Long, who had done so much to purge the Tory party of Wyndhamite sentimentality towards the Irish, pointed out that the number of evicted tenants to be reinstated had increased dramatically since the day when Dillon had spoken of a mere eight hundred.[114] The Lords naturally were very concerned about the principle of compulsion. The bill was only passed under the guillotine procedure and the Lords did their utmost to minimize the compulsory section and this provoked the Irish party to walk out on the last stages of the debate. In defending the Government's bill in the Lords, the Earl of Crewe had argued that many non-nationalist Irishmen supported the new proposals,[115] but, nevertheless, Birrell's decision to act obviously owed a great deal to Dillon's pressure. By June 1908, 1,655 evicted tenants had been reinstated—a figure which contrasted well with the figure of 284 for the 1903–6 period.[116] (Ironically the estates commissioners found that UIL members proved exceptionally reluctant to make way for the 'wounded soldiers' and most of those reinstated in the first year of the legislation owed their good fortune to the direct action of landlords.)[117] But this triumph did not satisfy the UIL leadership, indeed while the evicted tenants legislation was still being debated in London on 12 July Laurence Ginnell received instructions from Joe Devlin to return to his constituency.[118] Ginnell had long been involved in the evicted tenants question[119] and had tabled amendments to Birrell's bill, yet despite this important business Ginnell was asked to spread the area of operation of the cattle drivers.

On his arrival in the midlands, Ginnell was quick to point out that in Galway, Mayo and Roscommon his advocacy of cattle driving had

---

[113] Frederick Wrench to James Bryce, 1 May 1906. NLI MS 11013.

[114] Hansard, 22 July 1907, vol. 178, col. 1235.

[115] *HL*, 6 August 1907, col. 1698.

[116] *Irish Times*, 15 August 1908.

[117] Ibid. Report of the Estates Commissioners for the year ending 31 March 1908 and for the period from 1 November 1903 to 31 March 1908; with appendices (Cd 4277), HC 1908, XXIII, 175.

[118] *Roscommon Herald*, 20 July 1907.

[119] Ibid.; see for his secretarial work, TCD Dillon papers, 6806–6826.

been acted on more rapidly than in his constituency. 'Let me tell you it is the people of the west who are scattering the cattle like chaff before the wind.'[120] Ginnell was determined, however, that this time the west should not bear yet again the whole burden of Irish agrarian radicalism. He reported a conversation with the South Galway MP (W. J. Duffy) who had already 150 constituents summoned before the magistrates. 'I fear, said this gentleman, that the people of Leinster and your county are too much afraid of jail.'[121]

In this same speech, Ginnell publicly claimed that he had received instructions from the party leadership to return to Ireland. The sense of all this was clear, or so Ginnell argued: the party leadership were convinced of the need to step up the land war. This also fits in with the words of another prominent cattle driver, John Fitzgibbon: 'I did nothing on my own responsibility . . . I went to my leaders . . . I am not going to say what they told me but they told me enough. They gave me my instructions and blessed the cattle drivers'.[122] The police accepted Ginnell's and Fitzgibbon's version: 'At first there was some small doubt he had the standing committee of the UIL at his back, but proof was obtained in November that the standing committee were arranging all Ginnell's meetings. The inference is obvious.'[123] In the same report, H. F. C. Price noted: 'A rumour got abroad and it was openly stated that the government sympathized with the cattle driving. This though, of course, groundless had a demoralizing effect.'[124] Nevertheless, Irish agrarian radicals reasonably perceived a degree of hesitancy and division within official opinion. Ginnell was typically forthright; declaring that members of the government used such strong language in support of cattle driving that he would blush to report it in the presence of ladies.[125] But while agrarian radicals happily speculated about the divisions and weaknesses in the forces ranged against them, they would have done well to devote some thought to the divisions and weaknesses on their own side. The ranch war leaders attempted to draw on traditional Irish agrarian arguments. These involved a number of very definite assumptions about the Irish tenantry's historical case.

[120] Ibid.
[121] Ibid.
[122] *Irish People*, 18 April 1908.
[123] H. F. C. Price, Report on the general state of Ireland in 1907, loc. cit.
[121] Ibid.
[125] *Irish Times*, 27 August 1907.

The Ideology of the Ranch War

Laurence Ginnell, who was on the extreme left of Irish agrarian radicalism, was capable of saying at Delvin: 'The land is what most concerns the country people and a splendid substantial thing it is to fight for. It is well worth fighting for even if we had no historical claim.'[126] But, of course, the point is that there was a 'historical claim'. Because of it, men much less spontaneously radical than Ginnell, felt able to work with him, or at least, allow him a certain sympathy. A few days earlier at nearby Killalon, Ginnell himself had made a point of stressing this debt owed to history:

Our people were scourged and banished: they were scattered like noxious vermin for the sheer pleasure of destroying them. Not only in the remote past, but in our own time, by men still living has the satanic pleasure of throwing peasants out on the roadside been indulged in . . . Some of the descendants of these victims are in this crowd today. I am in the knowledge of it, and who will deny their right, who will give them anything but praise and encouragement when they look with longing eyes to try to recover these lands.[127]

Again in November, Ginnell reminded his audience: 'The Fetherstones and the Cookes cleared out happy families, and Nemesis like the bitterly wronged descendants of the hunted farmers are going to effect re-distribution.'[128] This was the core of the case for the cattle drivers: at last, the wrongs of history were to be avenged. But nationalism also insisted that Irish Catholics in general had been wronged by history; hence the key problem for the cattle drivers—how far were they justified in pressing their case when it clashed with the interests of other Catholic and Nationalist farmers? Ginnell had no doubt that the rural poor were justified in pushing their case as hard as possible. In his book *Land and Liberty* (1908) Ginnell argued that anti-British sentiment amongst Irishmen owed more to the famine clearances than, say, the Penal Laws or the Act of Union, thus neatly giving nationalist primacy to the cause of radical agrarianism.[129] This is why his speeches are full of advice to his followers to ignore the religious and political loyalties of the ranches. He told the crowd at Kilmaryle, Co. Roscommon on 28 July 1907 that it was necessary to

---

[126] *Roscommon Herald*, 2 November 1907.
[127] *Roscommon Herald*, 26 October 1907.
[128] Ibid., 23 November 1907.
[129] *Land and Liberty*, Dublin, 1908, 23.

oppose the 'rancher whoever he may be, at whatever alter he may kneel'.[130] At Navan, Co. Meath, in August he admitted that many of his rancher enemies were 'excellent Nationalists'.[131] Ginnell paid a personal price for his outspokenness: 'Why was he (Mr Ginnell) carped at in his own county except because he attacked the ranching system? He saw in that Church today when at Mass, men with whom he attended catechism in the Chapel of Delvin, and for what reason was he criticized? . . . Simply because he attacked the ranches; simply because he wanted to get the land back for the people.'[132]

As Ginnell's remarks imply, the Irish Catholic Church was placed under particular pressure by the cattle driving question. At a Connaught Provincial Session at Tuam in 1907 cattle driving was placed on the list of reserved sins for which absolution was reserved to the bishop.[133] The Archbishop of Tuam roundly declared: 'I would not give one sod to a man who would be a party to cattle driving. I don't think he is an honest man.'[134] Yet, as was public knowledge, Bishop O'Donnell of nearby Raphoe, was along with John Fitzgibbon, noted cattle driver, a trustee of the Irish party's funds—funds which Ginnell claimed to have been made available to support cattle driving.[135]

D. P. Moran of the *Leader* was also a critic of the policy of cattle driving. Frustrated by reading an article on the topic by the liberal Maynooth professor, the Revd Walter MacDonald—which Moran felt had not penetrated to the heart of the matter—Moran felt driven to conclude:

At its best the 'hazel' as a weapon of general use is two-edged. It strikes at more than the grazier's bullock. It involves neighbour against neighbour, Irishman against Irishman, and its muddling effect on ignorant minds concerning the meum et tuum might be very deplorable. In the Land League days the issues between rack-rented and insecure tenants, and more or less cruel, worthless and foreign landlordism, was fairly clear cut; but cattle driving as a general policy, is a different and more complex and more dangerous problem altogether.[136]

---

[130] PRO CO 903/13/16.
[131] *Irish Times*, 15 August 1907.
[132] *Roscommon Herald*, 20 July 1907.
[133] David Miller, *Church State and Nation*, 205–6.
[134] *Weekly Freeman's Journal*, 13 June 1908.
[135] *Irish People*, 27 February 1907.
[136] *Leader*, 18 January 1908; see also *Leader*, 11 January 1908.

Finally, the authority of the Parnell name—such as it now was—was available to the anti-cattle driving side. While still broadly in favour of land redistribution, J. H. Parnell declared publicly his opposition to cattle driving. He added a warning: 'I doubt if all the grazing lands were cut up and tilled these lands would bring in the quantity of money the cattle would.'[137]

But what of the new nationalist threat to the party, the Sinn Fein movement, which unsuccessfully challenged the official machine in April 1908, when C. J. Dolan resigned his seat to stand again in the Sinn Fein interest? There is some evidence that it flirted with agrarian militancy; but there is also evidence that its local leaders were as ambivalent as those of the Irish party on the issue. Certainly, there was a clear suggestion that the more sophisticated Sinn Feiners had their doubts about the rhetoric of cattle driving. Indeed, it is not too much to say that Sinn Fein seemed to be characterized by a rather sceptical attitude towards the whole tradition of Irish agrarian radicalism. Anna Parnell, the sharpest and most politicized of the Parnells, an early recruit to Dolan's campaign—who was treated rather roughly by her constitutionalist opponents, notably Richard Hazleton, author of one of the sickliest tributes to her late brother[138]—had set about demystifying this history with a vengeance. In late 1906 she published a savage review of Barry O'Brien's life of Charles Stewart Parnell[139] and followed this up in 1907 with the serialization of her devasting exposé *Tale of the Land League: a Great Sham* published in the *Irish People* and then celebrated in *Sinn Fein*:[140] not satisfied with her dismissal of Barry O'Brien's work, Anna Parnell moved on to describing Michael Davitt's *Fall of feudalism* as 'almost absolutely false about important points of Irish history'.[141] At the end of 1907, *Sinn Fein* also published a most interesting article 'Some notes on cattle and cattle driving'. In this essay, the secretary of the Castlerea branch of Sinn Fein made some points which parliamentary nationalists preferred to forget. This writer noted the massive decline in tillage acreage in Roscommon since 1851—from 5,858,951 acres in that year to 4,631,051 in the year 1901. But, he pointed out, in an interesting echo of Michael Davitt:

[137] *Irish Independent*, 7 January 1910.
[138] See Hazleton's prize-winning essay on Parnell, *IWI*, 8 October 1898.
[139] *Gaelic American*, reprinted *Irish People*, 16 February 1907.
[140] *Sinn Fein*, 16 October 1909.
[141] *The Peasant and Irish Irelander*, 5 October 1907; see also her comments in 20 October and 2 November issues.

It must not be assumed that the sub-division of the ranches would lead to any wholesale increase in the area of tillage. Our observation of tracts already divided into holdings of 20 acres and upwards shows that the incoming tenant takes as many grazing beasts as he can accommodate, and sometimes tills a patch sufficient to produce enough white cabbage and potatoes for his table use.[142]

This writer acknowledged: 'Some will ask what is all the trouble about so long as the small farmer is the grazier and hires his land for grazing.'[143] But the *Sinn Fein* piece insisted that the small farmers' general contribution to Ireland was much exaggerated: 'When his position is properly studied in relation to the nation it will be found he has been much overrated.'[144] Firin in the *Peasant* agreed: 'The average Irish farmer has a farm but not a country . . . the cry of the land for the people did not mean the land for the farmer alone. All the other sections of the community were included in it.'[145] It is clear from these articles that some of the more astute minds in Sinn Fein had their doubts about the policy of cattle driving. In particular, some of the cracks in the Irish party's vague philosophy of agrarian radicalism were clearly visible. For Sinn Fein it was of course, impossible to withhold support from the struggling peasantry: the cattle-driving campaign at least had the merit of being an alternative to parliamentary activity. It was to be supported but only for that reason. Enough has been said to show that cattle driving had its critics as well as its supporters. The 'Ranch War' was likely to create trouble for the graziers. But it was also likely to create trouble for the nationalist movement and John Redmond.

John Redmond and the Cattle Driving Question

The county of Longford was not necessarily the most likely place to produce a flare up of anti-grazing activity. Longford's activity in the United Irish League in its early days had been circumspect. The 'Longford notes' section of one provincial journal concluded: 'although the special object for which the League was founded, namely, the division of the grasslands, is not quite so urgent in County Longford as elsewhere, still the people recognize that the League is providing a common platform for all Nationalists, and that in fact it is

---

[142] *Sinn Fein*, 28 December 1907.
[143] Ibid.   [144] Ibid.
[145] *The Peasant and Irish Irelander*, 9 March 1907, 'The Farmer and the Nation'.

the National League in a new form.'[146] The same writer was rather
more positive about the anti-grazing aspect of the UIL programme a
few months later when he wrote: 'This grazing question does not affect
Longford as much as the other counties but nevertheless . . . there is
much good work to be done. If they had all these big farms of from 300
to 600 acres taken and divided up amongst the poorer farmers and
labourers, instead of having a diminished population, they would have
an increasing one.'[147] But this realization remained a latent one:
proven by the fact that the McCanns, the largest ranchers in the area,
had no difficulty in getting elected to local government office in
1899.[148]

But in the summer of 1907 Longford leapt to the forefront. The
previously-admired McCanns—'amongst the most popular men in
the community'—came under considerable fire. J. P. Farrell, the local
MP, played the decisive role in giving organization and leadership.
But the Longford excitement was of interest also for the light it threw
on John Redmond's leadership at the national level. Battle began
when on 7 July 1907, a public meeting was held in Newtonforbes to
demand the surrender of the ranches. On 8 August, a deputation of
'leading nationalists' of Killashee, Clonguish, Killoe and Drumlish
waited on the graziers holding land on the Douglas estate, and
demanded the unconditional surrender of the ranches in their
possession for the purpose of having them distributed amongst the
people who are the rightful owners. This deputation drove first to the
house of Michael McCann, with a force of police in hot pursuit. After
a somewhat unpleasant verbal confrontation with the unfortunate wife
of McCann, the deputation then proceeded to James McCann's
business premises in Newtonforbes. Here again they were baulked as
McCann refused to emerge to speak to them. But they had more luck
at their next port of call. At 'Martin's ranch', Harris Martin received
the visitors in a very courteous manner and expressed his intention of
giving up the farm for the benefit of the people but would not state
when he would surrender. 'The deputation left dissatisfied at this
undecided answer of Mr Martin's and told Mr Martin his answer
would be considered on his merits.'[149] Next, the deputation visited the
Percival ranch and were told that the Percivals were spending a week

---

[146] *Roscommon Herald*, 1 November 1898.
[147] Ibid., 11 April 1899.
[148] Ibid., 2 November 1907. Messrs McCann: isolated at Newtonforbes.
[149] *Longford Leader*, 10 August 1902.

in Dublin on business. It was at their final destination, the Pierce ranch that the deputation received its sharpest rebuff. The United Irish League organizer in the locality, Dermot Cogan told Arthur Pierce 'that all his neighbours were there to ask him to surrender these wasted ranches he held on the 11 months system, for the benefit of the people'. Mr Pierce responded by telling Cogan that he 'had a stiff neck to come and much such a demand', and added that he would only give up when he would be made to do it, and he further said 'that you or your league will never make me give it up'.[150]

With that, Pierce ordered the League and the police off his ranch. Pierce also gave a parting shot at the police who had allowed this confrontation to take place: 'it must be supposed that the police are anxious to have the ranches split up.' There is no doubt that the RIC men—many of them sons of small farmers—had divided allegiances on the matter. The harrassed Mrs McCann had found this out also. She had turned to the police and asked 'what should she say to these people?' But as long as the Leaguers did not resort to violence, the police were reluctant to act. 'The police quietly replied they would not interfere.'[151]

Following this UIL deputation a further escalation of the conflict was inevitable. A few days later, it happened: a cattle drive took place on the McCann's ranch. The crowd leapt the wall of McCann's property, McCann himself was pushed into a dike, the police forced out of the way and his bullocks made to wander. On 22 August, McCann's labourers walked off his land: 'The various labourers employed on these ranches practically struck work on Wednesday last, and walked out in a body with the cry of "land for the people" on their lips.'[152]

J. P. Farrell used his editorials in the *Longford Leader* to tell the young men of the locality: 'Of one thing our young men may rest certain, when the time comes for dividing these lands, the sloucher and the stay-at-home may stay at home then!!'[153] To make matters even clearer, Farrell added: 'As far as our influence goes not a sod will one of that class of cowardly backsliders get.'[154] It is hardly surprising that Farrell's message seems to have got through. The 'Longford Notes' of a nearby journal added a few days later observed: 'The UIL branch in Longford is growing into large proportions, and every

---

[150] Ibid.   [151] Ibid.
[152] Ibid., 24 August 1907.   [153] Ibid., 28 September 1907.
[154] Ibid.

meeting sees the addition of at least a dozen members, with the results
that the number of privates now in the ranks runs into hundreds.'[155]
The pressure of local ostracism—which would be directed, also at the
family of 'offenders'—could be excruciating. Some parents felt moved
to quite remarkable displays of family disloyalty. The father of one of
McCann's few remaining working employees was reduced to a
desperate plea addressed to the President of the local UIL. 'The boy is
away from me doing business for 12 years and was not in my house for
the last five years', wrote John Creed of Dilleary, and if that was not
enough he added, 'besides I am not on very friendly terms with him.'[156]
This impressive display of parental cowardice left the local League
officials quite unmoved. It was no doubt useful that John Creed felt it
necessary to grovel publicly before the League but he did not gain
thereby any reduction in the League's hostility. After all twenty-four
agricultural labourers at Percivals', McCanns' and Pearses' farms had
gone on strike without any prospect of employment. Those who
continued to work for McCann could therefore expect little mercy.

For the McCanns the whole affair must have been distressing. They
were largely isolated within a community in which previously they had
enjoyed considerable popularity. If they ventured on to the streets in
Longford they were likely to have mud thrown at them or bicycles
driven at them. When one of the McCanns entered a public house the
cry went up 'Here comes the bullock!' Their bread deliveries were
interfered with, and in general, life was made more difficult. To add
insult to injury, in the course of defending the McCann ranch one of
the police constables had had the misfortune to strike McCann—
mistaking him apparently for an assailant: 'When remonstrated with
by McCann, who said he was the owner of the ranch, the policeman
jocularly replied: "don't give a damn who you are: you'll go out of
this".'[157]

Finally, all business ceased at the public house the McCanns
owned in Newtonforbes. When one of the employees of the Longford
Arms Hotel actually ventured to take a drink there, both Frank
McGuinness and J. P. Farrell called on 'two well known members of
the Hotel company who were also members of the League branch to
ensure the dismissal of the erring employees'. There was even a

---

[155] *Roscommon Herald*, 12 October 1907.
[156] *Longford Leader*, 26 Octoebr 1907.
[157] Ibid., 24August 1907.

rumour—false at it turned out—that the McCann's race horse 'Prince Charles' had been killed by angry militants.[158]

Under this onslaught, McCann retained a good measure of self-possession. 'Mac' of the *Roscommon Herald*, successfully sought an interview with him in mid-September. McCann was reasoned and almost laconic in his responses:

'Haven't you that farm on the eleven month system?' queries our reporter. 'No I have not', was McCann's reply, and further, continued he, 'there was never anybody evicted off those lands—never to my memory'. 'Isn't that so, Billy?' said he, addressing an old man who looked well on the other side of the half-a-century, who was standing close by. 'Yes', retorted Billy, 'and I am over sixty years of age, and you hadn't the farm then and even that time there was no-one evicted.' 'Do you live on the farm Mr McCann?' asked our reporter. 'I do', was the reply, 'and I needn't tell you that I am getting unnecessary trouble from the natives'. 'How do you mean?' enquired our reporter. 'Well, it is difficult to get work done, and a man can generally do with the goodwill of the public better than with their illwill.'[159]

In September also, the police took the situation seriously enough to transform McCann's stables into a police barrack. Then on Sunday 19 September, the Clonguish UIL men carried out a cattle drive on the Percival farm at Newtonforbes, from which they drove 64 cattle. Once again the police performance was unimpressive. 'The drive was organized in real Irish style, and was performed in broad daylight, between ten and eleven o'clock on Sunday, and in the presence of six policemen who ran for their lives when the Clonguish boys came on with their drive, which they propelled with the aid of huge black thorns.'[160] The police here had some excuse. They were engaged in preparation for Redmond's visit to Longford which took place on the same day. It was to Redmond's meeting that the men of Clonguish—wearied no doubt by their cattle-driving exertions—made their way.

The Longford meeting was a genuinely stirring event. The town had prepared with great enthusiasm. 'If ever Longford looked its best it did so on Saturday night, for what with the illuminations, torches and bonfires, and bands the scene was something like fairyland.'[161] The *Freeman's Journal* called Longford's welcome for Redmond 'one of those welcomes that stir the pulses of even the most hardened campaigners in the field of Irish politics'.[162] As the demonstration opened, J. P. Farrell was delighted: 'He remembered the great Parnell meeting of '81 but he doubted if the meeting was bigger than this.'[163] Farrell made an unusually short speech, mainly devoted to praising Redmond. Then the new local leader, P. McKenna, who immediately preceded Redmond, dwelt at length on the merits of the cattle driving policy. Following this Farrell must have been expected to have been rewarded for his patriotic enthusiasms by his leader. In the event, John Redmond's speech was a profound disappointment to his audience. The words 'cattle drive', 'ranch' or indeed any other agrarian radical theme did not cross his lips, still less any of the roguish references to Farrell's 'umbrella' (a cattle driving implement) which were *de rigueur* on these occasions. A critic of cattle driving acidly observed: 'We are not suprised to learn that Mr Farrell's face was a study while Mr Redmond's speech was being delivered.'[164] Most of the speech was an attack on the overtaxation of Ireland by England. Redmond's remarks were both interesting and poignant:

This (excessive taxation) is the cause of emigration: in one shape or another it is the cause of every material grievance concerning Ireland. It affects every class. It affects the landlords, the tenants, the labourers. It affects also the Orange artisan in Belfast just as much as the Nationalists in Dublin, and I confess the fact that there has been no great, strong and vigorous and united movement in Ireland powerful enough to effect a remedy almost makes one despair of one's country. Here, if ever, there was a necessity for the union of all creeds and classes which would have secured a remedy.[165]

Redmond was here returning to one of his classic themes of the 1890s. Suggestively, his tone was unusually resigned and pessimistic. The fact that the union of creeds and classes had not been achieved forced him to adopt a somewhat defensive conclusion:

Do not suppose for a moment that I am not willing with open arms to welcome any Irishman, of any creed, or class or politics, who chooses to come in and give assistance upon this or any other Irish question. So far from repelling such men, I would welcome them with all my heart; but I am bound to honesty to say this, that my profound conviction is, that in the long run we must rely

---

[162] Quoted in *Longford Leader*, 21 September 1907.
[163] Ibid., 21 September 1907.
[164] *Irish People*, 21 September 1907.
[165] *Longford Leader* 21, September 1907.

upon our own movement, and that if we allow it to grow slack or be broken, or the action of the Irish parliamentary party suspended that it is not worth a pinch of salt. The moral I point, therefore, is this: support your party, insist upon its being a united and disciplined party acting as one man.[166]

In short, Redmond was saying that the failure of Irish nationalism to win a significant number of supporters outside its traditional Catholic base, implied the need for the maintenance of the unity of the party at all costs. The party remained as the substance of the nationalist cause, and without the party, 'it is not worth a pinch of salt'. This allowed a certain opening towards the cattle drivers but it was a very limited one. He made an allusion to the possibilty of Farrell being tried by a packed jury. Then he went on:

Make every branch of the United Irish League a citadel of the people's power. Act under the direction of your leaders. Go on as you did years ago and as your fathers did. Scorn all sacrifices and suffering that may, perhaps, be threatened to you by the ruling powers of the day. Why, what is a little imprisonment to an Irish Nationalist? My own feeling was that I was never worth my salt until I had slept on a plank bed (cheers). Let the young men be regardless absolutely of such consequences to themselves. Let their English masters see that they are in earnest, and will stand no nonsense upon the Irish question that we will have to be governed as free-born men by laws made by ourselves, as in the case of every part of the British empire except in Ireland.[167]

Indeed, even before he had finished his speech, Redmond then tempered the terms of his one militant declaration. He referred to the fact that if legislation was not fast enough they would use 'other methods of promoting reforms', with the obvious implication that until legislation was tried and failured, the 'other methods should not be resorted to'.[168] This was uninspiring stuff.

Farrell must have expected a rather more generous and specific celebration of his recent activities. He had, instead, been offered the very minimum a nationalist leader could offer under such circumstances: a condemnation of jury packing and a generalized insistence on the value of selfless patriotism and a spell of imprisonment 'for the cause'. J. P. Farrell, in the event, was prepared to swallow his personal disappointment and to continue to support Redmond. The *Freeman's Journal*, in an article specifically devoted to the Longford meeting, enthusiastically concluded: 'The Irish Party was never more united than it is today.'[169] But it need hardly be said that other observers were

---

[166] Ibid.   [167] Ibid.   [168] Ibid.   [169] Quoted in ibid.

far from convinced. William O'Brien's newspaper, the *Irish People*, commented that the meeting had been set up to force Redmond to endorse cattle driving: 'But in vain is the net set in sight of the bird. Mr Redmond was not to be caught napping. Not one word had he to say about the subject on which the meeting was most anxious to hear his views.'[170] J. P. Farrell had little choice but to make the best of it. He wrote: 'The leader of the Irish party was cool, calm and steady and never did he make a better impression on his followers than here.'[171] Fortunately, for Redmond, J. P. Farrell was one of nature's loyalists. Opponents of Redmond, were he declared, three years later, 'scalliwags' who did not know 'B from a bull's foot'.[172] But Laurence Ginnell did not share Farrell's amiable characteristics and his cattle driving preoccupations were to be a source of rather more discomfort for the party leadership.

Ginnell versus Hayden

To be fair, Redmond had been putting Ginnell's sense of loyalty under some strain. In August Redmond claimed that the enemies of nationalism would 'get their answer from every quarter of Ireland before the harvest is saved'.[173] The unionist *Irish Times* translated: 'In other words, Mr Redmond hopes to come back to power on the wave of agrarian agitation which is stirred up in the west and south of Ireland by the coming flood of impassioned political oratory.'[174] Later in the same month at Ballybofey, Co. Donegal, Redmond was more explicit: he argued that it was in the Irish party's power to secure within the next parliamentary session, a land bill for the settlement of the congested districts, the abolition of the zones and compulsory purchase at fair and reasonable prices. But he added, no Irish reform was every won without a fight.[175] Ginnell might reasonably have claimed that he was merely following Redmond's instructions as outlined in these speeches. As the *Irish Times* observed: 'it is only natural but necessary to assume that in preaching cattle driving the last six months, Mr Ginnell has done so with the approval of his parliamentary leader.'[176] Notwithstanding this assessment, Ginnell

---

170 *Irish People*, 21 September 1907.
171 *Longford Leader*, editorial 21 September 1907.
172 *Roscommon Herald*, 10 September 1910.
173 *Irish Times*, 17 August 1907.
174 Ibid.
175 *Weekly Freeman's Journal*, 5 September 1907.
176 *Irish Times*, 17 December 1907.

found himself under increasing pressure to withdraw from the 'battle'. The Westmeath MP spoke of this publicly at a meeting in Jordanstown, Co. Meath on 15 September which he explained 'might be his last opportunity of addressing the men of Meath'.[177] As part of the policy of 'fight' decided on at the National convention in May 1907, Ginnell had, he argued, been 'sent' from London to help the men of Leinster and Connaught. However, Ginnell acknowledged as a loyal soldier he was prepared to accept new orders. But his 'withdrawal' would 'naturally be regarded as a victory for the ranchers'.[178] Throughout October, some of Ginnell's friends continued to demand his 'return'. But they also went on the offensive: they opened fire on Redmond's loyal ally, J. P. Hayden.

On the 2 October J. P. Hayden had given evidence at a Boyle meeting of the Dudley Commission. His exchange with the landlord representative, Sir John Colomb, had been of some interest. Sir John had said:

Again, would you admit that hitherto the demand for the purchase and division of the grass lands has been justified on the grounds that it would be the means of relieving congestion in the west? Yes.

Does it not therefore come to this that if you say if you cannot force people into a locality where their presence may be unwelcome, that the future acquisition and division of grass lands is to be defended not for the purpose of relieving of congestion in the west, but for the purpose of providing land for people who have no land at all? Yes, to some extent.[179]

Sir John Colomb had accurately pinpointed the tension at the heart of UIL policy, but it is unlikely that Hayden's frank answers lost him any local popularity. On the contrary, Hayden emerged from his confrontation with the Dudley commission with his reputation as an agrarian radical temporarily enhanced. Some of the other nationalist witnesses were less fortunate. Patrick Webb, prominent veteran of the struggle on the de Freyne estate and comrade of John Redmond and John Fitzgibbon, emerged as the very type of shopkeeper-grazier[180] regularly denounced in UIL rhetoric—indeed, one earlier clerical witness had claimed that such men were not to be found in the ranks of

---

[177] *Roscomon Herald*, 21 September 1907.
[178] Ibid.
[179] Royal commission on congestion in Ireland; appendix to the nineth report, 'Minutes of Evidence . . . and Documents Relating Thereto', 213 (C 4007), 1908, xlii, 22.
[180] Congestion, comm. evidence app. tenth report, 231/234.

the organization.[181] Martin Finnerty, secretary of the East Galway UIL admitted to tilling only four acres on his sixty-acre holding. Lord Dudley observed reproachfully: 'It does seem extraordinary that while you hold such strong opinions on the value of tillage you do not till more.' Finnerty confessed: 'I admit I am wrong.'[182] T. B. Hibbett, another UIL activist, managed some 2000 acres of grassland and admitting to making 'money out of a system he condemned'.[183] Such embarrassments gave Irish unionists a rare moment of innocent pleasure. The *Irish Times* made the obvious point: 'The Commission has made one point clear: it has shown in plain English that some of the most active members of the United Irish League in the west harass their neighbours for being guilty of grazing while they do it themselves on a most extensive scale.'[184] At this point the *Times* did not accuse John Hayden of such inconsistency—but the very next day local nationalists were to advance precisely such a charge.

The 6 October monthly meeting of the Roscommon United Irish League—normally an uneventful affair—was the scene of great excitement: the Hayden family were accused of a land grab in the locality.[185] Nor did Ginnell's friends confine themselves to mere words. On 27 October John Hayden made a speech at Four Roads, against the grazing system. Two days later his sincerity was put to the test in a rather unusual way. The cattle on 'Gallowstown land' in Roscommon were unexpectedly driven on the 29 October. This escapade provoked intense excitement in Roscommon—for a portion of that land had been stocked by Hayden's brother. It was quite clear that the cattle drive was intended to embarrass Hayden further. As the *Roscommon Herald* gleefully concluded: 'The drive is the chief topic of conversation in Roscommon, as it occurred in an unexpected quarter, and those engaged in it completely outwitted all opposition.'[186]

A week later Hayden again expressed anti-grazing sentiments at an important meeting in North Westmeath. The speakers addressed the crowd at the gate of the prize Cookesboro Ranch, which comprised almost two thousand acres. Here, fifty years previously, local tradition

---

[181] M. D. Higgins and J. P. Gibbons, 'Shopkeeper graziers and land agitation in Ireland 1895–1900' in P. J. Drudy, *Ireland: land, politics and people*, 104, for a discussionof Fr. Flatley's evidence.
[182] Congestion, comm. evidence app. tenth report, 302.
[183] Ibid., 299.
[184] *Irish Times*, 5 October 1907.
[185] *Irish Times*, 5 October 1909.
[186] *Roscommon Herald*, 12 October 1907.

had it, some thirty or forty families had been evicted from the estate. According to one report 'what was once a rich, thickly populated area of rich, fattening land was converted into a miniature prairie'.[187] Laurence Ginnell was sufficiently self-confident to join Hayden on the platform; Ginnell could not resist the chance to embarrass his opponent: 'We welcome all converts but in common prudence we must keep an eye of them.' The same press report of the meeting observed: 'Some of his (Ginnell's) biting passages of satire on the suddenly converted supporters of the cattle driving movement were evidently keenly relished by the crowd.'

Hayden was certainly finding life difficult. At a Roscommon meeting a few days later he shared a platform with Willie Redmond and John Fitzgibbon. Again, all did not go smoothly. Hayden had just got into his stride, when he was rudely interrupted:

We are assembled here today to proclaim, as we have done in the past, our undying fidelity to the cause of our . . .

Mr Patrick Leonard—Is your brother going to give up any holding at Gallowstown, that he grabbed? (Uproar)

Mr Fitzgibbon—Put that man out.

Mr Leonard—They won't; the Haydens grabbed my home in Gallowstown, and I want to know now is your brother going to give it up?

Mr Hayden—Put that man out.

No man in the meeting responded to Mr Hayden's request.[188]

Tempers then became very heated. Leonard asked Fitzgibbon to read a note to the meeting in which the recent cattle drive on his grabbed holding was acknowledged. Despite the hostility of Hayden, Fitzgibbon and Willie Redmond who was also on the platform, Leonard refused to give way. Almost inevitably, blows were struck. William Byrne, the veterinary surgeon for Roscommon, who had been Redmond's host the previous night, jumped off the platform and assisted by four police dragged Leonard to one side. Leonard then addressed a large group of sympathizers during the entirety of Hayden's speech, which was hardly surprisingly a general homily on the need for nationalist unity in Roscommon. Leonard, on the other hand, was highly specific. It was a forceful exposé—well illustrated with intimate local detail:

<hr/>

[187] Ibid., 2 November 1907.
[188] Ibid., 9 November 1907.

Fellow-countrymen, you are all aware that my holding has been grabbed, and that I was put on the roadside and because I asked Mr Hayden today for a definite answer would his brother give it up, I was set upon by Mr William Byrne, veterinary surgeon for the whole county, getting a huge salary from the rates, and boasting today that he is against the eleven months men, and tomorrow you will see him sporting his figure with all the eleven months men at the hunts (hear, hear). My land was grabbed and John Hayden by his silence admitted it. If my charge was not true, why didn't he say so? The home of my people for generations is grabbed and why should not the grabber be condemned in Roscommon today as ever? (applause) Look up at the platform and see the company that is on it.[189]

There is some evidence that Ginnell exaggerated the significance of these local successes. Ginnell had embarrassed J. P. Hayden, one of John Redmond's few close friends in the party. Ginnell had also effectively defeated efforts to silence his own campaign. As he told an interviewer in mid November: 'I am quite satisfied with the way things are going. It would appear that I am no longer the son of Hagar; I was described as such some time ago.'[190] But that was the height of his achievement: he had not as yet decisively forced John Redmond's hand.

Not surprisingly J. P. Hayden had had enough of Ginnell. He refused to go to a Moyvore meeting where Ginnell was billed to speak. But this time Ginnell encountered opposition from the South Westmeath MP, Sir Walter Nugent. Nugent was nothing if not frank. He had obviously decided that this was his best course: Nugent praised Ginnell's courage and sense of conviction. But, Nugent pointed out, he did not see 'eye to eye' with Ginnell on all questions of public policy. Ginnell had helped to expose the ranching evil and important beneficial legislation was on the way. The speech concluded: 'He (Sir Walter) moreover believed that continued breaches of law, either technical or otherwise, would retard instead of advancing the passing of these reforms.'[191] The *Westmeath Independent* drily observed that despite all protestations of party unity the Moyvore meeting revealed 'we have members of Parliament standing on the same platform enunciating diametrically opposed political doctrines.'[192] Cattle driving, this editorial observed, was the outcome of no previous arrangement or foresight, it had been the 'creation of the

---

[189] Ibid.   [190] Ibid.
[191] *Roscommon Herald*, 23 November 1907.
[192] *Roscommon Herald*, 21 December 1907.

moment', or, in another phrase, 'the hazard of the hour'. Quite probably Redmond had never conceived that it should be part of the 'virile' campaign: yet cattle driving had led to 228 prosecutions by the end of 1907.

John Redmond's Reconsiderations

In the last months of 1907, John Redmond was in dispirited mood. Redmond publicly declared that he intended to compel the Liberal government to join Home Rule to the question of the reform of the House of Lords at the next general election. But then the Liberal leader, Sir Henry Campbell-Bannerman took a hand. The Prime Minister made it clear that he was not prepared to do any such thing. In mapping out the Liberal programme for the next few years, the Prime Minister as, the *Westminster Gazette* put it, laid down the mainlines of the controversy which was to take place. The great struggle into which the Liberal party was about to enter was to be confined solely to one issue. The question of Home Rule was not to be raised and consequently there was to be no mandate for dealing with it in the next parliament.[193] The Liberal government also appeared to offer little prospect of major land reform. Privately in September 1907, Augustine Birrell, chief secretary, had written to Sir Antony MacDonnell: 'Ginnell's speeches, though mischievious are not without a certain grasp of the situation. Are all the graziers in Meath on the eleven months system?'[194] In public, the chief secretary was, however, despite much Tory denunciation on this point, capable of adopting a firm 'law and order' position, for example, on 12 November 1907, in a Southampton speech, Birrell threatened to suspend the policy of reform unless cattle driving ceased.[195] Redmond's reaction was feeble and uninspiring. Speaking at Maryborough in mid October—by which time the reality of the Liberal position was openly acknowledged in the Irish nationalist press—he could hardly even muster the strength for a riposte. Instead, Redmond adopted what was an increasingly common device: a speech on England's historical record of oppression in Ireland—in this case, stress was laid on the 'strangling' of Irish industries.[196] But of current political analysis, Redmond gave his audience nothing. Such a trick was less than

---

[193] Quoted in *Irish People*, 28 December 1907.
[194] Quoted in *Irish People*, 19 October 1907.
[195] Birrell to MacDonnell, 2 September 1907 quoted in Hepburn, 'Liberal Policies', 492.   [196] *Weekly Freeman's Journal*, 16 November 1907.

effective. His critics accused him of failing to add a single 'new fact' to a discussion which had been worn threadbare by Irish debating societies for half a century—or, more concretely, of offering 'a hackneyed political dissertation in the abstract.'[197] In truth, Redmond's speeches in this epoch were often pallid and discursive; and this contrasted with Parnell's which had always been striking if disconnected. As the political reality became too depressing it would appear that Redmond retreated to the comfort of the formal debating society treatise of his youth. Redmond did however feel some pressure to clarify his position. In a Cardiff speech in early December, he outlined the historic injustices which had led to cattle driving. But he added carefully but unambiguously: 'Now don't take me as advocating this action. No one regrets more than I do that there should be breaches in the law even in a good cause.'[198] Effectively, Redmond admitted therefore that cattle driving had been carried on without his approval. But if Redmond was free from ambiguity, the reaction of the party press again was not. Despite the fact that the Cardiff speech was an important one, representing the start of a propagandist campaign by the nationalist leaders—the *Freeman* did not think it worthy of a line of comment. Those who wished to know Redmond's views on one of the burning questions of the hour, had to wade through his long speech to find the two rather cautiously framed sentences in which he distinctly dissociated himself from the cattle drivers.[199] In this context, it is not surprising that the party as a whole never seems to have debated the cattle driving question.[200]

It was not alone Redmond's 'moderation' on the cattle driving question which was controversial. His moderation on the devolution issue was also proving unpopular in some quarters. Speaking to an American interviewer of the Irish Council Bill in September 1907, Redmond said: 'If a comparatively small number of concessions had been made the Bill might have been fairly satisfactory. The majority of the present cabinet were quite ready to meet our wishes—they are avowed Home Rulers—but they could not do it without breaking up their government in consequence of the action of the Roseberyites in their cabinet—small in number, but very powerful.'[201]

---

[197] *Irish People*, 19 October 1907.
[198] Hepburn, op. cit., 507.
[199] *Irish People*, 7 December 1907.
[200] Ibid.
[201] *Irish People*, 18 September 1908.

The Standing Committee of the UIL reacted by declaring an intention to distribute a resolution to all the branches of the organization which was quite remarkable in tone. It spoke of the danger of 'unworthy compromise and the lowering of the national flag'. The same document called on John Dillon 'to return immediately to the National ranks where his absence leaves a gap which cannot be filled'. Dillon, it was said, accurately enough, will not make 'any overtures to O'Brien'. More surprisingly, although Dillon had taken a part in the framing of the Irish Council Bill he was acclaimed as the leader who would insist on 'Boer Home Rule as a minimum'.[202]

Faced with such open insubordination from his standing committee on the one hand, and Laurence Ginnell and his friends on the other, Redmond had little choice but to seek new allies. In this case, the new allies were obvious enough—the O'Brienites. William O'Malley MP, a Redmond loyalist, was quick to give an interview to the *Independent* in which he called for an end to cattle driving. O'Malley, who had been a notably sharp critic of O'Brien in the recent past, then went on to call for his return to the Irish party.[202] J. P. Farrell was—not surprisingly—bitter and confused by this development. He wrote to Dillon in some anguish: 'It seems that the cattle drivers are to be thrown over for Mr William O'Brien, although I am quite satisfied to take my share of the punishment, keep saying that the men who lend themselves to O'Brien and his movement revive Dunravenism and are killing the last hope of the rallying the young of Ireland to win in our day.' Farrell added significantly: 'I don't want you to reply to me on this point—I know your difficulties as well as my own but after this all I can say is God help Ireland!!!'[203] John Fitzgibbon also sympathized with Farrell's dislike of O'Brienism. At an executive meeting of the South Roscommon UIL, Fitzgibbon reminded those who would listen that in 1902 O'Brien had criticized the 'foolishness' of Fitzgibbon's fight on the de Freyne estate which, Fitzgibbon declared, 'without fear of contradiction . . . brought on the Land Conference and the Land Act of 1903'.[204] Those who were convinced by this claim—and there would have been many who were not—were then assured:

This was not the time for William O'Brien to pelt mud on the cattle drivers. Men who were activated by as pure motives as Mr O'Brien (cheers). He spoke

---

[202] Quoted in *Irish People*, 7 December 1907.
[203] J. P. Farrell to John Dillon, 18 December 1908, Dillon papers, TCD MS 6753/425.
[204] *Leader*, 21 December 1907.

of Lord Dudley's Commission and he said that the Report of that Commission would now be read by thousands of Englishmen and Scotchmen who never would have read a line of it, but for the cattle driving in Ireland (cheers). They were all anxious to give Mr Birrell a chance of legislating on the lines of the Commission's report.[205]

Despite this attack from a close friend of Redmond's, O'Brien was in a mood to oblige the leader of the Irish Party. He had been desperately casting around, without lasting success, for new friends—approaches to aristocratic Unionists and at the other end of the spectrum, Sinn Feiners,[206] had led to nothing. Redmond clearly hoped that O'Brien would be content to act as a counterweight to those radical nationalist and agrarian tendencies which threatened his own leadership. Much would depend on O'Brien's acceptance of this restricted definition of his new role.

[205] Ibid.

[206] R. Davis, *Arthur Griffith and Non-Violent Sinn Fein*, Dublin, 1974, 59–60. The pages of *Sinn Fein* in this period are ambiguous—critical of 'gombeen' parliamentary nationalism they are surprisingly sympathetic at points to figures like O'Brien and even Plunkett. But in the last analysis, they avoid anything which might be construed as an embrace of the ascendancy.

6

Factional Conflicts:
April 1908–December 1910

You often hear on Irish platforms that God made Irish land for the Irish
people (nationalist cheers). Yes, but did he make the land of Meath for
the men of Mayo or the land of Roscommon for the men of Galway?

Augustine Birrell, Hansard, vol. 183, 3 February 1908, vol. 578.

Patrick McKenna—I want the ranches.

A voice—Yes for yourself—the way you grabbed them in Westmeath.

Longford Leader, 8 October 1909.

AT the end of 1907 and the beginning of 1908 the debate about cattle
driving intensified sharply. J. P. Farrell and the Longford cattle
drivers were tried at the Wicklow assizes in December of 1907 but,
following an eloquent defence plea asserting the morality of cattle
driving by Tom Kettle, MP for Tyrone East, the jury failed to agree
and a *nolle prosequi* was subsequently entered at the spring assizes of
1908.[1] The government, in the shape of R. R. Cherry, the Irish
Attorney-General, put a good face on it by stressing that the McCanns
were still successfully carrying out their business[2]—but Judge
Curran's strong condemnation of the state of affairs in Longford
probably made considerably more impact on the public perception of
these events.[3] Laurence Ginnell did however manage to get himself
placed in gaol not, as chief secretary Birrell was at pains to point out,[4]
as a result of any action of the Irish executive. Ginnell had been
leading a cattle driving campaign which affected the estate of John P.
Kearney, situated on the border of Meath and Westmeath; this

---

[1] J. B. Lyons, *The Enigma of Tom Kettle*, 133–6.
[2] Hansard, 3 February 1908, vol. 183, col. 827. 'Now I happen to know the McCann case . . . I have no hesitation in saying that it has been grossly exaggerated,' Cherry declared.
[3] John Ayde Curran, *Reminiscences*, London, 1915, 242, 246–7.
[4] *Irish Times*, 18 March 1908.

particular property was under the protection of the Chancery division thus allowing Justice Ross—without jury—to give Ginnell a six-month sentence in the Land Judges Court.[5] Redmond, who was thoroughly fed up with Ginnell's attempts to embarrass and abuse his old friend Hayden, was less than dismayed by Ginnell's forcible removal from the scene. 'I really do not see that we are bound in anyway to get into a row with the government over this matter',[6] he wrote to Dillon.

On 15 January, the eighth annual meeting of the National Directory of the UIL was held in Dublin. The eighty leading Nationalists present adopted a resolution declaring that the national demand for a native parliament remained unaltered, expressing unshaken confidence in the Irish parliamentary party under the leadership of John Redmond, and congratulating the Nationalists in the country upon the response made by them during the autumn to the appeal of the Directory for a virile and vigorous campaign in favour of Home Rule. But behind this facade of unity there was much unease. The Directory of the UIL—'most of whom are delighted to see him taking a rest cure'[7]—passed a resolution denouncing Ginnell's committal for contempt of court. A resolution was proposed denouncing cattle driving by Martin O'Dwyer, one of the 'moderates' in the Templemore fight of 1902, but was withdrawn in favour of one by Michael Reddy MP calling for the breaking up of the ranches. The UIL's queasiness was reflected at a local level also, representative nationalist bodies in Meath and Westmeath divided bitterly over the wisdom of Ginnell's tactics.[8] Two days later, William O'Brien, foremost critic of the cattle drivers, formally returned to the divided party.[9]

In mid-January also, Stephen Gwynn MP argued in the *Spectator* that graziers were mere 'speculators' and the cattle driving involved no cruelty to the animals driven. J. Craig Davidson replied sharply that the graziers filled a very necessary place in the Irish cattle trade.[10] When the debate moved across the Irish sea to Westminster at the end of the month, Craig Davidson's argument was taken up in H. H. Asquith's speech. The chancellor of the exchequer described cattle driving as 'a serious blow to a flourishing and necessary Irish

[5] *Weekly Freeman*, 2 May 1908. This article reviews the whole affair following Ginnell's early release on health grounds.
[6] Redmond to Dillon, 4 March 1908, TCD Dillon papers, 6748/274.
[7] *Irish Times*, 16 January 1908.
[8] Ibid.
[9] See Lyons, *Dillon*, 299–301; *Mayo News*, 21 January 1908.
[10] *Irish Times*, 16 January 1908.

industry'.[11] Stung by Asquith's sharp condemnation from the government front bench, Redmond came unusually close to a justification of cattle driving. Redmond asked with apparent incredulity 'Does he (Asquith) mean to say Ireland is richer or better off with plenty of bullocks than if the land were tilled?'[12] Stressing that the origins of cattle driving lay in the famine clearances Redmond insisted: 'It is no use blinking the fact that until some further legislation is passed the land war in Ireland in some of its most acute phases cannot be said to be at end.'[13] John Dillon echoed this argument in a later debate: 'The cattle trade would not suffer if these grass ranches were divided. It would be improved and even if it did suffer he was for the people as against the cattle trade.'[14]

Dillon and Redmond were here merely expressing the standard line. The *Freeman*, for example, exclaimed: 'No; the rancher is not the backbone of the cattle trade, but, on the contrary, retards the trade.'[15] Belgium, it was pointed out, had no ranches but raised and fed three times as many cattle as Ireland in proportion to size and population.[16] The *Freeman* concluded one major editorial on the subject: 'Establish instead the farmer with the moderate sized holding, on which the mixed tillage and grazing system is practised, and on which the cattle mature early, and it will prove the saving of the cattle trade; and this system has the further advantage of giving employment in the land.'[17] Such arguments were the traditional mainstays of nationalist political economy. Even the *Freeman's* principal rival, the *Independent* concluded: 'When a distribution on equitable lines of the large ranches in this country was first suggested the objection was raised that it would injuriously affect the cattle trade. But when we consider the real economic bearings of the problem there does not seem to be any validity in that objection.'[18]

It was the House of Lords rather than the Commons which saw the most revealing exchanges on the cattle driving question—exchanges which went beyond the slightly stale encounters of the lower house. The Lords debate was inevitably characterized by much denunciation

[11] Hansard, vol. 183, col. 149, 29 January 1908.
[12] Ibid., col. 155.
[13] Ibid.
[14] Hansard, 23 November 1908, vol. 196, col. 1901.
[15] *Weekly Freeman*, 25 July 1908.
[16] Ibid., 5 October 1907.
[17] Ibid., 25 July 1908.
[18] *Irish Independent*, 18 May 1910.

of the governments allegedly flaccid approach to law enforcement by angry conservative and unionist peers. The Marquis of Londonderry gave a typical Ulster unionist speech calling for vigorous repression of the 'ranch warriors'. His predictable remarks were inspired by the traditional unionist conception of Irish nationalism as an elaborate conspiracy; thus Londonderry acknowledged that some nationalists denounced cattle driving but this, in his view, was not done out of any sense of conviction, rather, the critics of cattle drivers were insincere. They were motivated only be a fear that the cattle drivers might disrupt negotiations with the liberals.[18] But other Irish peers moved away from these blinkered and ungenerous obsessions; these speakers were rather more inclined to treat nationalist divisions as substantive and deep-rooted. The Earl of Donoughmore pointed out that the President of the Clooneyquin, Co. Westmeath branch of the UIL had been placed under police protection such was his unpopularity with fellow nationalists. Donoughmore added his own analysis:

I have been in Ireland during the whole of the recess ... I have come to the conclusion that in the vast majority of cases, cattle driving is not being carried on by the poor man who wants to get hold of the rich land, and in the part of the country where I made careful enquiries I was particularly struck by the fact that the cattle drivers are the sons of rich ... but healthy farmers.[19]

Donoughmore was followed in the debate by Lord Castletown, who also stressed the role of factional antagonism:

I know of a case of a Protestant farmer who was told that his cattle were to be driven. He told me that the people came down from the neighbouring village and went to the public house, where the whole thing had been arranged. They got so drunk they were unable to proceed with the cattle drive and eventually retreated after a scuffle. Many of these cases were settled by the men themselves. One man who was boycotted, instead of appealing for police protection, called on a large number of his friends and there was a fair fight between the two sides and the whole question was settled without any further trouble.[20]

Such tales had always been part of the landlord's armoury; nevertheless it is difficult to dismiss these speeches as simply antinationalist rhetoric. Lord Castletown was a Home Ruler, supporter of the Irish

---

[19] HL Hansard, series 4, vol. 183, 29 January 1908, col. 207.
[20] Ibid., col. 218.

language and believer in a peasant proprietorship,[21] unlike Lord Clonbrock who spoke in the same debate and who could be described as a 'fossilized bigot'[22] by the local nationalist press. Donoughmore and Castletown would have had no difficulty in multiplying their examples from the pages of the provincial nationalist press or indeed from the evidence given to the Royal Commission on Congestion. Nor did Lord Castletown spoil his case by refusing to acknowledge the area of genuine grievance. He pointed to the widespread frustration caused by expectation since the Wyndham Act that untenanted land, at any rate, would be redistributed; instead, in the period since 1903, in many areas graziers had, if anything, tightened their grip. Perhaps such shrewd and relatively sympathetic comment put new heart into William O'Brien as he considered a new attempt to commit the Irish party to the path of conciliation.

One month after O'Brien's return to the party, at the end of February 1908, Redmond gave an interview to the London correspondent of the *Freeman*. Suggestively the text appeared in the New York press but not in the *Freeman* itself. His thesis—that the Wyndham land legislation had increased the prospects of Home Rule and that the Tory party might be the party to introduce it—delighted O'Brien, and indeed, a much wider section of Irish opinion which was deeply disappointed with the 'Liberal alliance'. The *Irish People* gloated as the *Freeman* fell silent: 'We need hardly say we subscribe to every word which Mr Redmond has said.'[23] But was the O'Brienite journal laying too much stress on Redmond's amiable but imprecise remarks? Certainly O'Brien's next move revealed that he had once again miscalculated the balance of forces. As so often before, the impetuous O'Brien pushed the pace too hard. On 28 April 1908 he attempted to win the party back to the conciliation policy and forced a vote on the question. Redmond felt it necessary to side with Dillon, with the inevitable result that O'Brien lost the vote by 42 to 15. For O'Brien were the following MP's: E. Barry, E. Crean, J. Gilhooly, Harrington, Healy, G. Murnaghan, William O'Brien, P. O'Dogherty, J. O'Donnell, T. O'Donnell, C. O. Kelly, J. Phillips, A. Roche,

---

[21] For a generous view of Castletown's politics, see *Cork Free Press*, 17 June 1910. See also Castletown's self-description, Castletown to Redmond, 14 November 1909, NLI MS 15175 (3).

[22] *Connaught Leader and Loughrea Nationalist*, 24 July 1907; see also *WF*, 17 October 1908.

[23] *Irish People*, 2 March 1908.

D. D. Sheehan and T. F. Smyth. Against his line were W. Abraham, J. P. Boland, J. Clancy, T. Condon, J. Cullinan, W. Delany, Devlin, Dillon, W. Duffy, W. Field, M. Flavin, J. C. Flynn, S. Gwynn, J. Halpin, Hayden, R. Hazeleton, M. Hogan, J. Jordan, M. Joyce, T. M. Kettle, D. Kilbride, J. G. S. MacNeill, P. A. MacHugh, C. McVeigh, F. Meehan, P. Meehan, J. Muldoon, J. P. Nannetti, Sir Walter Nugent, K. O'Brien, P. O'Brien, James O'Connor, John O'Connor, W. O'Dowd, P. O'Shaughnessy, J. J. O'Shee, P. Power, D. Reddy, J. Redmond, W. Redmond, J. Roche and D. Sheehy.[24] The *Freeman*, with unusual mildness, commended the absence of 'acrimonious discussion' and insisted that the party had no desire to 'shirk the fair consideration of the vendor's side of the question', but nevertheless a decisive turning point had been reached.[25]

This failure of the *rapprochement* with O'Brien left Redmond in a difficult position. He seemed to speak with two voices. With one voice, he appeared to advocate at least a limited degree of co-operation with the government. With considerable logic, Redmond insisted that the Liberals must be helped to pass beneficial reforms such as the university bill and the housing of the working class in the towns of Ireland Bill. If the Tories moved in favour of coercion the Irish party could not vote against the government. But all this implied that the Liberals could in effect rely on Irish support. But at this point in the argument, Redmond appeared to contradict himself and to speak with another ovice entirely. For, and apparently in the face of his previous advocacy, Redmond called for a 'strong, willing, consistent and combative movement'[26] in parliament and in Ireland. Redmond, in fact, stated that Ireland should hasten a dissolution. He went so far as to write to the UIL's American organizer promising a 'most exciting'[27] agitation. But it seemed inconsistent to urge a dissolution so long as there were desirable Irish bills that Ireland could help the government to pass. Furthermore, it was legitimate to ask, if Ireland forced a dissolution, whilst making no bargain with the Tories, what then? What chance was there of the Liberals weakening their chances of coming back to power by putting Home Rule on the front of their programme?

On the other hand there was a definite pressure from the nationalist

[24] Ibid., 7 May 1908.
[25] *Weekly Freeman*, 2 May 1908.
[26] *Leader*, 25 April 1908.
[27] Redmond to J. O'Callaghan, 3 April 1908, TCD Dillon papers, 6747/291.

left. In early April, Tom Kettle, increasingly disappointed by the fruits of the Liberal alliance, threatened to resign his seat if Redmond did not turn the Irish vote against Winston Churchill in a sensitive Manchester by-election.[28] Kettle capitulated but following upon the resignations of C. J. Dolan, James O'Mara, and (from his position as senior party whip) Thomas Grattan Esmonde, the Tyrone MPs despair was a worrying sign. Then there was the question of the nature of Redmond's 'vigorous' movement. He spoke vaguely of it being easier in the autumn and winter to raise up a 'powerful movement' than it had been in the previous year. In Redmond's view, the land question was likely to 'afford plenty of opportunity and scope for vigorous agitation in the near future'.[29] Yet the only agitation in Ireland which might remotely have been described as vigorous was cattle driving. Men had gone to gaol for cattle driving, there had been extra police, and compensation for damages as a result of that movement. These damages were increasingly bitterly resented by 'innocent' nationalist ratepayers who had to meet them in cattle-driving localities.[30] Most observers felt sure that Redmond was opposed to cattle driving[31]—but his remarks nevertheless, seemed to leave the door uncomfortably open. For some it was a grim omen when on 25 April Laurence Ginnell was released early from prison on health grounds.[32]

The gap between O'Brien and Redmond was now to widen irreparably. For example, the final report of the Royal Commission on congestion in Ireland appeared at the end of May and was to be the occasion of controversy. On the main principles of the report, there was widespread agreement. Birrell told the cabinet: 'all the Commissioners report in favour of (1) the relief of congestion (2) compulsory purchase (3) the breaking up of the grass lands, and (4) a large increase of grants from the Treasury for the purpose of the relief of congestion'.[33] As Sir A. P. MacDonnell put it: 'I have signed the Report because I agree with the greater part of it, and because I am in hearty sympathy with the spirit of humanity and benevolence towards the

[28] Joe Devlin to John Dillon, 11 April 1908, TCD Dillon papers, 6272q/18.
[29] *Leader*, 25 April 1908.
[30] For details of the heavy costs of cattle driving, see John Ayde Curran, *Reminiscences*, 242–7. See also Redmond Barry to assistant under-secretary, 4 February 1908, CSO RP 1908/2433. H. F. C. Price to under-secretary, 4 February 1908, loc. cit.
[31] *Leader*, 18 April 1908.
[32] *Weekly Freeman*, 2 May 1908.
[33] PRO Cab 37/93/71. 2 June 1908. Augustine Birrell.

western peasantry which pervades it.'[34] But as Birrell commented there remained, none the less, a 'sharp difference of opinion between the majority of the Commissioners and Sir Antony MacDonnell. Unhappily it is a difference which excites the jealousy of two rival departments—the Land Commission and the Congested Districts Board.'[35] The *Freeman's Journal* explained to its readers:

Seven members of the Commission, incuding Lord Dudley, the Bishop of Raphoe, Sir Francis Mowatt, Walter Kavanagh and Messrs Bryce and Sutherland are in favour of maintaining the Congested Districts Board, broadening its constitution, increasing its funds and enlarging the area of its operations. Sir Antony MacDonnell recommends the complete abolition of the Board, and the Transfer of its functions in respect to Land Purchase, Migration and the enlargement of holdings to the Estates Commissioners and the surrender of its industrial development functions to the agricultural department, whose failure outside the sphere of agricultural instruction is notorious.[36]

There was, in fact, a further point of division. The majority of the commissioners advocated that the reconstituted Congested Districts Board should have a 'popular' element—that nine out of its twenty members should be nominated by the local nationalist county councils. John Fitzgibbon, chairman of the Roscommon county council, had already gleefully speculated on the possibilities for 'clientilist' politics thus opened up. Drawing attention to Fitzgibbon's calculations, MacDonnell noted:

If migration be the real remedy for congestion, and if there be, as there certainly is, an acute conflict between the claims for land of local 'landless' men and of 'congests' to be migrated from a distance it follows as a necessary consequence that it is not a popular Board which should be entrusted with the work. For local feeling will be in favour of the local 'landless' men and the elected members of the Board must reflect the feelings and opinions of their constituents.[37]

Immediately the two main tendencies in nationalism locked horns over the report and the MacDonnell criticisms. For the *Freeman* these were perhaps inevitably further evidence of Sir Antony's imperious

[34] Royal commission on congestion in Ireland, final report (Cd. 4097) HC 1908, xliii, 153.

[35] PRO Cab 37/93/71. 2 June 1908. Augustine Birrell.

[36] *Weekly Freeman*, 30 May 1908. See William O'Brien's statement, *Irish Independent*, 4 July 1908.

[37] Royal commission on congestion, loc. cit., 157.

elitist hostility towards the Irish democracy—the majority commissioners, on the other hand, were absolutely in the right. O'Brien's *Irish People* saw matters the other way. It supported Sir Antony MacDonnell's argument and indeed that made by Conor O'Kelly, MP for North Mayo, who, increasingly unpopular with Redmond, had had the courage to publish a 'note' to the report indicating agreement with the substance of Sir Antony's case.[38] O'Brien and his supporters felt that the Dudley Report was offering a bureaucratic solution to a problem which could only be solved by a change in hearts and minds—in other words, by the policy of conciliation. To the O'Brienites, the strengthening of the Congested Districts Board was the essence of the Dudley Report. The *Irish People* was sharply critical of the proposal to turn the CDB into what it called a 'gigantic corporation',[39] with more officials and an increased area to administer. In particular, it was opposed to the principle that no sales of land should take place in the enlarged areas without the Board's consent. Given the Board's previously unimpressive record it seemed absurd to place the solution of the problem in the hands of that body. Anyway these proposals were so radical and expensive: 'it is certain that legislation based on them will never become law'.[40] The *Irish People* summed up its case: 'There is really one way, and one way alone, in which it is possible to carry any considerable Bill for passing the Dudley Report into law or for the resumption of Land Purchase this year and that *is by a preliminary agreement with the landlords*'.[41]

As Birrell told the cabinet:

We have here all the materials for a furious controversy. Roughly speaking, the Congested Districts Board is a popular body, or at all events, contains popular elements within it, which make it by comparison a popular body in Ireland. It contains a Bishop and a Priest. This has conciliated popular sentiment. It has undoubtedly done a great deal of good, though I daresay at a heavy cost. It has found its way into the national life, and is frequently mentioned both in novels and plays; in fact, undoubtedly it has become in its way, a real national institution, unlike any of the other Boards in Ireland. But it has its enemies even in the Nationalist ranks. Co. Mayo, where both the Bishop and the Priest comes from, is generally believed to have received more than its fair share of what was going. Mr William O'Brien and his friends may

---

[38] Ibid., 110.
[39] *Irish People*, 30 May 1908.
[40] Ibid.
[41] Ibid.

be ranked as enemies of the Congested Districts Board, and friends by preference of the Estates Commissioners.[42]

Nevertheless O'Brien was particularly pleased by certain aspects of the report—most notably those where MacDonnell had clearly influenced the other members. The Royal Commission on Congestion in Ireland was an unusual document in that it gave considerable weight to the historical dimensions of the problem. The final report drew attention to what it called 'the most thorough measure of confiscation in Irish history'[43] when in 1653 and 1654 'a large portion of the native population in Ulster, Leinster and Munster, were banished to Connaught'. It also emphasized the devastating effect of the famine clearance (1846–52) in the region: 'many of the small farms swept away were uneconomic, but the sudden nature of the changes undoubtedly caused great suffering, and in many cases, left bitter memories'.[44] The sense of these pages was clear: one particular grouping, the 'congested' peasantry of Connaught, had suffered a grievous weight of historic injustice. It was the duty of legislation, therefore, to meet the grievances of this section of small farmers rather than promote the cause of the Irish rural poor in general. The cartoon caption on the front page of the *Irish People* (30 May 1908) summed up the argument: 'The royal commission on congestion in its report has definitely laid down that the untenanted land must be given to the congests from the west and not to the landless men and sons of farmers in the locality or, in other words, to the cattle drivers.'[45] In short, the landless men in the west led by John Fitzgibbon had been rebuffed—as had the midlands cattle drivers led by Farrell and Ginnell. The Dudley Report was not, however, government policy and all eyes now turned on the government to see its reaction.

Birrell, Redmond, and Land Reform

On 2 June Birrell presented his cabinet colleagues with a paper on the Dudley Report. His tone was urgent:

The game is up so far as the retention of land by the landlords is concerned; it is all a question of price, and in that question the British treasury is greatly involved . . . I cannot hope to get through the winter in Ireland unless I take a

---

[42] PRO Cab 37/93/71, 2 June 1908.
[43] Royal commission on congestion, loc. cit., 8.
[44] Ibid., 9.
[45] *Irish People*, 30 May 1908.

first step of some kind and give Ireland something to talk about ... a bill of course could not be proceeded with beyond a second reading, but it would be subject matter for discussion in Ireland between landlords and tenants, between the followers of Mr Dillon and the followers of Mr Wm O'Brien, and although I am not very sanguine about it, I still think it possible that some agreement might be come to between these parties, although doubtless any such agreement would be one not likely to recommend itself offhand to the British treasury ... [but] I cannot part with the question without reiterating the opinion I have already expressed more than once in the cabinet, that in my judgement the present situation in Ireland is one capable of very dangerous development, and that past experience teaches us that we do not in the long run secure economy by simply refusing to listen to Irish demands.[46]

A few days later in a Leeds speech, Redmond added weight to Birrell's warning with a demand for a compulsory land bill coupled with a threat that it it was not introduced the government 'will have to face risks and dangers in the coming time of winter which no wise minister could contemplate with equanimity'.[47] On 21 July Redmond sent Birrell an even more explicit message:

If the people once get it into their heads that the defects of the Land Act of 1903 are not to be remedied, and, above all, if they come to the conclusion that no fresh legislation is going to be immediately proposed dealing with the question of congestion and with the breaking up of grass lands, or if any proposal be made on the financial side of the question which would interfere with or stop the progress of land purchase throughout the country, it would be impossible for the national party to hold themselves responsible for the peace of Ireland.[48]

The next day Redmond confidently told Dillon: 'I am sure that after receipt of my letter Birrell will be anxious to talk to us on the land question.'[49] Yet Redmond can hardly have enjoyed dispensing these threats. In July and August two developments served to remind him that there were decided limitations to the usefulness—from his point of view—of agrarian militancy.

The first of these developments was the re-emergence of the Canadian cattle issue. O'Brien again accused the Irish party of a sluggish parliamentary response; in reply, on 31 July, Redmond issued

[46] The Dudley report on congestion, a cabinet paper by Birrell, 2 June 1908. Cab 37/93/71. Quoted by Hepburn, 527.
[47] Hepburn, ibid.
[48] Redmond to Birrell, 21 July 1908, TCD Dillon papers, 6748/376.
[49] Redmond to Dillon, 22 July 1908, TCD Dillion papers, 6748/377.

a public statement to the effect that he had been actively pursuing the matter privately with Winston Churchill at the Board of Trade.[50] Once again the Irish party appeared to flirt with agrarian radicalism only to retreat: the material interests of the great bulk of the Irish farmers proving to be a more than adequate counterweight. Firin explained in *The Peasant*: 'Speak to the average farmer nowadays as to the outlook of the country. He will immediately condemn the importation of Canadian cattle as tending to destroy the cattle trade.'[51] As the *Freeman*, in this instance abandoning the radicals, put it: 'The introduction of Canadian cattle would mean a loss to Irish landholders generally, but it is the small and middle-class farmers who would suffer most should they come.'[52] The *Irish People* extracted the utmost possible satisfaction from Redmond's loss of face: 'The men who only a week ago were intimating to an English Prime Minister that the Irish party has an open mind on the Canadian cattle question have been promptly obliged to retrace their steps and make at least a semblance of change from Mr Cullinan's "serve the Irish people right".'[53]

Even more irritating to Redmond was the provocative activity of Laurence Ginnell. In July, Ginnell, apparently fully restored to health, returned to the fray. Ginnell recommended that there should be no slackening in the cattle-driving campaign so long as there was a hazel in the hedges.[54] More generally he claimed that the government was moving towards an attempted settlement of the congestion problem in the west but was not prepared to do anything for his own followers. The difficulty surfaced in early July at a meeting of North Westmeath UIL executive, at which Ginnell clashed again with Hayden. Hayden argued that Chief Secretary Augustine Birrell was prepared to allow compulsory sale of untenanted lands in all parts of Ireland and not simply for the west alone. Ginnell insisted that Birrell's speeches suggested—in line with Dudley—that compulsion would be applied only in the west.[55] At this point, Ginnell's closest supporters felt compelled to make public their dissatisfaction with Redmond. The Rockford Bridge branch of Westmeath UIL, whose most prominent

---

[50] *Irish People*, 8 August 1908, 'Mr Redmond's Unstarred Question: A Lame Explanation'.

[51] *The Peasant and Irish Irelander*, 9 March 1907.

[52] *Weekly Freeman*, 1 August 1908.

[53] *Irish People*, 1 August 1908.

[54] *Weekly Freeman*, 25 July 1908.

[55] *Irish Independent*, 10 July 1908.

member was Ginnell's father-in-law and political ally, James King, passed 'a resolution of a most insulting character directed against Mr John Redmond'.[56] When David Sheehy attempted to squash the criticism at a meeting of the South Westmeath executive, he was refused admittance. Again, James King, who presided over this meeting, played the decisive role.

These clashes signalled Ginnell's growing unhappiness: an unhappiness which led to his more or less open espousal of Sinn Fein doctrine by the autumn of 1908.[57] Fortunately for Redmond, J. P. Farrell, Ginnell's natural ally responded by refusing to threaten party unity. While retaining his optimism that an eventual settlement would embrace his own local supporters, he generously acknowledged that the government would not be 'worth its salt' if it did not prosecute cattle drivers. He warned too against the exploitation of family disputes and ancient quarrels—going back more than sixty years—by the cattle drivers.[58] Farrell's attitude was suggestive indeed but there were other even more revealing signs of Ginnell's isolation. The ranch war's most recent scholarly historian has identified a 'militant clique' of four men—David Sheehy, J. P. Hayden, John Fitzgibbon and Laurence Ginnell—who were 'unequivocal in their promotion of militant forms of action'.[59] However, it is worth noting that by summer 1908 two of the four activists thus identified—David Sheehy[60] and John Hayden[61]—had already suffered embarrassing disclosures which raised doubts about the depth of their opposition to the grazing system. Sheehy, in the case of a friend, and Hayden, more excusably perhaps, in the case of a brother, seemed willing to make exceptions to the general rule of hostility to ranchers. John Fitzgibbon, excited by the prospect of an increase in his powers of patronage, was publicly moving towards a compromise with the government. (Birrell was soon to describe the 'Roscommon hero'[62] as 'quite the statesman now'.)[63]

In April Fitzgibbon gave an interview which specifically contradicted much of his own earlier aggressive rhetoric: he called for an end

---

[56] *Longford Leader*, 18 July 1908.
[57] *Irish Times*, 21 October 1908.
[58] *Longford Leader*, 11 July 1908.
[59] David S. Jones, 'Agrarian Capitalism and Rural Social Development in Ireland' (Queen's University, Belfast, Ph.D., 1978), 103–4.
[60] See Chapter 3 above.
[61] See Chapter 5 above.
[62] Birrell to Dillon, 21 December 1908. TCD Dillon papers, 6798/168.
[63] Birrell to Dillon, 31 January 1910. TCD Dillon papers, 679/171.

to cattle driving and looking to the future, argued that 'the fight for the land might become a fight amongst ourselves is the greater danger we have to face at the present time, and, therefore, let me warn you against this danger. There is no need to raise any clamour against intending migrants. There is no need of saying that the people of the parish must get all the land in that parish'.[64] (Four years later Fitzgibbon was to be publicly denounced for grass grabbing by Jasper Tully: 'What young man can expect a share of a grass farm—what "congest" looking hungrily at a waste ranch can expect redress—if a shopkeeper like Mr Fitzgibbon, with an ample income from the public taxes can huxter and gamble and grab in the land market as he has done?' Fitzgibbon confesses dolefully: 'People called me foxy, perhaps I am.')[65]

The growing moderation in UIL leadership circles on the cattle-driving question was reflected in the level and nature of that cattle-driving activism which continued. In the months of July, August and September the focus of the cattle-driving movement switched to Co. Clare. The number of cattle drives dropped form 297 to 97 in this quarter, but of these 41 took place in Clare;[66] more generally, one-third of all the agrarian outrages in Ireland took place in that well armed county. The Earl of Crewe lamented: 'I think we should all have said of Co. Clare what I daresay my noble friend the Secretary of State for India would say of such a place as Poona—if there is trouble there it is more deep-seated and worse kind than in any other part of the country.'[67] The country's MPs reacted with uncertainty to a movement over which they had little direct control. William Redmond insisted that cattle driving in Clare had been 'the spontaneous action of the impatient people themselves'.[68] The *Clare Champion* of July agreed: 'There is a well justified feeling—that while the rich counties of Ireland are reaping the benefits of the Land Act, Clare, owing to the stubborn reluctance of the landlords to sell on reasonable terms has to stand by and wait.'[69] The same editorial added: 'They are not waiting for MPs to advise them ... they are taking the matter in their own

---

[64] *Irish People*, 18 April 1908.
[65] *Roscommon Herald*, 18 May 1912.
[66] HL, vol. 194, 21 October 1908, col. 1084. Lord Denman.
[67] Ibid. On the question of arms in Clare see the comments in H. F. C. Price, 'Report on the general state of Ireland in 1907'.
[68] *Clare Champion*, 26 September 1908.
[69] *Clare Champion*, 19 July 1908.

hands.'[70] William Redmond seems to have responded to the local pressure, in September he had 'no word of blame for the cattle drivers'; though he admitted, 'he had done a lot of queer things in his life but he had never yet driven a bullock'.[71] James Halpin MP (Clare West) advocated cattle driving on one occasion at Touclea, but by October his vagaries were the subject of much caustic comment in the constituency. When, for example, 44 cattle drivers were sent to gaol on 30 September in Ennistymon, followed by alleged scenes of police ruffianism, Halpin was conspicuous by his absence; but then 'perhaps he had other engagements, more important, or at least less dangerous to fulfil'.[72]

Perhaps the most telling indication of the change of attitude in the UIL leadership was the growing blandness of John Fitzgibbon. Accompanying John Redmond on an American tour in the autumn of 1908, he was full of easy optimism. This emerged particularly clearly in Boston when both he and Redmond were being interviewed by an American reporter. Redmond was speaking about the pace of land purchase:

Q. How long in your opinion will it be before the entire land has been transferred?
A. Fifteen years at the outside.

At this point, Mr Fitzgibbon asked permission to interrupt in order that he might say that within the next five years the land would be transferred. 'I don't know what time will be taken to pay off the landlords,' said Mr Fitzgibbbon, 'but I am speaking of the time in which the transfer will be completed. At the present moment, the landlords are in a mood for selling.'[73]

Birrell's Land Bill

For this trend away from 'activism' in agarian matters amongst UIL leaders to continue, Redmond must have reasoned, it was vital that Birrell's proposed new legislation not disappoint when it was unveiled in November 1908. Birrell presented his new legislation as a technical, almost non-political exercise. He argued reasonably that the financial basis of the 1903 Act had broken down. The Wyndham Act had

[70] Ibid.
[71] Ibid., 26 September 1908.
[72] *Clare Champion*, 3 October 1908.
[73] *Irish People*, 10 October 1908.

however specifically stated that in such an event the Irish ratepayers had to meet the responsibility. Birrell's initial problem therefore was to confront the Treasury and to persuade them that the Irish ratepayers could not meet this burden. Of these negotiations, he later wryly recalled: 'It is not always an easy thing to get people to regard an Act of Parliament as absurd on the face of it, especially when you ask them to resume an obligation of many millions from which they are relieved by an Act of Parliament.'[74] Birrell was therefore in a rather weak position. His critics later argued that he could have extracted more from the Treasury. In reply, Birrell insisted that he had 'extorted' the maximum: certainly he fought against exponents of 'rigorous economy'.[75]

Birrell's legislative proposals provided that future sales were to be financed not in cash but in a new guaranteed 3 per cent stock to be issued to the vendors of estates at its face value. Birrell explained the Treasury's attitude to Dillon: 'Unless the landlords take stock, we cannot get the cash quicker than five millions a year. The Treasury are awfully alive to the fact that they stand to lose but they must fight for the least possible loss.'[76] The rate of purchase annuity was consequently raised to $3\frac{1}{2}$ per cent (3 per cent for interest and $\frac{1}{2}$ per cent for sinking fund) payable over a period of sixty-six years. The bonus for landlords continued to be paid in cash; Birrell had told the cabinet: 'I regard the bonus as the pulse of the land purchase machine'.[77] But it was no longer calculated at the flat rate of 12 per cent but at rates varying inversely with the number of years purchase of rent which the resale prices represented. The maximum bonus was fixed at 18 per cent of the price. This interference with the bonus serves to emphasize an important fact—obscured by Birrell's technical treatises on the money market—that the new legislation contained elements that were profoundly political in inspiration: interference with the bonus but also attacks on the zone system, universal compulsion and provision for landless men—all signifying a disruption of the conciliatory agreement made at the land conference in 1902–3.[78]

It was these controversial elements which temporarily reassured the radical wing of the Irish party. Having listened carefully to Birrell's

[74] *Weekly Freeman*, 26 August 1911.
[75] PRO Cab 37/100/113. Birrell's comments, 18 August 1909.
[76] Birrell to Dillon n.d. October 1908. Dillon papers, 6798/162.
[77] PRO Cab 37/100/113.
[78] Mullan, *The passing of the 1909 Land Act*, 149

speech introducing his bill in November 1908, J. P. Farrell reported to his followers that while Birrell had devoted much of his speech to defending the application of compulsion in the west, the chief secretary had gone further: 'and . . . in counties such as Longford the estates commissioners will have power to acquire all grazing and untenanted lands compulsorily and divide them'.[79] Farrell confidently concluded: 'The grazing question is settled in Longford.'[80]

For O'Brien, on the other hand, Birrell's new land bill was simply a disaster; Birrell, in his view, had been defeated by the Treasury with the result that his 'purchase blocking' legislation offered too little to landlords or tenants. O'Brien concluded: 'that the Act had been designed to save the Treasury of the richest country in the world from a present liability which could not exceed £100,000 a year.'[81] The poorer section of the tenantry were now being asked to buy their land at a higher rate of interest than the richer who had already bought.[82] In O'Brien's view, Birrell's proposal served to destroy the necessary atmosphere for conference plus business in other ways. For Birrell—despite the advice of the Royal Commission on Congestion—made apparent concessions to the cattle drivers.

The Unionist case against Birrell's proposed legislation may be easily summarized. The evidence of the O'Conor Don before the Dudley Commission was taken as proof that there was no need for compulsion even in the west—the problem having been located as the slowness of the Congested Districts Board and behind it, of course, the attitude of the Treasury.[83] But the deepest anger was reserved for two other proposals. The *Irish Times* noted: 'Outside Connaught the suggestion for compulsion would be ridiculous if its inspiration were not so sinister. Parliament is being asked to give unparalleled powers of compulsion to the Estates Commissioners at a moment when the real embarrassment consists in the huge and unexpected volume of voluntary transactions.'[84] The same journal added: 'The proposals for the reconstitution of the Congested Districts Board are so flagrant that Mr Birrell has not even tried to defend them.'[85] Like Sir Antony MacDonnell, the *Times* suspected that the popular element in the new

---

[79] *Longford Leader*, 28 November 1908.
[80] Ibid.
[81] *Irish People*, 10 October 1908.
[82] *Irish Independent*, 10 June 1909.
[83] *Irish Times*, 20 April 1909.
[84] Ibid.   [85] Ibid.

Congested Districts Board would curry favour with local landless men: 'We know perfectly well that these landless men—in other words, the sons of local farmers and League politicians—would have the best pull with the reconstituted board.'[86]

Birrell's bill had to be withdrawn because of lack of parliamentary time in the 1908 session but it was confidently expected on all sides that it would be reintroduced early in 1909. In part, no doubt because of the intensity of Irish unionist criticisms of Birrell's proposal, the Irish party leadership declared itself to be well satisfied. Not even the imprisonment of J. P. Farrell for a threatening speech at Clondra just before Christmas 1908 under a 'musty' statute of Edward III was allowed to disrupt relations with the Liberal government: Redmond contented himself with a declaration to the effect that the government's action was inconsistent given the amount of common ground shared with Farrell. 'Like Mr Birrell as between the cattle and the people, Mr Farrell choses the people. Like Mr Cherry he does not believe that ranching is a suitable system for the country.'[87] But there was to be no question of an officially sanctioned return to cattle driving. On New Year's Day 1909 David Sheehy explained the new line at a meeting in Trim, Co. Meath:

His advice to the people at the present time was that cattle driving would be injudicous. Why did he advise theme to give up cattle driving? They had been compelled to adopt the practice in order to get the lands divided amongst the people, but now a bill was about to be introduced by which these lands should be acquired compulsorily and by legal action, from the ranch owners.[88]

At the end of January, the police in Meath noted 'nearly all the eleven months farms have been taken and often at prices exceeding those of last year'.[89] In February Redmond formally rebuked the cattle drivers in parliament.[90] Not surprisingly the unfortunate J. P. Farrell was left outside this consensus. His expected spell in gaol gave him reason to doubt Birrell's good faith. Recanting his earlier optimism, he wrote to Dillon from Kilmainham: 'I strongly advise you not to depend too strongly upon Birrell's bill.'[91]

[86] *Irish Times*, 27 January 1909.
[87] *Weekly Freeman*, 2 January 1909.
[88] *Irish Times*, 2 January 1909.
[89] PRO Co 904/77/6.
[90] *Irish Times*, 25 February 1909.
[91] J. P. Farrell to John Dillon, 18 December 1908. TCD Dillon papers, 6753/425.

Serious trouble persisted only in areas outside the UIL writ. For example, in Galway (East Riding) Co. Inspector Smith reported at the end of March: 'a state of terrorism exists about Craughwell, Athenry and Kiltulla owing to the outrages committed by the local IRB organization'.[92] This development was 'peculiar', as the police admitted, 'in that the members go in for outrages in connection with agrarian disputes and this is not in accordance with IRB principles. There is no doubt that the leaders make money in the commission of these outrages.'[93] In this case, it appeared that a pre-existing secret society had joined the IRB without, however, altering its local ways. 'This organization embraces GAA men and Sinn Feiners and it is evident that these kindred associations are made a recruiting ground for the IRB'. In most areas, however, the police recorded a sharp dimunition in agrarian activism—even in the hottest spots of Co. Clare.[94]

In the meantime, O'Brien launched his last unavailing struggle to win the Irish party back to the conciliation policy. In the view of the O'Brienites, the Birrell Bill offered poor terms to the tenants, whilst its concessions to the cattle drivers served only to infuriate Irish Unionist opinion. In some desperation, O'Brien wrote to his old ally Lord Dunraven, asking him to state publicly 'that a reasonable understanding both as to land Purchase and Congestion was all along possible and is still possible to defeat the Treasury Scheme'. O'Brien added that 'the only alternative is that the landlords will simply be *compelled to decline to sell*'.[95] On 14 January 1909 O'Brien however had to admit to Dunraven: 'I am wholly in the dark as to how opinion goes in the country.'[96] Perhaps over-impressed by signs of tension between Redmond and Dillon,[97] O'Brien was soon in a more sanguine mood: in early 1909 he made one last appeal to the party. He decided to attend the National Convention of 9 February 1909 which had been called to consider Birrell's new Land Bill. O'Brien feared lest his speech be disrupted by Joe Devlin's increasingly influential, Catholic nationalist Ancient Order of Hibernians machine—which as O'Brien

[92] PRO CO 904/77/232.
[93] Ibid., 318.   [94] CO 904/77/5–9.
[95] O'Brien to Dunraven, 4 January 1908, University College, Cork, O'Brien MS, AR–6.
[96] O'Brien to Dunraven, 14 January 1908, University College, Cork, O'Brien MS, AR–51.
[97] O'Brien to Sophie O'Brien, 10 December 1908, University College, Cork, MS, BH–18.

liked to say would have excluded Parnell, as a Protestant, from membership.[98] The AOH had greatly expanded its support since 1905, and many of its Ulster activists, in particular, had understandably little time for O'Brien's 'toleration' of Unionism. The police explained: 'it appeals more strongly to the younger men and is more manifestly antagonistic to the Orange Society'.[99] Nevertheless, O'Brien was not fully prepared for the violence which actually took place. The 'Baton Convention' as it came to be known, was probably the stormiest meeting ever held by constitutional nationalists. It was a deeply embarrassing occasion for Redmond who had hoped to guarantee free speech. Instead a Belfast supporter of Devlin's, with a baton strung to his waist, threatened to 'slaughter' J. Gilhooly, MP for Cork NE, a mere two yards from Redmond's chair. Nor should this be treated as purely an unfortunate intrusion of Belfast crudity: it is all too often overlooked that the Belfast 'Mollies' who made such a mockery of the convention were supplemented by other allies from the South. As O'Brien noted: 'The special train of cattle drivers from Longford and Westmeath arrived with "the hazels" hitherto reserved for use on the flanks of the bullocks and brought a fresh accession to the (Hibernian) corps of occupation.'[100] The air was thick with taunts of 'down with the Russian Jewess!' O'Brien and his wife had been the target of anti-semitic abuse since his explicit adoption of the conciliation policy in 1903. Jasper Tully had argued that O'Brien, sold 'body and bone'[101] to the Jews, was a central figure in a conspiracy by which the Irish peasantry would be duped into over-paying heavily mortgaged Irish landlords and thus fill the coffers of those Jewish financiers who stood behind the landlords. In early 1909 these sentiments had revived in the *Longford Leader*, the newspaper owned by the imprisoned J. P. Farrell.[102] It is not surprising that the supporters of the incarcerated Farrell chose to take their frustrations out on the most 'legitimate' target available. For John Redmond, a strong opponent of anti-semitism, the loss of moral authority was considerable. It was a personal friend and political ally of Redmond's, Pierce Mahony, who wrote to O'Brien: 'I can not allow this time to go by without expressing the indignation with which I read of your

---

[98] W. O'Brien, *The Irish Revolution*, London, 1923, 117.
[99] PRO Co 904/77/2555.
[100] *An Olive Branch*, 445.
[101] *Roscommon Herald*, 10 January 1903.
[102] *Longford Leader*, 6 and 13 February 1909; see also 10 March 1909.

treatment at the convention. The saddest part of all ... that John Redmond having expressed the views he did in his opening speech should have allowed you to be howled down while he was in the chair.'[103]

O'Brien then resigned from the party for the last time. He retired to Cork where he retained a personal following and in March 1909 set about the launching of yet another new movement, this time to be called the All-For-Ireland League. Cork had also been the area where O'Brien 'conference plus business' policy has enjoyed the greatest effect, as O'Brien explained in his memoirs:

Cork headed, not only Mayo, but all the other counties in Ireland both as to the extent and as to the cheapness of its purchases—the average reduction for all Ireland being only 27.5 compared with Cork's 30.7 and 32.7, and the average number of years' purchase for all Ireland being 22.5, as compared with Cork's 21.3 and 20.7. What more conclusive proof could be given that the 'inflated prices' under the Act of 1903 were not inherent in the Act, but simply the consequence of the conduct of those who destroyed the plans for a systematic test of the Act, seeing that in Cork, where alone those plans got even a moderate share of fair play, no difficulty was found in not only realising the substantial equivalent of Ashbourne prices but bettering them by 4 per cent[104]

O'Brien, in short, had a secure base in Cork; but would he be able to expand outside it? John Fitzgibbon confidently argued that policies which were acceptable in a prosperous county like Cork were impossible in the west of Ireland.[105] At first glance, the most striking features of O'Brien's new movement were the negative ones. His newspaper the *Cork Accent* (later the *Cork Free Press*) claimed to be, and evidently was, 'anti-Dillon, anti-Radical, anti-*Freeman Journal* and anti-Molly Maguire'.[106] ('Molly Maguire' was O'Brien's term of abuse for the Hibernians.) All the manifestations of the dominant tendency in Irish nationalism and its ally 'new Liberalism', were denounced from a non-sectarian but also rather conservative stance. More positively, closer inspection revealed O'Brien's new movement drew its strength from a growing body of opinion which argued for a new initiative in Irish politics. From early 1908 onwards some Irish nationalists had asked themselves old questions about a Tory alliance with a renewed vigour. Symptomatic here, was the publicity given in

[103] Pierce Mahony to William O'Brien, n.d., University College, Cork, MS AR–7.
[104] *An Olive Branch*, 337/8.
[105] *Connaught Champion*, 10 December 1910.
[106] Joseph V. O'Brien, *William O'Brien*, 132.

Ireland to an article in the conservative *Liberty Review*, an organ of the Liberty and Property Defence League. This article was reprinted widely in the Irish press in the first days of 1908.[107] It argued for a Tory reconciliation with Irish nationalism as the way out of the party's apparently insoluble contradictions. The article called for the concession to Ireland of a Home Rule parliament with a strong House of Lords. It also called for the retention of some forty or so Irish MPs at Westminster 'There is yet time for Conservatives to adopt—under all possible safeguards—a policy of conservative Home Rule.'[108] Even D. P. Moran's the *Leader*, bitterly critical always of 'conciliation', dreamed of an alliance with 'the tariff reform' wing of conservatism to dish 'Asquith and Co.'[109] Former Irish party MPs, Jasper Tully[110] and J H. Parnell[111] supported this notion as did two current members of the party, A. M. Kavanagh[112] and S. J. Gwynn.[113] More generally as the *Times* had noted some years earlier: 'in the fiscal question as it affects Ireland—the nationalist public is strangely without interest'.[114] In truth the *Leader*'s sentiments were a product more of deep disappointment with the Liberals than justified enthusiasm for any section of the Tories, but the very existence of such widespread speculation indicated a deep unease about Irish party Liberal relations.

Nevertheless, the prospects for O'Brien's new movement were not especially bright. At the very least, O'Brien needed to retain the support of the fifteen MPs who had supported his pro-conciliation motion at the meeting of April 1908. But these MPs all came under formidable pressure to stay in line: the slightest public sign of O'Brienite sentiments was likely to get an MP into trouble. In particular, as the baton convention had revealed, the cattle driving wing of the party were prepared to be used as the 'enforcers' of the anti-conciliatory line. Events in Co. Longford were to provide further proof of this point.

On 15 July, a striking parliamentary question was posed by J. P. Phillips, MP for North Longford. Phillips, who had been an active

[107] For example, *Drogheda Independent*, 4 January 1908; *Mayo News*, 4 January 1908.
[108] Ibid.
[109] *Leader*, 25 November 1908.
[110] *Roscommon Herald*, 9 October 1909.
[111] *Irish Independent*, 7 January 1910.
[112] *Galway Express*, 1 January 1910.
[113] *Irish Times*, 17 April 1908.
[114] Quoted in *Mayo News*, 12 December 1903.

cattle driver in the early days of the campaign, asked the Chief Secretary for Ireland 'whether he will take proceedings to protect the innocent ratepayers for the future from the punishment imposed upon them by extra police taxation for crimes they not only take no part in, but detest and abhor, namely cattle driving, the acts of a few irresponsible parties and thoughtless young boys'.[115] The phrasing of this question inevitably infuriated the recently released J. P. Farrell, Phillips's fellow nationalist Longford MP. The *Longford Leader*, in a bitter article, denounced Phillips as a hypocrite and crypto-O'Brienite.[116] Phillips was called to explain himself before a meeting of the Longford UIL executive; the meeting, happily for Phillips, was held on 9 August, when J. P. Farrell could not attend for health reasons. Phillips explained that the controversial references to 'irresponsible parties' and 'thoughtless boys' had been purely tactical; the principal endeavour of his question, had been to expose the government's dubious strategy of tackling the cattle drivers by penalizing local ratepayers.[117] Phillips insisted that he was a 'cattle driver still',[118] but somewhat compromised this declaration by announcing that this activity should cease until the House of Lords actually rejected Birrell's bill. J. P. Farrell remained unmollified and his newspaper maintained its fire on Phillips.[119]

The argument continued to simmer in Longford UIL circles for the next six weeks. Then at the beginning of October followers of Phillips (who had been joined by Patrick McKenna) attempted to break up a UIL branch meeting at Newtonforbes—a branch which J. P. Farrell was in the process of 'reorganizing'. The stormy scenes which ensured were described locally as the most bitter since the Parnell split.[120] The outlines of the dispute are clear enough. Farrell's supporters decried the implicit disloyalty of Phillips's parliamentary question and claimed that Phillips and his supporters had abandoned the struggle against the graziers. Phillips and his friends denied all this and insisted that his conduct had been entirely consistent.[121] The dispute involved much washing of dirty linen in public—allegations about the

---

[115] HC, 5 series, vol. 11, col. 2287.
[116] *Longford Leader*, 24 July 1909.
[117] *Irish Times*, 10 August 1909.
[118] Ibid.
[119] *Longford Leader*, 14 August 1909.
[120] *Longford Leader*, 9 October 1907.
[121] *Longford Leader*, 16 October 1909.

high costs of Farrell's printing work for the UIL, for example[122]—and both sides felt the need to reduce tension to avoid further embarrassment. On 23 October, the factions officially declared[123] that peace had broken out, though the resentments and bitterness remained just below the surface.[124]

These events in Longford were not merely an amusing side-show; they revealed much about the balance of forces inside the Irish party. J. P. Farrell and his friends were strong enough to stop conciliatory opinion on the agrarian question gaining ground within the party. But, despite their eloquent pleas, they were unable to force the party leadership to take the side of the most militant ranch warriors; those who argued that cattle driving should be maintained until Birrell explicitly satisfied all the cattle drivers. In a parliamentary speech in September, Farrell made his position clear: 'notwithstanding the report of the Dudley commission, notwithstanding all that has been said about congestion, this question is not solely confined to Connaught'.[125] Criticizing Walter Kavanagh, the Carlow nationalist MP who as a member of the commission had supported the principal recommendations of the Dudley report, Farrell added: 'It is all very well ... to speak about the congest getting the preference over the landless men but who is the landless man? The son of the farmer. Is he not entitled to some other chance than the emigrant's ship?'[126]

Farrell can hardly have expected the House of Lords to pay attention to such an argument. As Birrell noted glumly on 26 October 1909 of his land bill as amended by the Lords, 'the Dudley Commission ... might as well never have sat, so completely are its main recommendations ignored'.[127] Birrell was prepared to move rejection of the Lords amendments *en bloc* whilst at the same time indicating certain possible areas of compromise. On 17 November, the Lords conceded ground in two important areas. They allowed compulsion outside the west (but only for the relief of congestion) and they accepted the addition of two permanent, paid members to the congested districts board. But they refused to yield on certain key points: the Lords sought to limit interference with the zones, they

---

[122] Ibid.
[123] *Longford Leader*, 23 October 1909.
[124] *Longford Leader*, 6 April 1917.
[125] Hansard, 17 September 1909, vol. X, col. 2523/4.
[126] Ibid.
[127] PRO Cab 37/101/144 The Irish Land Bill as amended by the Lords.

accepted compulsion only for relief of congestion and insisted that there was to be no special provision for landless men. They rejected also the presence of a strong 'popular' elected element on the congested districts board. In one final provocative move, they asked for a tribunal, including two King's Bench judges, to hear appeals against compulsory purchase. Birrell in return refused this idea of a tribunal but he gave way on the other points. The chief secretary chose to drop his proposals for interference with the zones rather than accept the Lords' limitation. Of particular significance, however, was Birrell's decision to drop his concessions to the cattle driving wing of the Irish party. Birrell had been fully aware of the case against the cattle drivers but had chosen in the earlier stages of the debate to take the cynical view that it was up to the Irish themselves to sort these factional disputes. On 23 November 1909 the agrarian radicals faced their moment of truth. Birrell announced his intention of accepting a Lords amendment which had the effect of placing the claim of the landless men *below* those of migrating congests and evicted tenants. Birrell presented his concession as essentially cosmetic. The chief secretary declared: 'I do not know that it makes really very much difference in the case, as it seems to me to make it plain that the sons of tenants are not to be provided for, but may be provided for when adequate provision has been made . . . for the relief of congestion and the evicted.'[128] But for the cattle-driving wing of the Irish party the concession was, of course, of the greatest significance; two active cattle drivers, J. P. Farrell[129] and W. J. Duffy[130] bitterly denounced Birrell's move. John Dillon inevitably added his voice to the weight of disapproval.[131] Farrell and Duffy both insisted that the chief secretary's earliest pronouncements had legitimately raised the hopes of the landless men, who were now at the last moment, to be thrown over. Both promised a renewed outbreak of cattle driving. Laurence Ginnell merely commented that the final outcome of the Birrell legislation had 'confirmed' his 'forecast'. It confirmed also the defeat of the ranch war of 1906–8; the landless activists who had backed Fitzgibbon, Farrell and Ginnell had failed to win legislative sanction of their claims. In disappointment, Farrell and Ginnell, brought together by the shared experience of defeat, launched a revival of

---

[128] HC, 5 series, vol. XIII, 23 November 1909, col. 58.
[129] Ibid., col. 602.   [130] Ibid., col. 74.
[131] Ibid., col. 66; see also *Irish Times*, 23 November 1909 for comment on the speeches by Farrell, Duffy and Dillon.

cattle driving in 1910[132] but to no avail. Taken in the round, Birrell's land bill of 1909 was easily presented as a victory for the Irish party—despite the last minute concessions to the Lords. Deprived of the elective possibility, Birrell was still able to use his patronage power to make the symbolic appointment of John Fitzgibbon to the congested districts board. The positive impact of Birrell's legislation on the progress of land purchase was unimpressive—as the chief secretary acknowledged when he brought in a new measure in 1913. But the purely political impact in the short term was considerable.

Towards Home Rule?

F. S. L. Lyons has written: 'Important though the 1909 Act was, it was carried though in an atmosphere almost of unreality, so preoccupied were both the English parties with the great constitutional crisis, so long impending and now at last precipitated when in 1909 Lloyd George brought in what seemed, for those days, a revolutionary budget.'[133] While such a comment hardly does justice to the sharpness of the debate provoked by the 1909 Act, it accurately pinpoints the sudden emergence not only of a major British constitutional crisis but also of new and exciting possibilities for the Home Rule party. As Lyons has put it: 'If the budget did produce the long-awaited crisis which would limit or end the veto of the House of Lords, then Home Rule might reasonably be expected to be a residuary legatee.'[134]

On its merits, the radical budget was unpopular in Ireland and not simply with the O'Brienites. John Redmond had little sympathy for reformist new liberalism—old age pensions he stigmatized 'as an extravagance and an extravagance that would not have been indulged in by an Irish parliament.'[135] The *Freeman* declared: 'the whiskey and tobacco duties are designedly and specially aimed at Ireland. They are treasury devices to get even with Ireland for her crime of having so many poor with rights.'[136] But despite these sentiments, Redmond felt that he could not go to the length of siding with the Lords to throw out the budget, because this would lead to the end of the Liberal alliance. Instead William O'Brien's All-For-Ireland League was allowed to gather the credit in the country on account of its unrelenting hostility to the budget. There was certainly plenty of credit going—the new

---

[132] *Longford Leader*, 4 December 1909. See the beginning of this realignment.
[133] Lyons, *Dillon*, 308.   [134] Ibid., 309.
[135] *Irish Independent*, 10 June 1909.
[136] *Weekly Freeman's Journal*, 8 May 1909.

farmer owners in Cork were less than enthusiastic when called upon to finance the measures of liberal progressivism.

In late November, J. J. Clancy summed up the Irish party's position on the budget; it was admitted, that even after the Irish party's best efforts, the measure was still 'unsatisfactory from the point of view of Ireland'.[137] Nevertheless, it was claimed that the party had 'substantially lightened' the burden of the budget. Pride of place in this exposition was given to the liquor licence duties: 'the exactions originally contained in the bill have been greatly modified'.[138] But such relatively unconvincing arguments did not constitute the nub of the case:[139] as Clancy insisted 'no Budget framed by English statesmanship with a single view to British affairs would ever fail to press onerously on this country'.[140] This assessment clearly implied the primacy of the Home Rule issue. But was Home Rule really on the agenda?

Fortunately for the Irish party the Lords fulfilled their threats and rejected the budget on 30 November. Such an action made a general election inevitable. It also allowed the Irish party to concentrate on the task of securing from the Prime Minister a public statement to the effect that the Liberal cabinet would regard Home Rule as an issue at the next general election. Asquith duly obliged by his speech at the Albert Hall on 10 December when he proclaimed his faith that the only solution of the Irish question would be the setting up in Ireland of a system of full self-government and that in the new House of Commons the hands of a Liberal majority would be entirely free in such a matter.[141]

The irony, of course, was plain enough and was pointed out at the time: in 1894 and 1895 Redmond had denounced precisely the strategy he was now promoting. The younger Redmond had argued that the aim of the nationalist strategy should be to bring about a wider change in English public opinion on Ireland; for the Lords could never resist a determined public mood in favour of Home Rule for Ireland. The way to bring about this change was by pursuing a thorough policy of conciliation of the Irish unionist minority. Redmond had by 1907–8 lost faith in such a strategy of conciliation. He had also come

---

[137] Ibid., 20 November 1909.
[138] Ibid.
[139] Lyons, *Irish Parliamentary Party*, 126.
[140] *Weekly Freeman*, 20 November 1909.
[141] Lyons, *Irish Parliamentary Party*, 127.

reluctantly to the conclusion that 'you can not rouse the British people on the question of home rule'.[142] This may well have been true—but if so, the consequences were far reachng. As William O'Brien—not unlike the Redmond of the 1890s—reflected prophetically at Cork in January 1910:

It (Home Rule) is no longer a question between the two parties, but between the two peoples, and unless we can make some impression upon the people outside Parliament all this intrigue and lobbying and selling Irish votes to one unscrupulous English party or another is all Parliamentary refreshment like strawberries and tea on the terrace—(laughter)—pleasant enough for the politicians but with equally little substantial results for Ireland (cheers). You might just as well go the whole hog, and hold out for an Irish Republic, because you have as much chance of getting it as you have of getting Gladstonian Home Rule by the present tactics of Mr Redmond and his followers or rather leaders.[143]

All such attempts, however, to remind Redmond of his former views, had little effect. When Lord Dunraven made an impassioned attempt to embarrass Redmond on this point, the *Freeman* confidently replied:

Because Mr Redmond doubted the success of such an attack in 1895, he cannot, Lord Dunraven argues, believe in its success in 1909. It would require a revolution, Mr Redmond said fourteen years ago. He was quite right; it did require a revolution to create the opportunity and the Lords themselves have obligingly provided the revolution. We are in for a revolution anyhow: either the people's control of their own taxation will be destroyed or the veto of the Lords will disappear.[144]

The Election of 1910

The critical test of public opinion on these issues came with the general election of January 1910. It is clear that the official Irish party machine suffered a significant number of reverses: eleven Nationalists independent of the offical party were returned, seven of them AFIL followers of O'Brien. This much is undisputed—but O'Brien and his supporters made a very much larger claim. One O'Brienite journal claimed that 'half the constituencies' in Ireland were in revolt against the 'dictation' of the UIL executive.[145] O'Brien in his memoirs gave a

---

[142] Quoted in J. A. Gaughan, *A Political Odyssey: Thomas O'Donnell*, Dublin, 1983, 293.
[143] *Weekly Irish Times*, 8 May 1909.
[144] *Weekly Freeman*, 18 December 1909; the *Western News*, 5 January 1910, was much less sure on this point.
[145] *Connaught Champion*, 7 January 1910.

long list of constituencies in which he claimed there had been 'plots' to remove independently inclined candidates. These had mostly failed—leading O'Brien to a remarkable conclusion which characteristically he did not flinch; defining official candidates as only those who had the full confidence of the UIL executive he argued that in these contests more votes were actually cast for independents— 'against whom the campaign of extermination had been waged'[146]— than official nominees.

There is no doubt that O'Brien is here overstating the case. Everything depends on what is here meant by 'independently' inclined: indeed O'Brien by his own admission included every MP who had exhibited even the slightest sign of heterodoxy. The great bulk of those he included had claimed in the election to be loyal Redmondites—even if this was disputed by Joe Devlin and the UIL executive in Dublin. O'Brien happily included as independents men whom the O'Brienite press had denounced for keeping their reservations about the official line private.[147] In other words, the category 'independent' was strained to the utmost; though, it is worth noting that in only a small number of cases does O'Brien seem to have awarded it for no reason whatsoever. The first point to be settled then is how many of these contests raised, however obliquely, the question of 'O'Brienism'? It is obviously not possible to regard O'Brien's memoir as an entirely reliable source. The investigation which follows draws on local and national press reports to produce a more accurate picture of a complex election.

The cases of Tim Healy and Tim Harrington are relatively uncontroversial. Both Healy (North Louth) and to a lesser extent Harrington (Dublin, Harbour) were major figures from the Parnell era who were fairly obviously identified with at least some of O'Brien's criticisms of the party. The challenges the two men faced were obviously not unexpected. Both Healy and Harrington were their 'own men', of course, and in no sense unaware of O'Brien's defects. Nevertheless in this contest of January 1910, they may be said to belong to his camp: Harrington in particular had written to Redmond in 1907[148] denouncing the sectarian exclusiveness of the Hibernians

---

[146] *An Olive Branch*, 468.
[147] *Irish People*, 21 October 1905 contains some choice comments on the cowardice of Sam Young of Cavan who none the less is listed as an 'independent'. Conor O'Kelly often came in for similar treatment; he too is listed as independent.
[148] Harrington to Redmond, 27 April 1907, NLI MS 15194.

and regretting that his old friendship with Redmond seemed to have cooled. Also in this category was Thomas O'Donnell[149] in West Kerry and Thomas Smyth in South Leitrim. Both men had voted for O'Brien in the key party vote on conciliation in 1908. The challenge to Smyth was complicated by a constituency scandal concerning his involvement as an auctioneer on the sale of 'boycotted' meadow lands.[150] O'Donnell, in particular, received much sympathetic coverage in the O'Brienite press.

Two other men who had voted with O'Brien were unsuccessfully challenged. Philip O'Docherty in North Donegal faced opposition from Charles Diamond of London at the UIL convention. In mid-Tyrone George Murnaghan, who had represented the area since 1898, was deposed as a nationalist candidate by John Valentine, despite having a considerable body of local feeling and the majority of the clergy behind him.[151] Murnaghan went on to fight the election none the less, thus splitting the nationalist vote and allowing a Unionist triumph. O'Brien, somewhat unscrupulously, seems to list this as a success for 'independence' against the UIL bosses.

Four other candidates may be added to the list of suspected O'Brienite's. Conor O'Kelly had voted with O'Brien in 1908 and signed the minority report of the Dudley Commission. He was therefore an object of suspicion despite all protestations of loyalty. As punishment he was moved from North Mayo, where was was perfectly happy, and made to fight South Mayo against the even more obviously 'O'Brienite' candidate John O'Donnell—a fight he lost. O'Donnell had close ties with O'Brien since the early days of the UIL in 1898 but it should be pointed out that though his election rhetoric was close to that of the All-For-Ireland League he had promised to take the pledge of loyalty to the party again.[152] In North Mayo, Daniel Boyle defeated the machine nominee Bernard Egan, who had earlier pushed Conor O'Kelly out of the chairmanship of Mayo County Council.[153] Fourthly, in Kerry East there was the case of Eugene O'Sullivan, a clear O'Brienite sympathizer, who displaced the sitting MP, John Murphy.[154]

[149] For O'Donnell, see J. A. Gaughan, *A Political Odyssey: Thomas O'Donnell*, Dublin, 1983, 58–76.

[150] *Leitrim Advertiser*, 20 January 1910; Garvin, *Evolution*, 93.

[151] *Weekly Freeman*, 8 January 1910; *Anglo-Celt*, 1 January 1910; D. Murphy, *Derry, Donegal and Modern Ulster*, Londonderry, 1981, 200; *Donegal Vindicator*, 21 January 1910.

[152] *Western News*, 29 January 1910; *CT*, 8 January 1910.

[153] Ibid.   [154] *Kerry People*, 8 January 1910.

O'Brien's list includes four MPs who do not seem to have been identified with his policies. Two of them, P. J. O'Shaughnessy (West Limerick) and J. P. Nannetti (College Green), actually voted against him in April 1909. The other two, J. R. Lardner (North Monaghan) and Sam Young (Cavan East) were absent. But their inclusion is not merely arbitrary; Nannetti[155] and Lardner[156] *had* notoriously bad relations with the AOH. Cheers for O'Brien were certainly heard amongst O'Shaughnessy's supporters in Limerick[157] while Sam Young's muted sympathy for O'Brien's ideas—which decidedly did not extend to a formal public endorsement—were fairly widely known.[158] O'Brien's list also includes one fairly obvious Healyite, John McKean (Monaghan South) though even McKean claimed all the while to be a loyal Redmondite.[159]

Two candidates were challenged by the UIL leadership on the basis of their alleged Sinn Fein sympathies. They were the patrician Sir Thomas Grattan Esmonde and the turbulent Laurence Ginnell. The case of Laurence Ginnell was complicated by his adherence to the practice of cattle driving long after it had ceased to be fashionable. Esmonde came under sharp attack solely on the Sinn Fein issue, though he had corresponded sympathetically with O'Brien.[160] One local critic noted: 'The man who . . . who asked us to follow him into an eighteenth century wilderness in which English institutions were not supposed to exist . . . is existing in an element into which it is impossible to transport the prosaic voters of North Wexford.'[161] Nevertheless Esmonde survived, as did Ginnell.

Ginnell found himself under siege from his ertswhile ranch war 'colleague', J. P. Hayden, MP for Roscommon. Hayden denounced Ginnell for Sinn Feinism, cattle driving and leaking the party's affairs to the press. However, Ginnell, despite lack of support in the town of Mullingar, had solid rural support and defeated the challenge of Patrick McKenna, the active Longford cattle driver of 1907. It is a remarkable fact that McKenna was greatly weakened during this campaign, by the charge—never effectively answered—that he himself

[155] James Connolly, *Worker's Republic*, 19 June 1915.
[156] Hepburn, 'Liberal Policies and Nationalist Politics', 593–4.
[157] *Limerick Leader*, 19 January 1910.
[158] *Irish People*, 21 October 1905.
[159] *Northern Standard*, 1 January 1910; *Anglo-Celt*, 1 January 1910.
[160] J. V. O'Brien, op. cit., 177–8, but note Esmonde's ingratiating letter to Redmond, 11 December 1909, NLI 15, 188.
[161] *Free Press* (Wexford), 1 January 1910.

was an 'eleven months' man, renting land at Kilpatrick in County Westmeath at £4.13 per acre.[162] The poll was the largest poll held in North Westmeath since 1886. Ginnell had a majority of 620 over McKenna who obtained 1,373 votes. But it is worth noting that even the volatile Ginnell still claimed to be a Redmond loyalist—arguing somewhat disingenuously that Redmond had never objected to anything Ginnell had said in or out of Parliament.[163]

There is finally no doubt that the priests joined the central leadership in opposing Colonel Arthur Lynch in West Clare. Lynch had published an article in the *Detroit Free Press* claiming—amongst other things—that only one of the Irish bishops was competent enough to be a member of Parliament. The local clergy were more than a little put out when this article surfaced in Ireland on the eve of the election: 'Their honour, as Irishmen was attacked in a foreign newspaper, and they would not be Irishmen if they did not resent it.'[164] However, the cry of 'unity' allowed Lynch to survive even this threat. The *Clare Champion* observed: 'The very memory of the Parnell split makes one shudder at the thought of another.'[165] The remarkable Colonel Lynch, Parnellite, soldier in the Boer War, war correspondent, psychologist and social philosopher lived to fight another day.

O'Brien's list of independents contains three names, 'Farmer' Hogan (North Tipperary), Haviland Burke (Tullamore) and Jeremiah Jordan (South Fermanagh) which are more or less inexplicable. All three faced challenges but there was nothing in their recent political behaviour to mark out any of these men as a real thorn in the flesh of the UIL leadership. O'Brien seems to have included two of them— Jordan and Burke—largely on the grounds that they were Protestants who faced opposition to their re-selection.[166]

It seems reasonable also to add to O'Brien's list of seats one constituency which he did not mention. In West Waterford, E. Arthur Ryan challenged J. J. O'Shee, the official UIL candidate for the seat. Ryan was not an O'Brienite; he pledged himself to 'sit, act, and vote'

---

[162] *Midland Reporter*, 13 January 1910, 3 February 1910; *Westmeath Examiner*, 8 January 1910.

[163] *Weekly Irish Times*, 8 January 1910.

[164] *Clare Champion*, 1 January 1910.

[165] Ibid.

[166] *Midland Tribune and Kings Co. Vindicator*, 1 January 1910. Burke *had* sent O'Brien an unusually friendly public letter on his first resignation. *Midland Tribune*, 14 November 1903.

with the Irish party. Nevertheless, he substantially accepted O'Brien's analysis of the key political issues of the day: in particular, he declared the Birrell Act to be a 'worthless measure'.[167] Arthur Ryan ran O'Shee very close indeed for the seat; proof yet again—as all the setbacks for the official machine were—that nationalist Ireland was unenthusiastic about the Liberal alliance, 'New Liberal' reforms—or at any rate their effects on taxation levels—and the Birrell land act. The general election had revealed 'much dissatisfaction'[168] in the *Independent*'s phrase. J. P. Farrell admitted that faction had had its triumphs— adding not unreasonably that in many areas ambitious men with 'large family connections'[169] had taken advantage of the chaos to make a name for themselves.

Redmond must have been relieved when the election campaign ended. He had fought the election on political principles radically different from those he had espoused in the 1893–1903 period—a fact which may have caused him a certain unease. Meanwhile, O'Brien's electoral success as an 'independent' nationalist leader compared very well with Redmond's own performance in the 1890s. Happily for Redmond the centre of interest soon shifted to Westminster. The results of the January election had given the balance of power to Redmond and the Irish party, for the Liberals and Conservatives were almost exactly equal in numbers. For some time, the death of the King in May led to a certain reduction in political strife. But the failure of the new King's conference proposal signalled a renewal of the veto struggle and a period of intense excitement followed. On 18 November Asquith announced in Parliament that there would be a new election. Redmond sat silent following the announcement. The reason for Redmond's silence, of course, was that as yet he had no assurance from the government as to the course they intended pursuing in the event of the General Election being won. He and his colleagues were determined that the government should only have their support at the polls on condition that once the veto in the Lords was destroyed the question of Ireland would immediately be taken up, and the Home Rule Bill passed with the least avoidable delay. It was not long, however, before these assurances were received and the Irish forces thrown enthusiastically into the electoral fight.

---

[167] *Munster Express*, 22 January 1910.
[168] *Irish Independent*, 28 January 1910.
[169] *Longford Leader*, 24 January 1910.

1910 had been a very good year for Redmond. His steady and persistent pressure on the government seemed to have brought the Irish within sight of complete victory. The very degree of intense hosility he received from the Tories increased his standing in Ireland. In consequence, he was able to face the second general election of the year with a great deal more confidence. In 1910 Redmond for the first time achieved a stature something akin to that of Parnell in 1886. He was seen to apply painful pressure on the very heart of British politics. After years of relative powerlessness this itself was a pleasure for the nationalist electorate. When in the dissolution debate of 1910 William O'Brien described him as the 'Dictator of England' and the 'destroyer of Ireland', it is reported that Redmond simply smiled broadly in response.[170] He well understood that to be acknowledged as the 'Dictator of England' by one of his bitterest nationalist critics could do him nothing but good in Ireland. He had even been able to achieve that objective which Parnell had formally set in 1881 but never really attained (or seriously sought to attain), the union of the Irish with the radical and democratic forces in British politics. Typically, in a December message to his constituency, William Redmond was full of optimism: 'In fact, he could not see anything which could prevent the passage of Home Rule after the election, because the House of Lords could hardly fail to agree with any measure passed in the House of Commons by a large majority. Their prospects were never better than they are now because with the veto of the House of Lords abolished the only obstacle to Home Rule would be removed.'[171]

In the second General Election of 1910, the Redmondite forces inevitably enjoyed a surge in their favour.[172] A notable victory was that achieved over Tim Healy who lost his seat in North Louth. O'Brien retained his strength in Cork but lost Kerry and Limerick. None of the fourteen candidates he fielded outside Cork was returned. By far the most important of these setbacks for O'Brienite supporters took place in Mayo: in Mayo West, O'Brien himself was outpolled three to one by William Dorris. Yet despite much Redmondite optimism, there remained a profound obstacle to the fulfilment of nationalist hopes. As the O'Brienite *Cork Free Press* declared:

When all is said and done the hostility of Ulster is the real obstacle in the way of Home Rule. If that were out of the way the English People would not

[170] *Freeman's Journal*, 7 March 1918.
[171] *Clare Champion*, 8 December 1910.
[172] Lyons, *Irish Parliamentary Party*, 177–9.

hesitate for a moment about delegating to Ireland large powers of self-government ... The government are pledged to bring in a bill, whatever may happen afterwards. It depends on Ulster whether that measure will be the herald of peace or whether it will only serve to embitter existing controversies.[173]

---

[173] *Cork Free Press*, 25 February 1911, quoted in B. Clifford, ed., *Reprints from the Cork Free Press 1910–16: An Account of Ireland's only Democratic Anti Partition Movement*, Belfast and Cork, 1984, 36.

Conclusion

Though Mr Redmond frequently declared that he stood where Mr Parnell stood, no one, for some time past, took him seriously in this— except that he meant he was a generation behind the times (in his interpretations of the aspirations of the vast majority of the Irish race).

J. E. Lane, Fermoy Sinn Fein, *The Southern Democrat*, 22 March 1918.

There is no reason to suppose the men in possession of the stage in 1917, will be any better than those who possessed it in 1892.

Anna Parnell, *Irish People*, 14 September 1907.

In May 1984 the Report of the New Ireland Forum, expressing the views of the principal constitutional nationalist political forces in Ireland, declared roundly: 'the positive vision of Irish nationalism ... has been to create a society that transcends religious differences'.[1] Recent historians of Irish nationalism have been a good deal more cautious in tone. In his *The Evolution of Irish Nationalist Politics*[2] (1981), Tom Garvin argues that, despite the secular and liberal leanings of many Irish leaders and theoreticians, their followers were frequently sectarian and conservative in outlook. D. George Boyce offers his *Nationalism in Ireland* (1982) as an attempt 'to explain why Irish nationalist ideology has failed to realise one of its most persistent goals: the creation of a comprehensive Irish nation embracing all creeds and classes of Irishmen'.[3] In any such discussion, the period 1890–1910 must take pride of place. It was a period when one major source of division in Irish society—for many *the* major source of division—the land question, seemed to be coming to an end. Lord Dunraven liked to say that this development ruled out the use of the word 'impossible'[4] in connection with Irish politics. At the very least, as John Redmond put it in one of those interviews which appeared in the world's press but not in the principal organ of constitutional

---

[1] Par. 4.6.
[2] Dublin and New York, 1981.
[3] London, Dublin and Baltimore, 1982, 10.
[4] *Irish People*, 7 November 1903.

nationalism, the *Freeman's Journal*: 'The cry of "Don't grant Home Rule" or the landlords will be robbed is no longer available to the Unionist cause.'[5]

In the mid-1880s Parnell had devoted much of his energy to meeting fears on precisely this point.[6] For Parnell had had his own quite distinctive opinions concerning the evolution of Irish nationalism. He had hoped that a generously financed land settlement would permit some form of reconciliation between the landlords and peasantry. In the 1890s, John Redmond, as the leader of the Parnellite minority had inherited this conception. Redmond's tactics of co-operation with moderate Unionists on the financial relations question and above all, the policy of toleration folowing the democratization of Irish local government (1898) reveal this clearly. As one of his biographers, W. B. Wells wrote of the Redmond of the late 1890s: 'his hope was for a *softening* of the class struggle'.[7] The dominant figure in the anti-Parnellite majority, John Dillon, and in this he was supported by Michael Davitt, opposed such notions vigorously. For Dillon, co-operation with those outside the nationalist bloc could lead only to an unacceptable dilution of faith. It is widely accepted also that Dillon feared that the resolution of the land question would significantly weaken peasant support for nationalism.

In a vivid phrase, he told Irish American Bourke Cockran that 'if the land purchase act of 1903 were allowed to work there would be an end of the national cause before six months'.[8] In the autumn of 1903 Dillon, basing himself on this view of the question, challenged Redmond's direction of Irish nationalism. Ironically, in later years, Dillon was prepared to take a different, rather more mild, position. In 1909, interviewed by Philadelphia-based journalist Hugh Sutherland, who asked: 'Has the redressing of the land wrongs obscured the political issue?' Dillon replied: 'The home rule sentiment is stronger than ever'.[9] In 1912 it was said of one of his own parliamentary speeches on Home Rule that 'John Dillon was at his best in showing how the beginning of better days in Ireland had not weakened the national demand'.[10] But in the critical years of 1903 and 1904 Dillon

---

[5] *Irish People*, 7 March 1908.
[6] Bew, *Parnell*, 78–84.
[7] W. B. Wells, *John Redmond*, London, 1919, 62. Emphasis added.
[8] O'Brien, *Evening Memories*, 484.
[9] *Irish World*, 31 July 1909.
[10] *Irish Weekly Independent*, 20 April 1912.

viewed land reform in a much more suspicious light. He engaged in a
series of bitter tirades against the Wyndham act and its supporters.

Against such preconceptions, Parnell had said in October 1881:

> So long as it is a continual source of dispute between landlords and tenants,
> how much rent is to be paid by the tenants and received by the landlords, I do
> not see how it is possible from the point of view of the government that they
> would give us autonomy. I think the land question has to be settled. If the land
> question were settled every other question would, I think, settle itself.[11]

For Redmond in 1903 the great opportunity to settle the land question,
envisaged in Parnell's statement, has at last come. All his actions show
his excitement at the prospect of a union of all creeds and classes to
pursue the goal of Irish self-government. For John Dillon the
Wyndham land act was not so much an opportunity as a snare. It
involved dialogue with traditional enemies; men who were still
opposed to Ireland's demand for self-government. It involved also the
risk that the peasantry might cease to see the Irish party as the sole
legitimate defenders of their material interests.

The land conference of 1902–3 and the subsequent legislation
therefore merely brought to a head what had been the fundamental
strategic difference within mainstream Irish nationalism since the
earliest days of the Land League in 1879. Many militants, especially
those with Fenian connections had argued that the land question
could not be solved while the link with Britain remained. From this
defective prognosis they deduced that the driving momentum of
unsatiated agrarianism was the most powerful force making for the
unsettlement of the union. In consequence, any attempt to settle the
land question by the British government was bound to be viewed with
grave suspicion regardless of the specific details. John Dillon and
Michael Davitt were therefore being perfectly consistent when they
opposed the 1903 legislation as they had opposed the Gladstone land
act of 1881. Equally consistent, however, was the alternative tradition
of Charles Stewart Parnell, John Redmond and William O'Brien. All
three men had set the land question in an entirely different political
context. They had argued unambiguously that the land question was
open to solution by the British parliament. The consequence of such a
solution could be an era of social peace in Ireland bringing about the
political reconciliation of Protestant landed classes (and their followers) with the Catholic masses. The accession of some of the

[11] Bew, *Land*, 63.

erstwhile unionist and upper class community to the Home Rule ranks would give that demand a new vitality. The Wyndham act created a genuine dilemma for Irish nationalism; either the path of reconciliation with the ascendancy, involving acceptance of land purchase and devolution proposals or the path of vaguely defined 'war', involving suspicion of land purchase and devolution. Weakened by the fear of another split; also by the affair of the 'Redmond price'[12]—but perhaps above all by the volatile behaviour of his most important allies William O'Brien and Tim Healy—Redmond allowed himself to be out-manœuvred and defeated by Dillon.

The traditional slogans of agrarian radicalism were, it seems, to be regarded as retaining all their own relevance. Yet here there is a striking paradox: Michael Davitt, himself the very embodiment of 'Land Leaguism', fully admitted in 1906 that the effects of the 'fall of feudalism' in Ireland were not those he had expected or worked for. Farmers had not turned to tillage; rural unemployment and under-employment was as marked as ever. Above all, the new owner occupiers refused to acknowledge any claims the 'national community' might have on the utilization of their new found property. Yet the Irish party retained its somewhat tattered agrarian credo. The consequences have never received enough attention. The party, or at any rate the active party, permitted itself to be used more and more as the agency for the expression of those agrarian grievances which remained. Indeed, while one section of the tenantry bought their land and thus weakened the appeal of agitation, another section, the landless men, had their claims legitimized. John Cullinan seemed to contemplate blithely the ruin of those farmers who had bought under the 1903 Act while Laurence Ginnell called for large-scale land redistribution to benefit the landless. New tactics, most notably cattle driving, were developed. Unsuccessful efforts were made to stifle Ginnell, the most vigorous cattle driver. In January 1910 Ginnell defeated Patrick McKenna's challenge to his seat; by December it was impossible to challenge him—partly, it was said, because of his popularity in Irish America. It is noticeable that while Ginnell personally may have suffered administrative attempts to silence him, his argument, *as arguments*, had never really been challenged within the UIL. Indeed the case for cattle driving was accepted by some of

---

[12] *Irish Weekly Independent*, 24 October 1903 for the most precise analysis of Redmond's predicament.

the most prominent leaders of the organization. In August 1910, for example, John Dillon took the trouble to attend the unveiling of a memorial for John Stenson, a young man shot dead by the police in a cattle-driving incident. According to Dillon:

Some people, excellent people, for the last two or three years have been very violent in their condemnation of cattle driving which poor Stenson fell in carrying out. I for my part have never been able to join in these condemnations (applause) because I have always regarded cattle driving in three-fourths of the cases—I don't say it has not been sometimes abused—but in three-fourths of the cases where it has occurred I have regarded cattle driving as the natural outbreaking of the people against an abominable system of extermination which has depopulated and laid waste the most fertile and fairest lands of Ireland and drove the people to madness.[13]

Dillon's position was, of course, ambiguous. He had recently voted for a salary increase for the police in the House of Commons. He had called on the nationalists of North Tyrone to elect Redmond Barry as Attorney-General; Barry, however, had prosecuted the cattle drivers. Dillon's equivocation in this matter was sharply attacked by William O'Brien and Tim Healy. 'Mr Dillon was one of the men who sent Mr Ginnell, Mr Kettle, Mr Sheehy, Mr Johnston, Mr Gwynn, Mr Farrell and all the other cattle drivers to preach the doctrine of the hazel and to make the people clear the ranches. But while doing this . . . he was very careful to keep out of danger himself',[14] one of O'Brien's newspapers angrily declared. 'A door', Tim Healy observed 'must be either open or shut'.[15] The continuation of agrarian militancy after 1903 generated considerable disunity within the nationalist bloc; Catholic nationalist was set against Catholic nationalist—it was not simply or even, in many places, mainly the landlord stratum who felt the heat. There was nothing in this that could not have been anticipated, a significant degree of disunity had characterized all major Irish agrarian activity since at least 1879. But it was depressing for Redmond that it should occur after the passing of legislation which he had hoped would settle the Irish land question.

More importantly, perhaps, the Irish party was thus condemned to live by an increasingly visible 'double standard' on agrarian matters. To understand this fully, however, it is necessary to register a

[13] *Roscommon Herald*, 20 August 1910.
[14] *Cork Free Press*, 17 August 1910.
[15] Ibid.

weakness in the existing historiography. Much of the writing on Irish rural conflict presumes a strong communal discipline which isolates those who offend against popular values. The most serious and substantial study of the ranch war (1906–8) is an example of work in this tradition. David S. Jones has presented a suggestive picture in which the acquisition of the graziers brought them into conflict with peasant farmers; Jones stresses also the blatant snobbery and elitism of the graziers and their failure to bolster the welfare of the peasant community.[16] Jones explains: 'The failure of ranchers to enter into mutual aid schemes and co-operative arrangements stemmed partly from the prosaic fact that the grazier could do without the assistance of local peasants.'[17] During the ranch war the graziers paid the 'price of aloofness'[18] and revealed their 'inability to secure even a modest degree of popular acceptance for their self-enriching endeavours.'[19] Jones has correctly located the source of antagonism between the graziers and the ranch war activists, but it is clear that his account—as some scholars have suspected[20]—exaggerates the degree to which the graziers were isolated from the rest of the community. A remarkably high proportion of the principal leaders of the ranch war either were or became graziers or were intimately related to graziers—John Hayden, John Fitzgibbon and Patrick McKenna all belong in this category. Others were guilty of attempting to call off the struggle against the graziers when it affected the interests of friends, associates or potential supporters in internal UIL disputes—W. J. Duffy,[21] 'Farmer' Hogan and David Sheehy fell into this category. Even the paid organizers of the UIL, who were traditionally more radical than the elected politicians, harboured their black sheep—T. A. Morris, the enthusiastic western organizer was to be embarrassed by a cattle drive on his own farm.[22] Local officials revealed a similar weakness of the flesh before the royal commission on congestion. It is important

---

[16] David S. Jones, 'The Cleavage between Graziers and Peasants in the Land Struggle 1890–1910', in Samuel Clark and James S. Donnelly ed., *Irish Peasants: Violence and Political Unrest 1780–1914*, Madison and Manchester, 1983, 374–417.

[17] Jones, op. cit., 409.

[18] Ibid.

[19] Jones, op. cit., 413.

[20] For example, Clark and Donnelly in their stimulating essay, 'The Unreaped Harvest' in *Irish Peasants*, 431.

[21] *Connaught Champion*, 5 January 1910.

[22] *Mayo News*, 1 February and 9 May 1908. See also Denis Johnstone to John Dillon, 12 February 1907, TCD Dillon papers, 6763/16.

not to exaggerate the case. J. P. Farrell and Laurence Ginnell both suffered imprisonment for their opposition to the ranching system, neither appear to have had grazing interests—though Ginnell's cousins certainly did have such interests they were not exempt from the attentions of the campaign.[23] The eleven-months system was bitterly disputed by many peasants who gazed on untenanted lands with much resentment. Nevertheless, and precisely because it 'provided an avenue of upward social mobility',[24] ranching was more despised in rhetoric than in practice. It is clear too that the rhetoric of peasant community versus the greedy capitalist farmer was often exploited for factional and competitive objectives.[25]

The political consequences for the Irish party were clear enough. In the era of Parnell and the Land League struggle (1879–82) against 'alien' landlords, the exploitation of the land question had been an unambiguous boon for constitutional nationalism. In the era of William O'Brien and the United Irish League (1898–1903) divisions within the tenantry, visible even during the Land League, were much more sharply evident; by 1903 both Mayo and Tipperary had yielded firm proof—if the inconsistency of Michael Davitt is not proof enough—that the fight against the grazier could never generate the rich popular resonance of the fight against the landlord. After the Wyndham act of 1903, the likelihood of a *united* movement of the Irish farmers receded even further. Yet the Irish party continued to promote a left of centre agrarian radicalism, which none the less stopped short of a full blown 'Ginnellism'. The key figure here was John Fitzgibbon. The Castlerea merchant first came to prominence in the 1890s as a loyal Redmondite wrestling with the contradiction between Redmond's conservatism and an upsurge of agrarian activism in the west. Despite his heavy involvement in agrarian militancy—notably the 'battle' on the de Freyne estate—Fitzgibbon seems to have envisaged

---

[23] See Patrick Shea, *Voices and the Sound of Drums*, Belfast, 1981, 33–4. I am indebted to Patrick Shea for clarification of the reference to Ginnell's social position given in his remarkable autobiography. In a personal communication (8 July 1984) Patrick Shea writes that Ginnell was of 'farming stock . . . his family would scarcely come into the rancher category'. Patrick Shea describes Ginnell's imprisonment by his father, an RIC man, in his memoir; in later years, Shea became Ginnell's relative by marriage.

[24] Jones, op. cit., 417.

[25] On this whole topic, see David Fitzpatrick, 'Class, family and rural unrest in nineteenth century Ireland', in P. J. Drudy ed., *Ireland: Land, Politics and People*, Cambridge, 1982, 37–76; and the same author's 'Unrest in rural Ireland', *Irish Economic and Social History*, vol. XII (1985), 100–2.

as early as 1903 that he could be co-opted into the agrarian machinery of the state via the congested districts board. He was inclined to outbursts of optimism which made him much more malleable than other 'land war' leaders. Symptomatically, on 6 March 1904 Fitzgibbon told a Castlerea meeting that one of the estates commissioners, Frederick Wrench, had assured him that all the large farms in Roscommon were to be 'split up'. Wrench, the most conservative of the estates commissioners, quickly issued a statement to the effect that he had never even met John Fitzgibbon![26] Four years later this same naïve combination—a desire to become part of the state machinery and a facile over-optimism—were to prove invaluable to Redmond. He exploited Fitzgibbon's weak spots to gain legitimacy for his call for an end to the ranch war. Fitzgibbon, one of the principal cattle drivers, rapidly became one of the principal peacemakers in the countryside. By 1910 Fitzgibbon—'quite the statesman now'[27] as Birrell described him to Dillon—had been appointed to a paid membership of the congested board by the chief secretary. In consequence, Fitzgibbon was given to even more florid promises of the demise of ranching in Connaught; promises, the force of which were somewhat diminished by the revelation of his own ranching involvements in May 1912. It is clear that Birrell's willingness to legitimatize, in a sense, the activities of men like Fitzgibbon was of the greatest political importance. In the general election of December 1910, John Fitzgibbon (elected unopposed in South Mayo) helped a relatively obscure provincial journalist, William Dorris, to a crushing victory over the nationally renowned William O'Brien. In the campaign much emphasis was laid on Fitzgibbon's new found power and prestige, John O'Donnell, ex-MP, O'Brien's most important Mayo ally, added a sour comment on this policy of bribery:

Was not John Fitzgibbon, who was pitchforked into South Mayo, which he no more represents than if he were an Indian Maharajah or the Grand Lama of Tibet—was not he a member of the Congested Districts Board? Had he not patronage and posts at his disposal, and would he not use his great and influential position to get ranches compulsorily broken up and the uneconomic holdings enlarged. Well, we shall 'wait and see', but we are likely to wait for a long time before the people see.[28]

---

[26] *Irish Times*, 8 March 1904.
[27] Augustine Birrell to John Dillon, 31 January 1910, TCD Dillon papers, 679/171.
[28] *Connaught Champion*, 23 December 1910.

This is the rhetoric of a defeated politician—O'Brien's humiliation in Mayo where he had invested so much political capital was the decisive end to his challenge to the UIL leadership—but it does accurately convey the flavour of the UIL campaign. The implication of this comment is evident: not only was the UIL infuriating those who had opposed the cattle drivers, it was raising unrealistic expectations amongst the rural poor. In particular, the Irish party had allowed the landless men to establish a moral claim on the nationalist leadership which was to survive until the mid-1940s—when the Fianna Fail Government under the direction of Sean Lemass and Sean Moylan finally announced it would no nothing more for this troublesome grouping, and thus extinguished the 'insidious assumption that every Irishman had a right to land'.[29]

This permits a general conclusion about the collapse of the Irish party. J. C. Beckett has argued of Redmond that 'during his long attendance at Westminster he had lost touch with the people in whose name he spoke, and he hardly understood the new forces at work in Irish politics'.[30] In a like-minded analysis, Tom Garvin argues that the Redmondite party became increasingly involved in imperial politics and thus increasingly out of touch with people at home.[31] This point is linked to the claim that even before 1914 other groups were able to outflank it on the issue of agrarian radicalism. This argument is difficult to sustain on electoral or any other evidence. Far from being cut off from the people, the Irish party echoed their concerns all too accurately.

There is another not dissimilar interpretation of the Irish party's fortunes. It was first advanced by William O'Brien in his frequently reiterated opposition of a 'sound people' and a 'repressive machine'.[32] Yet the striking feature of the Irish party's machine is its relative weakness. Healyites and O'Brienites were able to inflict several blows on it. As the secular and liberal *National Democrat* put it after the triumph of Healyite J. R. Lardner, MP in Monaghan, in 1907: 'A simple parish priest and a country solicitor have overthrown the whole force of the Irish party'.[33] In January 1910 O'Brienites performed very

---

[29] See Paul Bew and Henry Patterson, *Sean Lemass and the Making of Modern Ireland*, Dublin, 1982, 21–9, and David Fitzpatrick, 'Class family and rural unrest', 63.

[30] J. C. Beckett, *The Making of Modern Ireland 1603–1923*, London, 1966, 420.

[31] Garvin, *Evolution*, 89.

[32] William O'Brien to Lord Dunraven, 23 July 1904, NLI MS 8554.

[33] *National Democrat*, 17 July 1907.

creditably against the official candidates. It is also noticeable that those who enforced the party's line, for example, Hugh Martin's Belfast AOH toughs–who assaulted Anna Parnell and the Sinn Feiners in Leitrim in 1908; silenced the O'Brienites at the baton convention of 1909 and finally were defeated by Sinn Fein in 1917 in South Longford[34]–were not under the direct control of the Redmond leadership and had their own priorities (the settling of scores in Ulster) which the party as a whole had little interest in catering for. The same point applies to their 'Baton' convention allies, the cattle drivers; they might turn the O'Brienites into 'honorary ranchers' for the day at the baton convention but they were never within sight of committing the Irish party to their perspective. The physical repression of conciliatory opinion was an outlet for the emotions of frustrated zealots; it was not an example of the smooth functioning of a well-organized party apparatus. Rather than viewing the party as a bureaucratic straitjacket enclosing the basically 'sound' body of mass opinion it seems more reasonable to see the party as shot through by the same ambiguities and complexities which afflicted the people. In retrospect, the Irish party's principal failure appears to have been in the field of political education. The abolition of the ranches was always just around the corner. Even more improbably, the Ulster question would be comprehensively settled at regular intervals by some speech or article of Redmond's. Nationalists were in general remarkably slow to see that in the Home Rule crisis of 1912-1914 the Ulster Unionists were not bluffing in their threat of armed resistance to Home Rule.[35]

For some years this policy of eternal optimism was reasonably successful in maintaining the Irish party's electoral hegemony. The land question might remain unresolved as Birrell's unsuccessful attempt to introduce new legislation in 1913 revealed. The Ulster Unionists might continue to threaten civil war in the event of Home Rule. Nevertheless, on the outbreak of the First World War, Home Rule was at least placed on the statute book with an amending bill which implicitly pointed towards some kind of partition settlement.

---

[34] *The Harp*, 5 May 1917.

[35] Notably Redmond's article in the *Reynolds News*, 12 January 1911, which was widely declared on the nationalist side to have resolved the Ulster question. For some of the earliest notes of alarm see the article by 'C' in the *Leader*, 8 November 1913. But in the same journal, later that month (23 November 1913) Carson's squads are dismissed as 'neglible quantities' . . . 'which probably create more derision and laughter amongst the Orangemen, than they do fear amongst us.'

Above all, the Irish party continued to win elections; when E. J. Grahame defeated the official party nominee in King's County in December 1914 he was careful to lay emphasis on his complete loyalty to Redmond.[36] On the eve of the Easter Rising of 1916 the Irish party easily crushed a challenge from 'dreamers' and 'ultra nationalists' in a North Louth by-election.[37] Within a few weeks, other 'dreamers' and 'ultra nationalists' launched the rising in Dublin–with remarkable speed the rising and the execution of its principal leaders gave legitimacy to a new challenge to the Irish party. In late 1914, a prominent UIL leader, Thomas Halligan, chairman of the Meath county council, ridiculed Sinn Feiners for having never risked 'a night's sleep'[38] for Ireland; after 1916 such jeers were stillborn. In the first by-election (Cork West) in nationalist Ireland after the rising the Irish party candidate, Daniel L. O'Leary, was indeed the victor, but this can hardly be interpreted as a late example of the 'smooth'[39] working of the party machine, still less the continued political appeal of Home Rule.[40] Daniel O'Leary's most important clerical supporter, Father McCarthy, declared roundly that he 'had as much sympathy with Sinn Feinism as anyone'.[41] The party's main opponent, Frank Healy, was castigated not for his Sinn Fein links but for being a 'false' Sinn Feiner, whilst his association with William O'Brien, on the other hand, was the subject of caustic comment–Father McCarthy noting at a Ballinaskagh meeting that William O'Brien had sought recruits for the British army in Cork, at least a week before John Redmond asked for one. Such an ultra-nationalist rhetoric must have deprived John Redmond of any comfort he might otherwise have derived from a UIL victory. The rapid change in political temperature is undeniable. The Irish party for so long the undisputed embodiment of nationalist aspirations was soon to be replaced by Sinn Fein, the umbrella organization of those forces which made or subsequently supported the Rising. Yet many observers expected or hoped that the Sinn Fein movement would be repelled by an increasingly conservative and satiated countryside–as so many urban romantic, republican movements (tinged with social radicalism) had been repelled in nineteenth-

[36] *Irish Independent*, 10 November 1914, also 10 December 1914; *National Volunteer*, 23 January 1915; *Midland Tribune*, 23 January 1915.
[37] *Drogheda Independent*, 4 March 1916.
[38] *Weekly Freeman's Journal*, 28 November 1914.
[39] As in Lee, *Modernisation*, 160.
[40] Robert Kee, *The Green Flag: Ourselves Alone*, vol. 3, London, 1982, 17.
[41] *Cork Examiner*, 8 November 1916.

century Europe. This is the site of a most interesting problem. Why did the Irish party's many victories on the land issue, which had helped to establish a nationalist peasant proprietorship, not stand more to its credit in the difficult days of 1917 and 1918? As A. C. Hepburn has noted of explanations of the Irish party's collapse:

The 'chain of causation' goes unquestioned: the frustration stirred by the third home rule bill crisis caused the 1916 Rising, which in turn re-aroused the patriotic fervour of the Irish people, who did not rest until the British government was driven from Ireland. A slightly more sophisticated version of this theory sees the above developments as having been 'forced' in the hot-house conditions of war. Indeed, much of this argument is irrefutable. But it does not explain why a nation of peasant farmers acted out the dream of Patrick Pearse . . .[42]

In February and May 1917, the UIL suffered, in North Roscommon and South Longford respectively, major electoral defeats in rural nationalist heartlands, defeats which were the harbingers of its total eclipse. How is this to be explained? British agrarian policy in war time Ireland was particularly vulnerable; officially, state policy favoured tillage within an effort to increase self-sufficiency. Redmondite loyalists tended to see this as a vindication of the party line, but to most nationalists the agencies of the state seemed to be unenthusiastic.[44] The stringencies of war-time finances appeared to involve a slowing down of the work of land purchase and redistribution, the congested districts board, for example, announced an end to the work of compulsory purchase. At other times–or so it seemed to nationalists–it was hinted that peasants who wanted some land from say, the estates commissioners, ought best to prove their fitness by joining up.[45] Even before the Easter Rising, the Irish party had to spend an increasing amount of time apologizing for its failure to settle finally the land question.[46]

Significantly, the party did everthing possible in 1917 to stress its

[42] *Liberal policies*, 825.
[43] See David Sheehy's address to the Meath UIL executive, *Meath Herald*, 2 Janaury 1917.
[44] *Connaught Telegraph*, 9 March 1915; *Nationality*, 20 April 1918; *Sligo Champion*, 6 February 1915; *Roscommon Herald*, 16 March 1918; *Freeman's Journal*, 20 February 1917.
[45] *Honesty*, 23 October 1915. Despite his formal opposition, William O'Malley MP admitted the strength of the government case. *Glancing Back*, London, 1933, 129.
[46] See, notably, John Dillon's speech at Thurles in August 1915. *Irish Weekly Independent*, 7 August 1915. 'One of the most difficult things Ireland had to suffer owing to the war was the postponement of the final settlement of the land question.'

record of achievement on the land issue, but found that it was no longer a vital resource of strength. Acknowledging the party's apparent agrarian radicalism, the pro-Sinn Fein journal *New Ireland* none the less felt that it missed the point: the key issue in early 1917 was Ireland's right to nationhood.[47] The evidence suggests that having outflanked the party on this issue, Sinn Fein was able to outflank the party on the agrarian left, but perhaps more suggestively also on the right. Sinn Fein's key organizer in North Roscommon, Father Michael O'Flanagan, had achieved prominence in 1915 as the eulogist at the funeral of the Fenian O'Donovan Rossa; but also, and equally significantly, as an agrarian radical critic of the sluggishness and ineffectiveness of the Congested Districts Board,[48] the very agency which one of its nationalist members, John Fitzgibbon, had argued would have completed its work of land redistribution by 1915.[49] While fighting North Roscommon, O'Flanagan was full of sympathy for the land hungry and the cattle drivers,[50] and few could deny his credentials—first established in a bitter public conflict in Sligo in October 1915 with T. W. Russell, still vice-president of the department of agriculture. But in South Longford, three months later, it was the UIL, with J. P. Farrell again to the fore, which proclaimed most openly its anti-ranching intentions, while the principal grazing interest in the area, the McCanns, with delicious irony, helped the Sinn Fein candidate defeat their erstwhile cattle driving antagonist of 1907, Patrick McKenna, who stood in the UIL interest.[51] It is no surprise to find the police noting a year later that the anti-ranching agitation had not 'caught on' in Longford.[52]

Sinn Fein, in other words, played both cards. In Clare, Sinn Fein made a calculated decision to initiate a cattle driving campaign;[53] in

---

[47] *New Ireland*, 10 February 1917. For evidence of the party's attacks on the rancher at this point, see *Roscommon Messenger*, 9 January 1917; 23 January 1917.

[48] *The Leader*, 21 November 1915.

[49] *Roscommon Messenger*, 9 and 16 April 1910.

[50] See O'Flanagan's interview with Keven O'Shiel reprinted in *New Ireland*, 10 February 1917. This should be complemented by O'Shiel's later assessment of O'Flanagan, *Irish Times*, 23 November 1966. The earlier piece stresses O'Flanagan's radicalism, the later article stresses his (post-1918) 'responsibility'. For further information on O'Flanagan's career, see the priest's own account in *Westmeath Independent*, 19 January 1918; *Sligo Champion*, 16 October 1915, 28 June 1918; *Nationality*, 24 March 1915.

[51] *Longford Leader*, 12 May 1917.

[52] PRO CO 903/19, 5.

[53] David Fitzpatrick, *Politics and Irish Life*, 156; see also M. Brennan's memoir, *The War in Clare 1911–21*, Dublin, 1980, 33.

Cork, on the other hand, O'Brienites, traditionally opponents of cattle driving, flooded into the ranks of the new anti-party nationalist movement.[54] The counties where turbulent agrarianism was a key issue in 1917-18 are easily identified. In Munster, they were Clare, Kerry and Tipperary (North Riding). In Leinster, they were King's County, Queen's County and Meath. In Connaught, traditionally the most difficult province, they were Mayo, Roscommon, Galway and Sligo. It appears from this list, that in many areas of the country Sinn Fein exploited rural radicalism to its own advantage, but it is also clear that in the majority of the counties of nationalist Ireland agrarian militancy was at a low ebb—after all Irish agrarian offences in 1917-18 numbered a mere 519 against 948 in 1907-8—and that this did not stop a strong commitment to Sinn Fein. It is evident that Sinn Fein's political success was a truly national phenomenon, while its cattle drive campaign was merely a regional one;[55] nor need this be surprising, many currents flowed into Sinn Fein. The UIL's evasive policy had created diverse sources of discontent—even if such irritations were subdued, though often with some difficulty, while the party retained its nationalist legitimacy and its organizational control. The party had all along maintained an ambiguous relationship with cattle driving and other forms of peasant self-help. They had exploited it at certain points and condemned it at others. They were in no position to complain when Sinn Fein—sanctioned by the 'blood sacrifice'—took over grass roots agrarian radicalism and turned it against its original progenitor, but nor could they complain, when those who had always opposed cattle driving joined the ranks of the new movement. According to Laurence Ginnell, the only Irish MP to join Sinn Fein, John Redmond was reduced to describing the Irish farmers as 'the most ungrateful sort of people in Europe'.[56]

Nevertheless, an attempt of sorts was made to work a red scare against Sinn Fein. Some supporters of the Irish party argued that 'the small farmers who give their support to the new movement are encouraging a dangerous system and one that might possibly later on react against themselves'. Every effort was made to stir up the spectre of communism, or at least land nationalization. The late P. A. MacHugh's newspaper *The Sligo Champion* analysed Sinn Fein's agrarian activism thus:

[54] Brendan MacGiolla Choille, *Intelligence Notes, 1913—16*, Dublin, 1966, 147.
[55] For this information see PRO CO 904/JCA 13425; PRO CO 903/19, 1–45.
[56] See Laurence Ginnell's Sinn Fein pamphlet, *The Land Question*, Dublin, 1917, 8.

A reign of terror similar to that of the Bolshevisks was inaugurated in some districts. The right to private property was ignored. Lands were taken over by force without previous agreement as to an equitable price ... There was no recognised principle in accordance with which it could be known in advance what lands were in danger and what lands were immune. Everything was left to the honesty, prejudice or greed of the members of the local committees ... Nearly every town in Ireland has its Trotzky if only suitable opportunity came.[57]

There is some evidence that such attacks led to some tactical readjustment by Sinn Fein. Moves were made to cool the ardour of the land hungry; T. V. Honan, President of the East Clare Sinn Fein Committee, warned against an obsession with the land question.[58] This new line was implemented with reasonable success. Local Sinn Fein branches condemned 'uncontrolled commandeering of land'[59] while attempting to ensure a more orderly land agitation was maintained.[60]

But beyond forcing the occasional tactical adjustment there is little evidence that the Irish party's critique of Sinn Fein's agrarian policies had any real effect. Such a critique was always compromised by two factors. In the first instance, there were inevitably some party supporters–especially in the west–who none the less sympathized with Sinn Fein cattle drivers. The *Ballina Herald* editorialized revealingly: 'We observe ... that the North Mayo Sinn Fein executive are moving in the matter of getting the land distributed. We differ on many points from Sinn Fein but on this matter of distributing the land amongst the uneconomic holders we are cordially with them.'[61] In the second instance, there were plenty of former O'Brienites around, who having transferred their allegiance to Sinn Fein, were still capable of reminding Dillon of his own dubious agrarian record. The *Westmeath Independent*, for example, agreed with John Dillon's charges against Sinn Fein that, mixed up with legitimate agrarian activism, there were 'excesses'. But, recalling Dillon's 'opposition' to the Wyndham land act and the O'Brienite policy of conciliation–'which would have transferred the land of Ireland to the people of Ireland, including the grass ranches long before now, if it had been given the opportunity to work'–it turned sharply against Dillon: 'It is insulting to hear Mr

[57] *Sligo Champion*, 2 March 1918.
[58] *Saturday Record* (Clare), 16 March 1918.
[59] *Midland Reporter*, 16 March 1918; *Western People*, 9 March 1918.
[60] Ibid.
[61] *Ballina Herald*, 4 March 1918.

Dillon and the press behind him, challenge Sinn Fein about this happening or the other, and endeavour to hold the real national movement responsible for the legacy of trouble of which he had so principal a share in committing to the farming classes in Ireland through the smashing up of the Wyndham land act.'[62] Yet the main reason why a 'red' scare failed to work against Sinn Fein was probably a simple one. Even its constitutionalist opponents did not really believe its agrarian radicalism represented anything fundamentally new or disturbing; after all, even in 1918 Arthur Griffith's *Nationality* was slightly to the right of ex-Irish party MP Laurence Ginnell on the issue of land redistribution.[63] Anyway as Griffith had always insisted: 'The man who declared he wanted national freedom in order to promote social reform did not understand the meaning of the nation.'[64] Indeed, the most provocative of Irish agricultural historians, Raymond Crotty, has suggested that since 1906 there had been growing disenchantment in rural bourgeois circles in Ireland with 'the increasingly radical United Kingdom'; with the threat of conscription of their sons on the agenda, in 1917 this disenchantment turned to pro-Sinn Fein feeling.[65] The *County Cork Eagle*, which remained loyal to the party, was contemptuous of Sinn Fein's agrarian radical credentials: 'You can see there is no general inclination by the Sinn Feiners to share their farms with their landless neighbours; nothing of the sort!'[66] In East Galway, the police reported an ancient vice: land seized ostensibly for tillage was in fact used for grazing.[67]

Just as the Irish party leaders in 1917-18 denounced Sinn Fein's lack of realism on agrarian matters so they denounced its coercive–if typically inconsistent–rhetoric on the Ulster question. Here again the party's previous line on this issue made it difficult to do this effectively. On Ulster as on the land question, Sinn Fein could afford to be both more 'extreme' and more 'moderate' than the party. The militancy came from Sinn Fein President, Eamon de Valera, who apparently felt a mild contempt for northern nationalists who had been relatively slow to rally to the Sinn Fein cause: 'the melt had been

[62] *Westmeath Independent*, 20 March 1918.
[63] Charles Russell, *Sinn Fein and Socialism*, 1919 (Cork Workers Club Historical Reprints no. 19), 31.
[64] *Sinn Fein*, 26 April 1913.
[65] R. Crotty, 'The Irish Land Question' in the *Tablet*, 7 November 1981, 1089; cf. also Garvin, *Evolution*, 212.
[66] *Co. Cork Eagle*, 9 March 1918.
[67] For East Galway, see PRO CO 903/19/12.

broken in these people',[68] he declared at Elphin. Shortly after his personal triumph in the East Clare by-election of June 1917, de Valera observed in Dublin: 'All the papers shouted out that Sinn Fein wanted to coerce Ulster. He did not believe in mincing matters, and would say that if Ulster stood in the way of obtaining Irish freedom, Ulster should be coerced (cheeers). Why should it not?'[69] The next day, de Valera gave an interview to Louis J. M'Quilland, special correspondent of the London *Daily Express*. M'Quilland raised the issue of the coercion of Ulster, but de Valera refused to be moved: 'I regard the Ulster Unionist as my brother, and if my brother stepped in the way of Ireland's freedom I would endeavour to sweep him from the path.'[70] In early September at Cootehill, County Cavan, he went even further: 'We say to these planters ... if you continue to be a garrison for the enemy ... We will have to kick you out.'[71] In the same month, Arthur Griffith in a Belfast speech gave the Orangemen some six months to change allegiance, otherwise Sinn Fein would deal with them. Griffith and de Valera seemed to be taking an equally demagogic line, and there seems to be no ground for the belief of some contemporaries that de Valera was in some way more moderate on Ulster than Griffith.[72] The real difference of emphasis was with Sinn Fein Vice-President, Father Michael O'Flanagan. In June 1916 Father O'Flanagan had declared:

If we reject Home Rule rather than agree to the exclusion of the Unionist party of Ulster, what case have we to put before the world? We can point out that Ireland is an island with a definite boundary ... National and geographic boundaries hardly ever coincide ... if a man were to try and construct a political map of Europe out of its physical map he would find himself groping in the dark. Geography has worked hard to make one nation of Ireland; history has worked against it. The island of Ireland and the national unit of Ireland simply do not coincide.[73]

The following month, the pro-Sinn Fein, *Irish Opinion* published the views of 'RJS' who argued, from a pro-Sinn Fein stance, that the Irish party had failed to grasp the 'true inwardness of Ulster Unionism'. He stated bluntly: 'If Irish unity is to be a new experiment and not a

  68 *Roscommon Herald*, 6 February 1918.
  69 *Weekly Irish Times*, 7 July 1912.
  70 *Weekly Freeman*, 21 July 1917.
  71 Ibid., 28 September 1917.
  72 J. Bowman, *De Valera and the Ulster Question 1917–73*, Oxford, 1982, 334.
  73 *Freeman's Journal*, 19 June 1916.

historical restoration, it ought to be asked humbly as a favour and not demanded proudly as a right.'[74] In September of the same year O'Flanagan argued: 'I agree that the "homogeneous Ulster" of the Unionist publicists is a sham and a delusion. But if there be no homogeneous Ulster, how can there be a homogeneous Ireland? A more acccurate description of Ireland for the past two hundred years would be an economic and social duality.'[75] A year later, in early September 1917, O'Flanagan gave a further exposition of his views. This was of particular significance because his earlier statement of 1916 on the Ulster issue, pre-dated his emergence to a position of national importance in 1917. But in the course of a lecture entitled 'Orange and Green' at Town Hall, Omagh, in one of the heartlands of anti-partitionist sentiment, O'Flanagan showed that he had lost none of the old heterodoxy. Indeed, his speech may well have been perceived as a veiled comment on de Valera's aggressive stance. Following a rather unconvincing attempt to distance himself from O'Brien's doctrine of conciliation, O'Flanagan came to the nub of the matter using the analogy of Ireland under the Union:

Now, is there any other method we could try on the Orangemen? I confess I don't like the word coercion, whether it be applied in Ireland or in Belgium or in any other part of the world. Forty million of (British) people have tried to coerce four millions, and they have failed. The relative proportion of the forces was ten to one, and the ten failed to coerce one—so, also I believe that if three million tried to coerce one million they would fail, too. Therefore I can see no hope of solution in coercion. You might try to get along for a time, as England under the Union struggled to get along, but in the end, if the process was coercion, it would fail; and I for one hope to God that it would. (Applause)[76]

Sinn Fein's line on Ulster was therefore wildly inconsistent. (The militant line rather than the moderate appealed to most of the movement's supporters—the editor of *Irish Opinion* was swamped by letters bitterly critical of 'RJS'.) The Irish party sharply attacked both de Valera's aggression—'God help the Orangemen of Ulster if de Valera and Griffith come to deal with them',[77] Dillon commented

[74] *Irish Opinion*, 15 July 1916.
[75] *The Leader*, 2 September 1916, for a discussion of Michael O'Flanagan in the context of recent developments within Irish nationalism, see Paul Bew and Henry Patterson, *The British State and the Ulster Crisis*, London, 1985, 128–9.
[76] *Fermanagh Herald*, 8 September 1917.
[77] *Weekly Freeman*, 28 September 1917.

sarcastically—and O'Flanagan's 'partitionism', but few were impressed. Having avoided the complexity of the Ulster question for so long it was almost impossible in the emotional years of 1917–18 for the constitutional nationalists to give the Irish electorate a lucid education on the subject.

For this reason alone, William O'Brien's reputation deserves some re-evaluation. When Birrell had offered devolution in 1907 William O'Brien had been alone in arguing that it should be accepted, despite the exceptionally limited powers offered, because it provided a thirty-two county framework for co-operation with the Unionists. O'Brien, as he was frankly told by the sympathetic independent Orange leader, Lindsay Crawford, did 'not fully comprehend . . . the difficulties of the Ulster position'.[78] It is clear that he under-estimated the depth of Unionist opposition to Home Rule-which was solidly based on the uneven development of Irish capitalism and the ideology of two Irish nations[79]—however generous the nationalist formulation. But it should not be forgotten by those who see him from a nationalist point of view solely as a misguided idealist,[80] that his policies were designed—by showing ample evidence of nationalist good faith towards the Protestant community—to create the conditions in which British intervention against the most unbending of the Unionists, if necessary, might be effectively attempted.[81] Nor should it be forgotten that the policies which were actually followed led to a bitter confronta-tion in the 1916–21 period in which northern Catholics and national-ists were the principal losers.[82] O'Brien's positive schemes for Irish unity and reconciliation may have had little substantial basis,[83] but this negative critique, from an intelligent pro-Home Rule position, revealed much about the pitfalls of UIL strategy. As the *Irish People* put it in 1905: 'The essential mistake of Mr Redmond or rather of those who dictate his policy, is in thinking that in the present posture

    [78] Lindsay Crawford to William O'Brien, 5 March 1909, University College Cork, O'Brien MS AR 34.
    [79] See on this point, Paul Bew and Henry Patterson, 'The Protestant–Catholic conflict in Ulster', *Journal of International Affairs*, vol. 36, no. 2, Fall/Winter 1982/3, 225.
    [80] As, for example, in Joseph V. O'Brien, *William O'Brien*, 246–7.
    [81] Sheehan, *Ireland since Parnell*, 248–9, Wells, *Redmond*, 114.
    [82] This may be the reason why, as Eamon Phoenix points out, Cahir Healy, the most formidable northern nationalist of the post-partition generation, retained such admiration for O'Brien's strategy. *Irish Times*, 9 June 1982.
    [83] Revealingly, the *Morning Post*'s Irish correspondent noted that Ulster Unionists saw O'Brien as a 'force of good' but could not accept an Irish parliament on any terms. Quoted in *Connaught Champion*, 23 December 1910.

of affairs, Home Rule is to be secured by parliamentary intrigues and rows. A united party of power, strength and independence is an important factor but is not the only one.'[84] Against this narrow parliamentary conception of politics, the O'Brienites at least had had the courage to face the brutal reality (and political significance) of secretarian division in Irish society.

The consequences of the Irish party's failure is evident. Despite 'the virtual solution of the land question by Wyndham's Act in 1903',[85] as one authority has perhaps slightly overstated it, there was no wider Catholic–Protestant *rapprochement*. The Parnell tradition was appropriated by those who identified with its intransigent nationalist elements but who had at the same time little understanding of the 'conciliatory' strand in his politics designed to minimize internal Irish conflicts: as Charles Townshend has put it, 'Thus a figure like Parnell was brought and kept within the nationalist pantheon by the device of commemorating a few suitably extreme (if unusual) phrases, especially those from his final embattled year, while quietly burying the inconvenient bulk of his aristocratic-conservative nationalism.'[86] This point may be illustrated most concisely by reference to the fate of Parnell's most famous speech, the words of which are engraved on his statue in Dublin. In January 1885 in a Cork speech, Parnell had declared: 'no man has a right to fix the boundary to the march of a nation. No man has a right to say his country, "Thus far shalt thou go and no further", and we have never attempted to fix the *ne plus ultra* to the progress of Ireland's nationhood and we never shall.'[87]

In the period covered in this study, two competing interpretations— one conciliatory, the other militant—fought out a battle for supremacy in Irish politics. At its high point, the conciliatory principle was embodied in William O'Brien All-for-Ireland League and it was one of O'Brien's MPs, M. J. Nagle who gave the most characteristic analysis of Parnell's words in a speech at Clonakilty, Co. Cork:

He had more experience of the English people than the average Irish member of Parliament, and he would say that the only hope for Home Rule coming speedily was to have a union of all classes and creeds in Ireland (loud

---

[84] *Irish People*, 28 October 1905.
[85] P. N. S. Mansergh, *The Irish Question 1890–1921*, London, 1965, 103.
[86] 'Modernisation and Nationalism: Perspectives in Recent Irish History', *History*, vol. 66, June 1981, 234.
[87] Lyons, *Parnell*, 260–1.

applause) ... The moment they satisfied the English people that they (the Catholics) were prepared to receive with open arms their Protestant fellow countrymen everything they demanded would be granted. Amen (applause). God grant the day was not far off when all creeds and classes could stand on the common platform; when they would see realised and materialised Parnell's great saying—'Who can place a boundary to a nation's forward march?'.[88]

Against this, has to be set the arguments of Eamon de Valera over seven years later: 'Remember Parnell said "No settlement shall be final. No man has a right to set a boundary to the onward march of a nation." (Loud and continued cheering). More than that. In America Parnell declared his aim was to break the last link that bound Ireland to England (cheers). If similar circumstances had prevailed in Parnell's day as do today, Parnell would use our methods (cheers).'[89] By the time de Valera had uttered these words there could be no doubt which assessment of the Parnell tradition and therefore of modern Irish nationalism had won out. Two generations were to pass before mainstream Irish nationalism was again to show signs of grasping the importance of Parnell's advocacy of the principle of conciliation,[90] even then it was often to be combined with the arguably less sophisticated assumption that it was the duty of the British state to manufacture Irish Unionist consent to the arrangements for a 'new Ireland'.

[88] *Cork Free Press*, 16 June 1910.
[89] *Southern Democrat*, 4 January 1918.
[90] Paul Bew and Henry Patterson, *The British State and the Ulster Crisis*, London, 1985, 128. See also, Barry White, *John Hume: Statesman of the Troubles*, Belfast, 1984, 282, for further explicit contemporary utilization of these Parnellite themes.

Bibliography

PARLIAMENTARY PAPERS: OFFICIAL PUBLICATIONS

Royal Commissions

Royal Commission appointed to inquire into the Estates of Evicted Tenants in Ireland, the proposals for reinstating them etc. (Cd. 6935), HC 1893–4, xxxi.
This commission is cited as the Evicted Tenants' Commission.

Royal Commission on the Procedure and Practice and Methods of Valuation followed by the Land Commission, the Land Judges Court and the Civil Bill Courts in Ireland, under the Land Acts and the Land Purchase Acts, Minutes of evidence (Cd. 8859), HC 1898, xxv.
This commission is cited as the Fry Commission.

Royal Commission on Congestion in Ireland, Minutes of evidence, and appendices and Documents relating thereto.

Volume 1 (Cd. 3267), HC 1906, xxii.

Volume 2 (Cd. 3319), HC 1907, xxxv.

Volume 3 (Cd. 3414), HC 1907, xxv.

Volume 4 (Cd. 3509), HC 1907, xxxvi.

Volume 5 (Cd. 3630), HC 1907, xxxvi.

Volume 6 (Cd. 3748), HC 1908), xxxix.

Volume 7 (Cd. 3784), HC 1908, xl.

Volume 8 (Cd. 3839). HC 1908, xli.

Volume 9 (Cd. 3845), HC 1908, xli.

Volume 10 (Cd. 4007), HC 1908, xlii.

Volume 11 (Cd. 4089), HC 1908, xlii.

Final Report (Cd. 4079), HC 1908, xlii.

Parliamentary Select Committee

Report from the Select Committee on Land Acts (Ireland), together with the proceedings of the Committee, Minutes of evidence, Appendix and Index, HC, 1894 (310), xiii.
This Committee is cited as the Morley Committee.

Other Reports

Report by Mr W. F. Bailey, Legal Assistant Commissioner, of an Inquiry into the Present Condition of Tenant Purchasers under the Land Purchase Act, HC 1903 (92), lvii.

Special Report of the County Inspector RIC, Galway East Riding, as to the State of the Riding in the Month of October, 1907 (Cd. 3949), HC 1908, cxi.

Report of the Estates commissioners for the year ending 31 March 1908 and for the period from 1 November 1903 to 31 March 1908; with appendices (Cd. 4277), HC 1908, xxiii.

Parliamentary Returns
Census of Ireland 1901, HC 1902 (Cd. 1190), cxxix.

Return of Untenanted Lands in Rural Districts, distinguishing demesnes in which there is a mansion, showing: Rural District and Electoral Divisions; Townland; Area in Statute Areas; Valuation (Poor Law); Names of Occupiers as in Valuation Lists, HC 1906 (250 c.

Return of the Number of Cases of Boycotting and of Persons Boycotted in Ireland on certain dates in the years 1902 to 1908, HC 1908 (89) xc.

Return by Counties and Quarterly Periods of the Number of Cattle Drives reported by the Royal Irish Constabulary to have taken place in Ireland from 1 Janaury 1907 to 30 September 1908, HC 1908 (310), xc.

Return giving, by counties and provinces, the area, the Poor Law Valuation and purchase-money of lands sold, and lands in respect of which proceedings have been instituted and are pending for sale under the Irish land purchase acts, also the estimated area, Poor Law Valuation, and purchase money of lands in respect of which proceedings for sale have not been instituted under the said acts (Cd. 4412), HC 1908, xc.

Return of the Number of Cases of Boycotting and of Persons Boycotted in each County in Ireland on certain dates in the years 1905 and 1909, HC 1909 (57), lxxiii.

Classified Return of Agrarian Outrages of an Indictable Character reported throughout Ireland in 1906, 1907, 1908, 1909, HC 1909 (70) lxxiii. Agricultural Statistics of Ireland, HC 1910 (Cd. 3964). Return showing the Names of the Judicial and other Commissioners, of the Legal and Lay Assistant Commissioners in connection with the Irish Land Commission holding office on 1 January 1912, HC 1912–13 (33) ci. Agricultural Statistics of Ireland, HC 1913 (Cd. 6987), lxxvii.

Census Returns
Census of Ireland 1901 Part II, General Report.

Irish Official Sources

Agricultural Statistics of Ireland 1847–1926 (Department of Industry and Commerce). Stationery Office: Dublin, 1928.

NEWSPAPERS AND JOURNALS

Miscellaneous

An Phoblacht (Dublin)
Bottom Dog (Dublin)
Daily Express (Dublin)
Evening Mail (Dublin)
Factionist (Dublin)
Felon Setter (Dublin)
Freeman's Journal (Dublin)
Gaelic American (New York)
Harp (Dublin)
Hibernian (Dublin)
Honesty (Dublin)
Irish Catholic (Dublin)
Irish Farmers' Gazette (Dublin)
Irish Independent (Dublin)
Irish Opinion (Dublin)
Irish People (Dublin)
Irish Times (Dublin)
Irish War News (Dublin)
Irish World (New York)

Justice (Dublin)
Leader (Dublin)
Melbourne Advocate
Morning Post (London)
National Volunteer (Dublin)
Nationist (Dublin)
New Ireland (Dublin)
New Way (Dublin)
New York Times (New York)
Parnellite (Dublin)
Peasant and Irish Irelander (Dublin)
Pall Mall Gazette (London)
Phoenix (Dublin)
Sinn Fein (Dublin)
Spectator (London)
Times (London)
United Irishman (Dublin)
Workers' Republic (Dublin)

Provincial Papers (cited by initials after first occasion)

Anglo-Celt
Ballina Herald
Ballinrobe Chronicle
Ballymoney Free Press
Carlow Sentinel
Clare Champion
Connaught Champion
Connaught/Leader and/Loughrea Nationalist
Connaught Telegraph
Connaught Tribune
Cork Eagle
Cork Examiner
Cork Free Press

Cork Herald
Donegal Vindicator
Drogheda Independent
Dundalk Democrat
Fermanagh Herald
Free Press (Wexford)
Galway Express
Galway Vindicator
Kerry People
Kerry Sentinel
Killarney Echo
Kilkenny Journal
Kilkenny Moderator
Leitrim Advocate

226   *Bibliography*

Limerick Leader
Longford Leader
Mayo News
Midland Reporter
Midland Tribune
Munster Express
Nationalist and Leinster Times
Nenagh Guardian
New Ross Standard
Northern Standard
Northern Whig
Roscommon Herald

Roscommon Journal
Roscommon Messenger
Saturday Record (Ennis)
Sligo Champion
Southern Democrat
Tuam Herald
Waterford News
Western News
Westmeath Examiner
Westmeath Independent
Wexford Constitution
Wexford People

SELECT DOCUMENTS

Baylen, J. O., ed., 'What Mr. Redmond Thought. An unpublished interview with John Redmond', December 1906. *Irish Historical Studies*, Vol. 19, 1974–5.
Hepburn, A. C., ed., *The Conflict of Nationality in Modern Ireland*, London, 1980.
MacGiolla, Choille B., ed., *Intelligence Notes*, Dublin, 1916.
MacMinn, J. R. B., ed., *Against the Tide: A Calendar of the Papers of J. B. Armour, Irish Presbyterian Minister and Home Ruler, 1869–1914*, Belfast, 1985.
O'Riordan, M., ed., *Frederick Ryan: Sinn Fein and Reaction*, Dublin, 1984.

CONTEMPORARY WORKS

Barker, Ernest, *Ireland in the Last Fifty Years*, Oxford, 1917.
Barlow, Jane, *Irish Ways*, London, 1911.
Birrell, A., *Things Past Redress*, London, 1937.
Bodkin, M. M., *Recollections of an Irish Judge*, London, 1914.
Bonn, Mortiz, *Modern Ireland and her Agrarian Problem*, Dublin, 1906.
Brennan, Michael, *The War in Clare 1911–21* (Dublin, 1980).
Bulfin, William, *Rambles in Eirinn*, Dublin, 1927.
Connolly, J., *The Workers' Republic*, Dublin, 1951.
Curran, John Ayde, *Reminiscences*, London, 1915.
Davitt, Michael, *The Fall of Feudalism in Ireland or the Story of the Land League Revolution*, London and New York, 1904.
Dunraven, Earl of, *Past Times and Past Times*, vol. ii, London, 1922.
Dunraven, Earl of, *The Outlook in Ireland*, Dublin, 1907.
Ginnell, Laurence, *Land and Liberty*, Dublin, 1908.
Gwynn, D. R., *Life of John Redmond*, London, 1932.
Gwynn, Stephen, *A Holiday in Connemara*, London, 1909.
Healy, T. M., *Letters and Leaders of my Day*, London, 1928.

Horgan, J. J., *Parnell to Pearse*, Dublin, 1948.
Iwan-Muller, E. B., *Ireland Today and Tomorrow*, London, 1907.
Kettle, Andrew, *The Material for Victory*, ed. L. J. Kettle, Dublin, 1958.
Lynch, A., *Ireland: Vital Hour*, Dublin, 1915.
Lynch, A., *My Life Story*, London, 1924.
Leech, H., Brougham, *The Continuity of the Irish Revolutionary Movement*, London, 1913.
Lucy, Sir Henry, *Diary of the Unionist Parliament 1895–1900*, London, 1910.
Mackail, J. W. and Wyndham, Guy, *Life and Letters of George Wyndham*, London, 1925.
McCarthy, Michael, *Five Years in Ireland 1895–1900*, Dublin, 1903.
McCarthy, Michael, *Irish Land and Liberty*, London, 1911.
McKnight, Thomas, *Ulster as it is*, London, 1896.
O'Brien, William, *An Olive Branch in Ireland*, London, 1910.
—— *The Irish Revolution*, London, 1923.
—— *The Responsibility for Partition*, Dublin and London, 1921.
O'Connor, T. P., *Memoirs of an Old Parliamentarian*, vol. ii, London, 1929.
O'Donnell, F. H., *History of the Irish Parliamentary Party*, London, 1910.
O'Malley, William, *Glancing Back*, London, 1933.
Paul-Dubois, L., *Contemporary Ireland*, Dublin, 1906.
Phillips, W., Alison, *The Revolution in Ireland*, London, 1923.
Plunkett, H., *Ireland in the New Century*, London, 1904.
Redmond-Howard, L. G., *John Redmond*, London, 1910.
Robinson, H., *Further Memories of Irish Life*, London, 1924.
—— *Memories Wise and Otherwise*, London, 1923.
Sheenhan, D. D., *Ireland Since Parnell*, London, 1921.
Spender, Harold, 'John Redmond: An Impression', *Contemporary Review*, vol. 43, April 1918.
Shea, Patrick, *Voices and the Sound of Drums*, Belfast, 1981.
Sullivan, T. D., *Recollections of Troubled times*, Dublin, 1905.
Sutherland, Hugh, *Ireland: Yesterday and Today*, London, 1904.
Wells, W. B., *John Redmond*, London, 1919.

SECONDARY SOURCES

Alter, P., *Die Irische National Bewegung Zwichen Parlament und Revolution: Der Konstitutionelle Nationalismus in Irland 1880–1918*, Munich, 1971.
Beckett, J. C., *The Making of Modern Ireland 1603–1923*, London, 1966.
Bew, Paul, *Land and the National Question in Ireland 1858–82*, Dublin and Atlantic Highlands, New Jersey, 1978; *C. S. Parnell*, Dublin, 1980.
Bew, Paul, Gibbon, Peter, and Patterson, Henry, *The State in Northern Ireland 1921–72: Political Forces and Social Classes*, Manchester and New York, 1979.
Bew, Paul and Patterson, Henry, 'The Protestant–Catholic Conflict in Ulster', *Journal of International Affairs*, vol. 36, 1982–3.

Bew, Paul and Patterson, Henry, *Sean Lemass and the Making of Modern Ireland*, Dublin, 1982.

Bew, Paul and Patterson, Henry, *The British State and the Ulster Crisis*, London, 1985.

Bowman, John, *De Valera and the Ulster Question*, Oxford, 1983.

Boyce, D. G., *Nationalism in Ireland*, London, Dublin and Baltimore, 1982.

Canny, N. P., 'Fusion and Faction in Ireland', *Comparative Studies in Society and History*, vol. 26, 1985.

Clark, Samuel, *Social Origins of the Irish Land War*, Princeton, 1979.

Clark, Samuel and Donnelly, James, ed., *Irish Peasants: Violence and Political Unrest*, Madison and Manchester, 1983.

Clarkson, L. and Goldstrom, J. M., ed., *Irish Population, Economy and Society: Essays in Honour of K. H. Connell*, Oxford, 1981.

Clifford, Brendan, ed., *Reprints from the Cork Free Press*, Belfast and Cork, 1984.

Comerford, R. V., *The Fenians in Context: Irish Politics and Society 1848–82*, Dublin and Atlantic Highlands, New Jersey, 1985.

Coogan, O., *The War in Meath 1913–23*, Dublin, 1983.

Crotty, R., *Irish Agricultural Production: Its Volume and Structure*, Cork, 1966.

Curtis, L. P., 'The Anglo-Irish Predicament', *Twentieth-Century Studies*, vol. 4, 1970.

Curtis, L. P., 'On Class and Class Conflict in the Land War', *Irish Economic and Social History*, vol. VIII, 1981.

Curtis, L. P., 'Incumbered Wealth: Landlord Indebtedness in Post-famine Ireland', *American Historical Review*, LXXV, 2, 1980.

D'alton, Ian, 'Southern Irish Unionism: A study of Cork Unionists, 1884–1914', *Transactions of the Royal Historical Society*, 5th series, vol. 23, 1972.

Daly, Mary, *A Social and Economic History of Ireland*, Dublin, 1981.

Davis, R., *Arthur Griffith and non-violent Sinn Fein*, Dublin, 1974.

dePaor, L., ed., *Milestones in Irish History*, Cork, 1986.

Deutsch-Brady, Chantal, 'The Cattle Drive of Tulira', *Journal of the Galway Archaeological and Historical Society*, vol. 34, 1974–5.

Drudy, P. J., ed., *Ireland, Land, Politics and People*, Cambridge, 1982.

Fanning, Ronan, 'The Unionist party and Ireland 1906–10', *Irish Historical Studies*, vol. XV, 1966.

Fitzpatrick, David, *Politics and Irish Life 1913–21, Provincial Experience of War and Revolution*, Dublin, 1977.

Fitzpatrick, David, 'Unrest in Rural Ireland', *Irish Economic and Social History*, vol. XII, 1985.

Foster, Roy, *Charles Stewart Parnell: The Man and his Family*, Hassocks, 1976.

Foster, Roy, 'Parnell and his People: The Ascendancy and Home Rule', *Canadian Journal of Irish Studies*, vol. 6, 1980.

Garvin, Tom, *The Evolution of Irish Nationalist Politics*, Dublin and New York, 1981.

Gaughan, J. A., *A Political Odyssey: Thomas O'Donnell*, Dublin, 1983.

Gibbon, Peter, *The Origins of Ulster Unionism*, Manchester, 1975.

Gray, John, *City in Revolt*, Belfast, 1985.

Griffith, K. and O'Grady, T., *Curious Journey: An Oral History of Ireland's Unfinished Revolution*, London, 1982.

Henry, R. M., *The Evolution of Sinn Fein*, Dublin, 1920.

Hepburn, A. C., 'The Ancient Order of Hibernians in Irish Politics 1905–14'; *Cithara* X, 1971.

Hepburn, A. C., 'The Irish Council Bill and the Fall of Sir Antony MacDonnell', *Irish Historical Studies*, vol. xvii, no. 68, 1971.

Hoppen, K. T., *Elections Politics and Society in Ireland 1832–1885*, Oxford, 1984.

Jalland, Patricia, *The Liberals and Ireland*, Brighton, 1980.

Johnstone, W. J., 'The Land Purchase Problem', *Journal of the Statistical and Social Inquiry Society of Ireland*, vol. XI, 1906.

Kee, Robert, *The Green Flag*, London, 1972.

Kolbert, C. F. and O'Brien, T., *Land Reform in Ireland*, Cambridge, 1975.

Laffan, M., 'The Unification of Sinn Fein', *Irish Historical Studies*, vol. XVII, 1971.

Lee, J. J., *The Modernisation of Irish Society 1848–1918*, Dublin, 1973.

Lyons, J. B., *The Enigma of Tom Kettle*, Dublin, 1983.

Lyons, F. S. L., *The Irish Parliamentary Party 1890–1910*, London, 1951.

Lyons, F. S. L., *John Dillon*, London 1968.

Lyons, F. S. L., 'The Political Ideas of Parnell', *Historical Journal* XVI, 1973.

Lyons, F. S. L., *Culture and Anarchy in Ireland 1890–1939*, Oxford, 1979.

Lyons, F. S. L., *Ireland since the Famine*, London, 1971.

Lyons, F. S. L., 'The Irish Unionist Party and the Devolution Crisis 1904', *Irish Historical Studies*, vol. VI, 1948–9.

Mansergh, P. N. S., *The Irish Question*, Dublin, 1965.

Miller, David, *Church, State and Nation in Ireland 1898–1921*, Dublin, 1973.

Miller, Kerby, *Emigrants and Exiles: Ireland and the Irish Exodus to North America*, Oxford, 1984.

Moody, T. W., *Davitt and Irish Revolution 1846–82*, Oxford, 1982.

Moody, T. W., ed., *Nationality and the Pursuit of National Independence*, Belfast, 1978.

Murphy, D., *Derry, Donegal and Modern Ulster*, Derry, 1981.

McMinn, J. R. B., 'Liberalism in north Antrim 1900–14', *Irish Historical Studies*, vol. XXIII, 1982.

Norman, E. R., *A History of Modern Ireland*, London, 1971.

O'Brien, Conor Cruise, *Parnell and his Party*, Oxford, 1957.

O'Brien, Conor Cruise, *States of Ireland*, London, 1972.

O'Brien, J. V., *William O'Brien and the Course of Irish Politics 1881–1918*, Berkeley, California, 1976.

O'Broin, L., *The Chief Secretary Augustine Birrell in Ireland*, London, 1969.

O'Broin, L., *Revolutionary Underground. the Story of the Irish Republican Brotherhood 1858–1924*, Dublin, 1976.

O'Broin, L., *Protestant Nationalists in Revolutionary Ireland*, Dublin, 1985.
O'Day, Alan, *The English Face of Irish Nationalism*, Dublin, 197.
O'Day, Alan, *Parnell and the First Home Rule Episode*, Dublin, 1986.
O'Tuathaigh, Gearóid, ed., *Community, Culture and Conflict*, Galway, 1986.
Patterson, H., *Class Conflict and Sectarianism*, Belfast, 1980.
Patterson, H., 'Independent Orangeism and Class Conflict in Edwardian Belfast', *Proceedings of the Royal Irish Academy*, vol. 90 C, no. 1, 1980.
Phillips, W. Alison, *The Revolution in Ireland*, London, 1923.
Pomfret, J. E., *the Struggle for Land in Ireland*, Princeton, 1930.
Staehle, H., 'Statistical Notes on the Economic History of Irish Agriculture 1847–1913', *Journal of the Statistical and Social Inquiry Society of Ireland*, XVII, 1950–1.
Thompson, Francis, 'Attitudes to Reform: Political Parties in Ulster and the Irish Land Bill of 1881', *Irish Historical Studies*, vol. XXIV, 1985.
Townshend, Charles, *Political Violence in Ireland; Government and Resistance since 1848*, Oxford, 1983.
Townshend, Charles, 'Modernisation and Nationalism: Perspectives in Recent Irish History', *History*, vol. 66, 1981.
Vaughan, W. E., *Landlords and Tenants in Ireland 1848–1904*, Dundalk, 1983.
Walker, B. M., ed., *Parliamentary Election Results in Ireland 1801–1922*, Dublin, 1978.
White, Barry, *John Hume, Statesman of the Troubles*, Belfast, 1984.
Winstanley, Michael, *Ireland and the Land Question 1800–1922*, London, 1984.

UNPUBLISHED THESES

Barrett, Richard, 'The Policies and Political Character of the Parnellite Party' (University College, Dublin, MA, 1983).
Bull, P. J., 'The Reconstruction of the Irish Parliamentary Party, 1895–1903: An Analysis with Special Reference to William O'Brien' (University of Cambridge, Ph.D., 1972).
Foy, Michael, 'The AOH: An Irish Politico-Religious Pressure Group 1884–1975' (Queen's University Belfast, MA, 1975).
Jones, David S., 'Agrarian Capitalism and Rural Social Development in Ireland' (Queen's University Belfast, Ph.D., 1978).
Jordan, Don, 'Land and Politics in the West of Ireland, 1846–82' (University of California, Ph.D., 1980).
Gailey, Andrew, 'The Unionist Government's Policy towards Ireland 1895–1905' (University of Cambridge, Ph.D., 1982).
Hepburn, A. C., 'Liberal Policies and Nationalist Politics in Ireland 1905–10' (University of Kent, Ph.D., 1968).
Loughlin, J. P., 'Gladstone, Irish Nationalism and the Home Rule Question 1882–1893', with particular reference to the Ulster Problem (Trinity College, Dublin, Ph.D., 1983).

Moore, Gerard, 'Anti-Semitism in Ireland' (University of Ulster, Ph.D., 1984).
Mullen, R. G., 'The Origins and Passing of the Irish Land Act of 1909' (Queen's University Belfast, MA, 1978).
Phoenix, Eamon G., 'The Nationalist Movement in Ireland 1914–28' (Queen's University Belfast, Ph.D., 1983.)
Shannon, Catherine, 'Arthur Balfour and the Irish Question 1874–1921' (University of Massachusetts, Ph.D., 1975).
–'Local Government in Ireland: The Politics and Administration' (University College, Dublin, MA, 1963).
Warwick-Haller, S., 'William O'Brien and the Land War in Ireland 1877–1903' (University of Kent, Ph.D., 1980).

Index

Index

238

Mayo 9, 17–18, 35–7, 39–40, 43–7, 57, 60,
79, 83–6, 93, 113–14, 135, 146, 167, 175,
187, 196, 200, 208–9, 215–16
Mayo, Earl of 97, 106
Mayo News 85–6, 113–14
Meath 9, 25 n., 70, 73, 78, 104, 135, 149, 159,
163, 167–8, 184, 212, 215
Meehan, F. 172
Meehan, P. 172
'Memories of Kilmainham' 2 n.
Midland Tribune 113, 115
Mitchell, Edward 123
Modderspruit, battle of 61
Monaghan 197, 210
Moore, George, *Hail and Farewell* 26 n.
Moran, D. P. 124, 149, 188
Morley, Lord, *Life of Gladstone* 139
Morning Post 220 n.
Morris, T. A. 207
Mowatt, Sir Francis 174
Moyland, Sean 210
Moyvore 162
Muldoon, J. 172
Mullally, E. 82–3
Mullingar 75, 197
Munster 9, 55, 74–7, 79–80, 82–3, 113, 115,
176, 215
Murnaghan, George 171, 196
Murphy, John 196
Murphy estate 92

Nagle, M. J. 130, 221
Nanetti, J. P. 172, 197
National Democrat 210
Nationalist 83
Nationalist and Leinster Times 116
Nationality 217
Navan 19, 149
Nebraska 38
New Ireland 214
New Ireland Forum 202
Newport 41
New Ross 10, 65
Newtownforbes 152, 154–5, 189
New York 19, 42
New York Times 69
Nineteenth Century 23, 28
North Antrim Land Association 88
Northern Whig 6, 88–91
Nugent, Sir Walter 162, 172
Nugent-Everard, Col. 97

O'Brien, Kendal 80, 82–3, 172

O'Brien, Patrick 61, 172
O'Brien, R. Barry 103; *Life of Charles
Stewart Parnell* 150
O'Brien, William: and UIL and militant
agrarianism 17–18, 35–9, 41–9, 52, 54–
7, 64–5, 71, 73–6, 78, 83–5, 92–4, 158,
165–6, 206, 208; and conciliation policy
17–18, 53–4, 57, 59–60, 73, 96–7, 99,
102–3, 107–8, 117–18, 120–1, 128, 135,
165–6, 171–2, 185–6, 204–5, 211, 216,
219–22; political judgement of 45, 48,
53, 72; and party reunification 46, 48,
52–4, 67–9; relations with Redmond 46,
68–9, 70–4, 92–4, 96, 103, 106, 108–13,
117, 122–3, 166, 171–3, 177–8, 187, 194,
200, 205; suffers nervous tension 78; and
Special Commission (1888) 86; and
T. W. Russell 87, 107; and land legislation 99–100, 102, 106, 117–18, 129–30,
135–6, 177, 183, 185, 187–8; and sale of
Redmond's estate 108–10; resignations
from Irish party 111–16, 187; differences with Davitt on nationalist destiny
128; and Irish Council Bill 131, 220; and
Sinn Fein 166, 215–16; returns to Irish
party 168; and Dudley Report 175–6;
and 'Barton Convention' 185–6, 211;
and AFIL 187–9, 192–4; and 1910 elec-
tions 194–200, 209–11; and Ulster 200,
220–1; recruits for British army 212;
otherwise mentioned 12, 27
O'Connell, Father Michael 41, 85
O'Connor, James 172
O'Connor, John 172
O'Connor, T. P. 94, 131
O'Conor, Charles Owen (the O'Conor
Don) 30, 50–1, 53–4, 57–63, 84, 127, 183
O'Docherty, Philip 171, 196
O'Donnell, Bishop 44, 149
O'Donnell, F. H. 65, 66
O'Donnell, John 39, 56, 171, 196, 206
O'Donnell, T. 171, 196
O'Dowd, W. 172
O'Dwyer, Martin 168
O'Flanaghan, Father Michael 214, 218–20
O'Grady estate 92
O'Growney, Father Eugene 5
O'Hara, Father Dennis 145
O'Hara family 40
O'Kelly, Conor 46, 63, 171, 175, 195 n., 196
O'Kelly, J. J. 51, 57, 67, 112–13
Oldham, C. H. 29
O'Leary, Daniel L. 212